TREKONOMICS

TREKONOMICS

MANU SAADIA

pipertext

Published by Pipertext Publishing Co., Inc., in association with Inkshares, Inc., San Francisco, California
www.pipertext.com
www.inkshares.com

Edited and designed by Girl Friday Productions
www.girlfridayproductions.com
Cover design by Jennifer Bostic
Cover art by John Powers

ISBN: 9781941758755
e-ISBN: 9781941758762
Library of Congress Control Number: 2016931451

First edition
Printed in United States

*To Lazare, our chief engineer,
and to my father, Yossef Saadia.*

CONTENTS

"I have shown how the ideas of progression and of the indefinite perfectibility of the human race belong to democratic ages. Democratic nations care but little for what has been, but they are haunted by visions of what will be; in this direction their unbounded imagination grows and dilates beyond all measure. Here then is the wildest range open to the genius of poets, which allows them to remove their performances to a sufficient distance from the eye. Democracy shuts the past against the poet, but opens the future before him."

—Alexis de Tocqueville, *Democracy in America*

"It no longer seemed so important whether the world was Adam Smith or Karl Marx. Neither made very much sense under the new circumstances."

—Isaac Asimov, *I, Robot*

FOREWORD

BY BRAD DELONG

"Live long and prosper." "Beam me up, Scotty." "The needs of the many outweigh the needs of the few, or the one." "Fascinating." "Make it so." "Logic is the beginning of wisdom, not the end." "I'm a doctor, not a bricklayer." "Highly illogical." "You can stop it!" "Stop it? I'm counting on it!"

Over the past half century *Star Trek* has woven itself into our sociocultural DNA. It provides a set of powerful, striking, and beneficial ideas that help us here in our civilization think better. Even those of us who are economists.

Why should the imaginary dreams of science fiction help us think better?

Back in 1759, the man who was to become the first economist, young Adam Smith, a Scottish moral philosopher on the make, wrote in his *Theory of Moral Sentiments* of how "a stranger to human nature, [seeing] the indifference of men about the misery of their inferiors . . . [would conclude that] pain must be more agonizing, and the convulsions of death more terrible, to persons of higher rank, than to those of meaner stations."

There is no such alien stranger. Smith is telling us of somebody who does not exist. It's a very short eighteenth-century science-fiction story. Why? Because we love to tell one another false stories, to converse about imaginary people, be it in philosophical treatises or in television serials. It is what we do as humans.

▲

If an alien intellect, vast and cool and unsympathetic (or vast and warm and sympathetic), were to scrutinize us from afar, it would inevitably conclude that telling each other false stories is a major part of what we are, and it would wonder why we communicate—or miscommunicate— in this way.

Everyone is engaged in dream-work. Everyone chatters about their imaginary friends. Some are ascribing agency, motivation, and intelligence to patterns of societal forces that are the emergent properties of distributed interactions. Others are writing—or filming—fiction.

Our fictions are, collectively, the dream-work of humanity. We dream these dreams to amuse ourselves, but also so that we will be more sane when we awake.

No wonder, then, that investors and economists also gab about imaginary friends, frenemies, and unfriends with names like "Ms. Market" and "confidence" and "global risk tolerance" as they try to understand things called "asset prices." They too are doing dream-work.

But in some ways the most profound thinking, the deepest dream-work, is being done by science fiction. That's because science-fiction writers and fans are explicitly aware that what they are engaged in is humanity's dreaming.

The Prime Directive of *Star Trek: The Original Series* was a way to process America's 1960s misadventure in Vietnam. I first recognized that *Star Trek* was a very different kind of show back in the 1960s, when at the end of "Arena," Kirk neither killed nor civilized nor brought democracy to the Gorn, but let him go to make his own destiny.

Gene Roddenberry mostly wanted to find a way to get people to pay him to make up stories, so that he wouldn't have to take a job that required a lot of heavy lifting. But he also wanted to tell particular stories. The stories he wanted to tell were those that would be the dream-work for a better future.

He wanted to tell stories of a progressive humanity. He wanted to tell stories about people in a better future in which governmental institutions were smart enough to stay out of Vietnam and people weren't obsessed with leaky roofs and food shortages. He wanted to tell stories in which racial prejudice was as silly and stupid as it, in fact, is. He wanted to tell stories in which it would be normal for a woman to be if not number one at least number two as first officer of a starship. He wanted to tell stories in which everyone—even the disposable Red Shirts—was an officer, a trained and well-educated professional treated with dignity and respect by her peers and superiors.

In turn, Gene Roddenberry's successors—showrunners, writers, actors, set designers, and all the rest—took on the same project: to do the dream-work of a better future. As North Atlantic civilization bobbled the historical opportunity that was the collapse of the Soviet Empire, *Star Trek VI: The Undiscovered Country* and *Star Trek: Deep Space Nine* pointed to better directions. Gene Roddenberry made *Star Trek* a collective dreaming about a better future, and not just a Western or a medieval romance with lightsabers, whooshing spaceships, and exploding planets bolted onto it.

Four hundred years ago, in almost all human societies, being rich relative to your neighbors mattered a lot. If you weren't rich, you were malnourished—perhaps not getting the nutrients for your immune system to function well, perhaps not getting the calories you needed to reliably ovulate, and probably losing at least one tooth with every baby. And, you were short. In the eighteenth century, Adam Smith's England was the richest society in the world, yet the orphans sent to sea by the charity that was the Marine Society were close to eight inches shorter than the aristocrats' sons sent to Sandhurst to become army officers. Plus, your roof leaked.

Today, in the prosperous North Atlantic, food-related public-health problems are no longer predominantly problems of malnutrition and caloric scarcity but rather problems of overabundance. And it is not just in food that those of us in the developed world's bubble have abundance. You only have to go down to Long Beach and look at the containers being unloaded to convince yourself that our current economic problem is not one of need.

Roddenberry's dreams, *Star Trek*'s dreams, help us to think through what it would be like to have a society of abundance, of logic and reason, and of inclusion. A world in which the fearsome Gorn might really be the good guy and in which mortal enemies can become allies. As Ayelborne forecasts to Captain Kirk in "Errand of Mercy": "You and the Klingons will become fast friends. You will work together."[1]

For those of us who are fans, it has been (and still is) a wild fifty-year ride. And for those of us who are not, I believe it really matters to listen to *Star Trek*'s dream-work, and to step into that ongoing fifty-year conversation.

---

1.   *Star Trek: The Original Series*, 1x26: "Errand of Mercy."

So with enthusiasm and admiration, I present to you Manu Saadia, and *Trekonomics*.

Brad DeLong, Berkeley, January 2016

INTRODUCTION

"DREAM NOT OF TODAY, MISTER PICARD"[2]

I grew up frightened. Nuclear war and concentration camps were my childhood monsters. It might sound overblown today, but dread and anxiety were very real. Looming disaster was a constant motif. I was born in 1972, a child of the Cold War and of the oil shock. Perpetual economic crisis and the Warsaw Pact's missiles cast long shadows over our heads. Even in my sheltered enclave of Paris, the threat of war, nuclear or otherwise, was palpable. It was like a background hum, never quite strident but nonetheless perceptible. Some were more aware of it than others. Kids certainly took it to heart.

The year I turned nine, my grandfather took it upon himself to tell me all about his arrest by the Gestapo and his time at Buchenwald. Needless to say, that did not help. The particulars of the story are what one would expect: torture, the cattle car, hunger, cold, forced labor, death. It was a lot to take in.

---

2. *ST:TNG*, 6x20: "The Chase."

In my overactive and somewhat precocious mind, I reached the sobering conclusion that neither my parents nor my relatives, nor even France and its mighty atomic arsenal, could ever protect me from mutually assured destruction. They were as powerless as I was against the rolling thunder of the world. And I was *right*.

These are the things you do not want to be right about at eight or nine.

You can easily understand why the Death Star was not my thing. It hit too close to home. *Star Wars* was too dangerous and had too many villains.

Star Trek, on the other hand, was different. I first saw *Star Trek: The Motion Picture* in Paris, at the age of eight. And if you had given me the choice, I would have jumped at the chance to live in the world of *Star Trek*. Watching the *Star Trek* movie was like being let into a gigantic space laboratory where adults were doing very cool and important things. In a sense, the *Enterprise* crew's leisurely yet rational technobabble-soaked demeanor made their lives and their work more approachable. In *Star Trek*, science and reason triumphed over danger. Their world was definitely better equipped for harmony than ours.

Star Trek presented my terrified eight-year-old self with the mind-blowing idea that in the future things would get better. *Star Trek: The Motion Picture* was my starting point, the moment in time when my mind finally awakened to the possibilities of the world, that there was something, a future maybe, to look forward to.

More than anything else from my childhood, this is what has stuck with me my entire life. When my wife and I got married, we convinced the befuddled judge to say, "Live long and prosper." To this day, the greatest sense of wonder I experience from *Star Trek* comes not from the starships and the stars, new life and new civilizations, but from its depiction of an uncompromisingly humanist, galaxy-spanning, utopian society.

Which means that one huge question has haunted me since I was a boy. Is *Star Trek* possible?

I committed very early on to live by the precepts of *Star Trek*, in the faint hope of hastening its coming somehow. That commitment was easy, as *Star Trek* blended effortlessly with the kind of secular Judaism passed on to me by my parents. Learn as much as humanly possible, solve problems for others, fight injustice wherever and whenever you can, try to be a mensch. Heal the world—*Tikkun olam*, as we say in Hebrew.

The task proved much more daunting and complicated than I ever could have envisioned. For one, like many before me I failed miserably at inventing faster-than-light engines. Yet I remain convinced that a better world is indeed within our grasp and that *Star Trek* gives us a road map for our shared future. Indeed, some of it is already happening right now, among us, in real life.

RENDER UNTO *STAR TREK* . . .

Everybody knows *Star Trek*. Everybody has heard of Leonard Nimoy's Vulcan salute and of the transporter ("Beam me up, Scotty"). You don't have to be a convention-going, costume-wearing fan to be familiar with *Star Trek*. In the fifty years since its first airing on NBC, the show, all 716 episodes of scripted TV, has become an icon, a cornerstone of popular culture, an American monument.

We owe a lot to *Star Trek*. It has had a tremendous impact in the real world. It has made it a better place. You cannot say that of many other TV or film franchises. As far as changing the world goes, *Star Trek* stands alone.

The list of practical technologies that came out of *Star Trek* is almost endless: ion propulsion, telepresence, portable diagnostic sensors, noninvasive medical imaging and surgery, transparent alumi-num, natural-language interaction between humans and computers, translations in real time, cybernetic prosthetic implants . . . There is not a month that passes without a research group or a start-up claim-ing to have come up with this or that *Star Trek* device.

Star Trek is famously responsible for the cell phone. Dr. Martin Cooper of Motorola was a fan of the original show and really wanted a portable communicator that would work just like Captain Kirk's. *Star Trek* gave its name to the first space shuttle, the *Enterprise*. *Star Trek: The Next Generation* showed one of the first instances of a software-defined, touch-sensitive contextual user interface, also known in plain English as the iPhone. And all that in the late 1980s.

It never ceases to amaze me that mere TV entertainment, and of a subgenre widely regarded as juvenile if not downright unserious, could spur such world-altering feats of engineering. At its best, *Star Trek* is a source of constantly renewed inspiration for engineers, scientists, and entrepreneurs—a true, demonstrable engine of progress, and, ulti-mately, a force for good in the world. And that is before even consider-ing the most profound of all *Star Trek* speculations, the one thing that has gotten the least attention by virtue of being the most obvious, and because it is much harder to re-create in a lab or to release as a prod-uct: the economics of *Star Trek*, or what I call *trekonomics*.

WHAT IS TREKONOMICS?

The world of *Star Trek* is an economic utopia.

Economics is the art and science of managing, producing, and exchanging resources as a society.

Economics exists because goods and resources are never in infinite supply. As a result, both individuals and society as a whole must make choices regarding the allocation of limited goods and resources. These choices can be made through multiple mechanisms, such as prices, markets, or central planning. But regardless of form or system, the fateful fact remains that *choices have to be made*. This is precisely what the great British economist John Maynard Keynes called "the economic problem," or, in the words of another famous Englishman: you can't always get what you want.

Trekonomics solves Keynes's economic problem, if only fictionally. In *Trek*'s universe, most if not all of the real-world conditions that drive economic behaviors essentially disappear. In *Star Trek*, currency has become obsolete as a medium of exchange. Labor cannot be distinguished from leisure. Universal abundance of almost all goods has made the pursuit of wealth irrelevant. Superstition, crime, poverty, and illness have been eradicated. For all intents and purposes, the United Federation of Planets is a paradise.

Star Trek's amazing world of carefree abundance appears on the screen as a by-product of incredible technological progress. Faster-than-light starships, transporters, replicators, holographic projections, and humanoid robots are *Star Trek*'s arsenal of prosperity. From the standpoint of economics, however, these do not matter one bit.

What really matters, and what makes *Star Trek* uniquely utopian, is the *social distribution* of these impressive technologies. What distinguishes the United Federation of Planets is not so much that it invented the replicators, these magical machines that can produce almost anything on demand, but rather that these replicators are free and available to all as *public goods*. Think about it this way: if the benefits of replicators, monetary or otherwise, only accrued to those who own and operate them, then *Star Trek* would not be *Star Trek*.

The other striking aspect of trekonomics is anthropological, for lack of a better word. Again, it goes back to Keynes's economic problem. A world where an evenly distributed cornucopia is both the norm and the policy profoundly changes its inhabitants. Just like money, the compulsion to work to ensure one's survival has simply vanished. Thanks to the free availability of robotic helpers, human labor has been rendered obsolete. *Star Trek* explores at great length what happens to motivations and psyche under such conditions of post-scarcity.

For one, competition among people is completely transformed. Reputation and honors, the esteem and recognition of one's peers, replace economic wealth as public markers of status. But these are largely optional, as there are no material penalties or disincentives for those who do not seek nor attain higher status. We usually see the best and the brightest of *Star Trek*'s society on the show, the small elite of heroes and overachievers who boldly go where no one has gone before. Do not be fooled: Starfleet captains and their crack officers are the outliers. That is why they are so exciting and relevant for TV drama. In the background, however, the vast majority of the Federation's citizens are not nearly as driven or exceptional. Or rather they are, but in a more pedestrian way. They all go about their daily lives without much concern or worry, safe in the knowledge that they shall never want for anything.

The world *Star Trek* built raises multiple economic problems. For instance, what happens to innovation and scientific progress without the hope of financial rewards? Similarly, how can a society where all is freely available avoid the tragedy of the commons, the trap of resource depletion caused by unchecked overconsumption? *Star Trek* does not shy away from these questions. Several episodes of the show deal openly with the challenges of organizing and regulating its own utopia.

THE INVENTION OF TREKONOMICS

Trekonomics did not come about fully formed. Through the lens of economics, there are in fact two distinct *Trek*s. There's *The Original Series* on the one hand, including the films up to *Star Trek III: The Search for Spock*; and, on the other hand, the post-economic, utopian world outlined in broad, comical strokes in *Star Trek IV: The Voyage Home*, and then fully fleshed out in the subsequent TV shows and movies. The first *Star Trek*, call it *Star Trek* 1.0, is heavily indebted to author Robert Heinlein, while version 2.0, *The Next Generation* and beyond, derives many of its basic elements from Isaac Asimov.

The difference between the two *Star Trek*s arises from within the universe's internal, fictional chronology. *Star Trek: Enterprise*, the last produced series of the franchise, is set in the twenty-second century. *The Original Series*, the first iteration of the show in the 1960s, is set in the twenty-third century. *The Next Generation, Deep Space Nine*, and *Voyager*, made in the 1980s and 1990s, all take place in the twenty-fourth century.

Through that grand saga of the future, the pace of technological innovation does not slow down. We go from the rustic quarters and galley kitchens of the early starships to civilian families, bars, holographic entertainment (the holodecks), and even an arboretum on Captain Picard's *Next Generation's Enterprise*. That *Enterprise* is an interstellar cruise ship with some science, diplomacy, and policing duties on the side. The *Love Boat* in space, with a shmear of galactic patrol. The show is a highlight reel of these few moments of tension and heroism that occasionally occur on an otherwise leisurely and uneventful journey.

That *Enterprise* holds something that its predecessors did not: replicators. That fact alone makes all the difference. Replicators can materialize anything out of thin air, on demand and for free. They can produce food, clothing, objects, even weapons (if the ship's safety protocols are disabled). They are the ultimate economic machines, a metaphor for robots and automation. Their presence indicates that by *The Next Generation*'s date (or "stardate," as the captain's log voice-overs state at the opening of each episode) the share of human labor in society has shrunk down to almost nothing. Jean-Luc Picard's world, the twenty-fourth-century Federation, has very little in common with Kirk and Spock's world.

The center of gravity of this book is therefore *Star Trek*'s twenty-fourth century. This is not to discount the importance of *The Original Series*. It was in fact groundbreaking. It contributed the key building blocks for trekonomics: the characters' altruism and their inclination toward science, as well as the uniquely utopian tone of the series, its optimistic vision of a humanity pacified at long last.

THE ISLAND OF UTOPIA

By a fortuitous coincidence of the calendar, 2016 is not only the fiftieth anniversary of *Star Trek*; it is also the five-hundredth anniversary of Thomas More's *Utopia*. That short epistolary novel spawned the literary tradition that bears its title. Science fiction, and therefore *Star Trek*, is its legacy.

Utopia literally means "not a place" or "nowhere" in Greek, which signals the speculative nature of both the book and the genre. In Thomas More's landmark work, Utopia is a fictional island in the middle of the Atlantic Ocean. Its inhabitants live happy lives in their perfectly organized yet hypothetical nation. In keeping with the philosophical program of the Renaissance, Thomas More rediscovered Plato's *Republic* and adapted it for his time and place. However, in contrast to Plato's classic opus, *Utopia* was a story rather than an abstract prescriptive treatise.

Utopia was inhabited by fictional people who embodied the author's discourse. By disguising his blueprint for a harmonious polity in narrative garb, Thomas More invited readers to identify with the characters and their circumstances. He walked them through the island's fictional society, so to speak, instead of presenting them with a ready catalog of schemas and plans. While the story could be mined for More's views on the ideal form of government, it read above all as a satire and critique of his contemporaries.

Thomas More's lasting invention was to paint the island of Utopia as a *better place* whose existence was chiefly a potential in the minds of readers. That dramatic artifice, More's bolt of pure genius, helped define a tradition that spanned several centuries. It produced some of the most provocative and popular works in the history of ideas. From its inception, *Star Trek* shared the same levity and playfulness as those tales from the past. It rightfully belongs in that noble literary tradition.

While it owes much to the utopian genre, *Star Trek* is also, primarily, science fiction. It is known the world over for its starships, its aliens, and its extrapolations of technology. Its overriding contract with the audience is to probe the consequences of progress.

The problem for *Star Trek* was that although science fiction is the progeny of utopian literature, it had early on broken with utopia, its intellectual forebear. Mary Shelley's *Frankenstein* epitomized that departure from the idyllic comforts of Utopia. At the dawn of the Industrial Revolution, *Frankenstein* captured the awe and the terror of the machines humans had unleashed upon the world. Such was the power of Shelley's creature that, to this day, dystopia, the "bad place," remains the dominant story in science fiction.

The enduring resonance of Shelley's template may explain why *Star Trek*'s brand of economic utopia has very few precursors or antecedents *in science fiction itself*. *Star Trek* presents intelligent machines and technological change as unequivocally beneficial, instead of threatening or even apocalyptic. In that, it stands largely athwart its own genre—science fiction—and in many ways it stands out from the rest of popular culture.

CAPITAL IN THE TWENTY-FOURTH CENTURY

Science fiction and economics share an oft-overlooked kinship. Both are preoccupied with change, and predictions about change. The future is their province, but not just any future: the future of society. One approaches it through narrative flourish, the other through mathematical tools. Both, however, derive their conclusions from careful observation of the world as it is. And both usually fail. As atomic physicist Niels Bohr once said, predictions are hard, especially about the future. But the very manner in which they fail matters, because they force us to think about our present condition in a new light.

Good science fiction such as *Star Trek* is great fun. Yet, at the same time, like economics it is meant to be deadly serious. Its mission is to explore the "new life and new civilizations" that lie ahead of us. What are the economic, social, and even psychological consequences of technological change? What will become of us humans, and what *can* we become in a world that runs on automatons?

Indeed, the rapid rise of automation in our everyday life is generating deep and legitimate anxieties. Many recent books have investigated the economic consequences of the coming of intelligent robots. Their conclusions are fraught and worrying. Countless people are already losing their livelihoods to automatons, and even the more specialized professions, from doctors and surgeons to financial analysts and engineers, stand to be mercilessly replaced as machines continue on their current trajectory of exponential improvement.

These anxieties are entirely about the political economy of technological progress. Who will reap the benefits of such wondrous inventions? Are we headed toward an even more unequal and oligarchic society? *Star Trek* hints that among the many potential paths forward there is at least one that is not uniformly bleak and dystopian. *Star Trek* proposes the prototype of a society where the replacement of human labor goes hand in hand with an even distribution of wealth. The franchise remains tantalizingly vague on the policies needed to reach such a harmonious and blissful outcome. There is no step-by-step guide on how to get there in *Star Trek*, except maybe to build a faster-than-light spaceship and to encounter pointy-eared, benevolent aliens, the Vulcans. And voilà!

For fans and interested observers alike, the first impulse is to treat that missing piece of the show as Dr. Martin Cooper did with the cell phone. It is the can-do spirit of the enthusiast—let us try to make it work with what we have now at our disposal. That is not illogical, given the proven success of that approach in the realm of technology. Unfortunately, developing policy prescriptions is not nearly as straightforward as inventing new machines, if only because the global economy is a very complex and dynamic system. One cannot as easily reverse engineer the future of society as a gadget or a gizmo.

WHAT'S IN THIS BOOK?

Everything has been written about *Star Trek*. The physics of *Star Trek*, the technology, religions, philosophy, political science, the history of the various shows, the actors, Gene Roddenberry, and so on. There are hundreds upon hundreds of books about every minute aspect of the franchise. And yet, surprisingly, despite that avalanche of works, scant attention has been paid so far to the economic theory behind

Star Trek's vision of the future. This is the book I really wanted to read but could not find anywhere.

Therefore, my primary objective is to describe the economics of *Star Trek*. The idea is to take a step back: instead of trying to reverse engineer the future one piece of technology or one policy fix at a time, I attempt to take *Star Trek* at its own word, to give credit to its economic imagination. Exploring how to get there makes very little sense without a clear picture of what it's like once we get there.

Furthermore, to my great surprise, in the process of researching and writing this book, the question of possibility gradually dissolved. It turned out that *Star Trek*'s main economic thesis, that machines can eventually free us of the drudgery of work, is almost as old as the Industrial Revolution itself. It is not at all crazy. On the contrary, it seems rather reasonable in light of the trajectory of the past two centuries. Human activity has quickly moved away from the purely physical toward the mental and the symbolic. Meanwhile, more or less autonomous machines have taken on the task of transforming raw materials on an unimaginable scale. *Star Trek*'s utopia is nothing more than the world that awaits us on the other side of that great social metamorphosis, provided that we decide to distribute our newly acquired freedom evenly and that we avoid boiling our planet.

The first chapter deals with the glaring absence of currency in the *Star Trek* universe. How does the Federation function without the pricing mechanism? What is lost and what is gained by renouncing money as both a unit of account and as an information signal? In a society where the "economic problem" has been overcome, money is of very limited usefulness.

The second chapter is interested in the status of human labor in *Star Trek*. It describes the paradoxical fact that while there is no need to work in *Star Trek*'s utopia, everyone seems incredibly busy. What existential meaning can be derived from work when sentient mechanical beings can make anything better and more efficiently than humans?

The third chapter focuses on the replicator, the machine that enables *Star Trek*'s post-scarcity. The replicator serves as a metaphor and a stand-in for automation, as well as the fictional endpoint of the Industrial Revolution. The replicator's place in *Star Trek*'s society rests entirely on the political decision to make it free and available to everyone as a public good.

The fourth chapter takes on the issue of natural limits to economic growth. If there is to be post-scarcity, that is, infinite social wealth, how can such a proposition be even remotely consistent with the old notion that natural resources are limited? Notable examples of technological substitution help demonstrate that *Star Trek*'s society does not break economic theory.

The fifth chapter investigates the question of negative externalities. While *Star Trek*'s society is indeed capable of managing common resources, alien species are much less inclined to do so. The chapter presents an analysis of a *Star Trek*–inflected prisoner's dilemma game to demonstrate that even the most rational and well-governed of societies is powerless when confronted with an uncooperative foreign actor.

The sixth chapter offers readers a breather. It proposes a brief intellectual history of *Star Trek* and trekonomics. Strangely enough, Isaac Asimov's oeuvre aside, the abolition of human labor is seldom an object of science fiction. Trekonomics is essentially a reworking and a deepening of Isaac Asimov's main inventions (he famously coined the term *robotics* in 1941, at the tender age of twenty-one).

Chapter 7 discusses human behavior and human nature. *Star Trek* characters such as Spock and Captain Picard have nothing in common with twenty-first-century humans. They can freely devote their lives to science and justice precisely because they are free from economic necessity. The remarkable weirdness of the shows' beloved protagonists illustrates how, under conditions of post-scarcity, most economic behaviors and psychology (naively taken as immutable and natural) disappear.

The penultimate chapter is all about the greatest alien species in all of *Trek*: the odious and disgusting Ferengis—that is, us. The Ferengis are the capitalists and merchants of *Star Trek*'s galaxy. Yet even they, the most hardened of profit-seeking species, can change. All of *Star Trek*'s third show, *Deep Space Nine*, is the story of how the Ferengis abjure their old traditions and become Keynesian social democrats.

Chapter 9 reveals how *Star Trek*'s cornucopian society is already here, albeit local and unevenly distributed. Expanding prosperity, combined with the spread of global public goods, the rise of "free" stuff, is bringing our world ever closer to trekonomics. The challenge is distribution rather than technology.

PORTRAIT OF THE AUTHOR AS A YOUNG FAN

You seldom meet people who develop a love for science fiction in their later, more serious years. Maybe because science fiction exerts special and enduring powers of enchantment over children. For those of us who catch the bug early, science fiction plays a pivotal role in who we become as grown-up citizens. It is a teacher and a moral compass. It shapes lifelong pursuits.

I was introduced to *Star Trek* and science fiction by one of those rare persons who had embraced fandom in adulthood. As I mentioned earlier, I can trace it all back to that day in 1980 in Paris, when a friend of my father's took me with her to see the newly released *Star Trek* movie. Her name was Dina Gertler. She was a psychoanalyst, a colleague of my dad's. Like him she had immigrated to Paris from Israel, but by way of Hungary. She was a Holocaust survivor. Science fiction had not made her, but she claimed it had saved her.

My parents were not exactly thrilled. To them anything that began with "Star" was bound to be super violent American crap. That is why they had denied me the chance to go see *Star Wars* back when I was five. And they still had to be convinced for *Star Trek*. Lucky for me, they trusted Dina's professional judgment. Her considered opinion as a therapist was that *Star Trek: The Motion Picture* was not going to cause any lasting psychological damage. On the contrary, she argued that it would be very beneficial, that it would heighten my budding interest in science and technology. Basically, she sold them on *Star Trek* by playing the good-grades card. I remember her joking afterward that my parents were boring and didn't know any better.

Up until that point my exposure to science fiction had been minimal, limited to France's national treasure, Jules Verne, and playground echoes of *Star Wars*. *Star Trek: The Original Series* was not shown on French TV, and besides, we did not have TV at home (another one of my parents' anti-imperialist decrees).

Star Trek: The Motion Picture, then, was my first encounter with Kirk, Spock, and the ship itself. The *Enterprise*, revealed in all its glory by Douglas Trumbull and John Dykstra's special effects, was the most amazing and majestic starship I had ever seen on a screen (obviously, I had been forbidden to experience the total sensory assault that is *Star Wars*' opening sequence).

When the movie was over, I really, really did not want to leave the bridge of the *Enterprise*. I had to make that experience last. I still remember that very precise feeling, equal parts wonderment, recognition, and melancholy: this was the place I had been looking for, this was where I wanted to live, this was where I belonged. I had found my promised land. Pity it was all fiction and make-believe.

Afterward, seeing my unbridled enthusiasm for the movie, Dina proceeded to feed me science-fiction books on a regular basis. They were both French translations and English originals, with gaudy covers and names that did not sound like the kind of stuff you were supposed to read in school, especially if you were trying to be a good student.

It is not like science fiction was an escape from the material circumstances of my daily life. My parents were as solidly middle-class as Parisian intellectual professionals could be. Sure, they had their quirks and their absurd demands. All parents do, and kids abide if only to get them off their backs. But my daily life was fine and uneventful. There was very little to escape.

The thing was, we were Jewish. Irreligious and miscreant, as expected in a household headed by Freudian analysts, but Jewish nonetheless. My dad was from Israel, a foreigner, an immigrant, a stranger in a strange land. There was no stigma or overt racism attached to that, especially in our rarefied, cosmopolitan milieu. But still, I had a funny name, and I looked just a tad too Mediterranean not to stand out. Every time a teacher or one of my friends' moms garbled my name or asked me to spell it out loud, even with the best of intentions, I was reminded that in their eyes I was not from here.

This may sound inconsequential to grown-ups, but kids do not take words lightly, and they are logical to a fault. So if my name raised eyebrows repeatedly and consistently among a wide sample of the natives, then it followed logically that my name was indeed odd and foreign. And if my name got such treatment, then what about all the rest? The accumulation of minuscule slights is quite an education. It warps you as surely as direct, frontal assaults of bigotry. From that experience, you grow with two demonstrably true yet contradictory realities: I am and I am not from here, this is and is not my hometown, this is and is not my culture or my country.

To me, diving headfirst into *Star Trek* and science fiction was the opposite of an escape. It was a revenge fantasy, the kind that kids and members of minority groups tell themselves to cope with the complete unfairness of the world. Thanks to science fiction I could renounce my French citizenship in all but the paperwork. I had pledged my allegiance to the future. Origins, skin color, the shape of your ears, none of that stuff mattered on the bridge of the *Enterprise*. Only your brains and your talent. Country? Pfff. There were no countries in *Star Trek* or Asimov! Outdated and irrelevant, a barbaric idea and a temporary annoyance. Besides, I was not from here, I was from the future, and it was an immeasurably better place. So it did not exist, so what? Neither did the place of my supposed foreign origin, the one unwittingly ascribed to me by the casual and ordinary racism of the locals. At least the future was a place of my own choosing. It was the land of imagination.

From the get-go, fandom was a refuge, a way to deal with the anxiety of not fitting in, of growing up ever-so-slightly different. I can only assume it is a rather common occurrence. But fandom was definitely not a social activity or a way to make new friends. These were the early eighties, I was in France, science fiction was completely marginal. Beyond *Star Wars*, kids my age couldn't care less, and my parents sneered at it.

The only other person I knew who was a fan was Dina, and she was a mystery to me. Because of the tattoo on her forearm, I had an inkling that she had survived the war and the camps, but I did not know the specifics. I knew about the tattoos because my grandfather had one, too (although he was not a science-fiction fan at all).

She was from Budapest, that I knew. She spoke several languages and seemed to be well read in all of them. She laughed a lot. She had a crystalline, generous, innocent laughter. Every time she would come to dinner at our place, she would bring new books for me.

Much later she told me more about her life. You see, she was of a different breed than you and me. She was a superhero, a true one, not some ridiculous comic-book invention.

By birth she was a member of that strange tribe, the Hungarian Jews. No community of a comparable, minuscule size had nurtured more Nobel Prize recipients and giants of the arts and sciences than the prewar Budapest Jewry. It is an oddity that so much of the modern world, from the atom bomb to astronautics and game theory to modern computing, would be the brainchild of so few people.

Dina was only a therapist. She had not brought about the nuclear age nor had she broken new artistic ground, but she definitely shared the same otherworldly will to live and intelligence as her fellow Hungarians. She had survived the war in Budapest and Auschwitz as a teenager. She had been a nurse on the front lines during Israel's War of Independence. She had lived in the United States for a while, and then had settled in France. Amid all that commotion, she had found the time and the energy to read everything and to become a psychoanalyst. As far as life goes, it doesn't get any more hard-core than hers.

That does not explain why she was such a fan of science fiction or what had led her to it. Science fiction alone could not have righted the wrongs she had suffered, nor could it have made them disappear. What kind of hope or wisdom did someone of such high culture, a Holocaust survivor, find in *Star Trek*?

I have very little to go on. Maybe it was not about hope at all. She passed away a long time ago, and I never got a chance to ask her. This book, concerned as it is with the economics of a fictional better world, is also and above all a belated meditation on that unanswerable question.

CHAPTER 1

"...MONEY WENT THE WAY OF THE DINOSAURS"[3]

THE ABSENCE OF MONEY IN STAR TREK

Kirk, Spock, McCoy, and the gang are flying back to Earth from planet Vulcan aboard a clunky Klingon bird-of-prey. They are to face a Starfleet court-martial for disregarding orders and destroying the *Enterprise* in their quest to rescue Spock in the previous movie. Upon approaching sector 01, aka the solar system, they pick up a distress signal from Earth on all frequencies. A mysterious alien probe is disrupting the planet's power grid and is slowly vaporizing its oceans by emitting an incredibly powerful electromagnetic pulse.

Spock gets to work at the science console and quickly realizes that the probe is in fact broadcasting some kind of distorted cosmic whale chant in an attempt to contact the local humpbacks. The only problem

---

3.   *ST:VOY*, 5x15: "Dark Frontier, Part I."

is that humpback whales had been hunted to extinction a couple of centuries back, and as a result there is no cetacean to answer the call from outer space. *Presto*, the *Enterprise* crew undertakes time-warp travel to 1985 San Francisco in search of a few specimens in order to save twenty-third-century Earth from destruction.

That is the premise of *Star Trek IV: The Voyage Home*. It has no villain to speak of, no space battle of any kind, and very little of the usual *Star Trek* technobabble. It is quite literally a fish (or rather, a cetacean) out of water comedy. Dropped among the barbarians—us—Kirk and the crew are befuddled, disoriented, and borderline impotent. And to top it all off, they are specifically forbidden to use most of their formidable powers lest they fatally alter the course of human history. *The Voyage Home* is a modern-day version of *Gulliver's Travels*. It reinvents the old Enlightenment trope of the well-meaning explorer who must grapple with the idiosyncrasies of the not-so-exotic tribes he encounters. Our society's mores are examined under the prodding gaze of beloved fictional twenty-third-century characters. The story gives us a chance to discover how Kirk, Spock, McCoy, and the others really see us. Or, rather, how we see our own world through the eyes of our better, wiser, and more technologically and socially advanced selves.

Following Kirk and Spock, we meet Dr. Gillian Taylor, a young marine biologist who takes care of the humpbacks at the fictional Sausalito Ocean Institute. They catch her at a particularly fraught moment: because of lack of funds, the two whales are about to be released into the wild, and one of them is pregnant. From then on, Gillian holds the audience's hands and stands as our stunt double and our advocate. She comes across as a lovable loser: a smart, honest, and passionate scientist backed into a corner by the blindness and ignorance of her contemporaries. In real life, she would be a *Star Trek* fan herself.

She strikes up a friendship with the two strangers, who eagerly volunteer their help to save her whales. She is weary of empty promises; she has had her share of bitter disappointments. Understandably, she has a hard time taking Kirk and Spock seriously. After all, they are a piece of work. They seem to be living in Golden Gate Park (where they previously landed their cloaked ship), and Spock wears a white robe and a bandeau to disguise his alien, pointy ears, and he speaks and acts like a weirdo. In not so many words: losers, broken by life, just like her.

Gillian takes Kirk out to dinner at an Italian restaurant. James Tiberius turns on the trademark charm he usually lavishes upon unsuspecting alien females. He desperately needs to convince her to let him take the whales. He goes so far as to break the Prime Directive and tells Gillian the whole truth: that he is a space captain from the future and that he must bring back the humpbacks to the twenty-third century in order to save the world once again. Yet, when the time comes to pick up the tab, it turns out that the captain, however chivalrous (or smarmy, depending on your appreciation of Shatner's acting chops), is just another intergalactic bum. "Don't tell me, they don't use money in the twenty-third century?"[4]

Indeed we don't. Cue the grins.

FEDERATION CREDITS

This is great fodder for comedy. It also happens to mark an epistemic turn in the *Star Trek* canon. After *ST IV: The Voyage Home*, the absence of money in the future becomes a cornerstone of the *Star Trek* universe. This is the pivot point when the *Star Trek* franchise, at the tail end of the Reagan years and the Cold War, becomes truly utopian. It

---

4.   *Star Trek IV: The Voyage Home.*

may play for laughs in the film to go along with its jocular Swiftian vibe, but it is no laughing matter. Here are characters from a most revered science-fiction franchise, a mainstay of prime-time TV syndication and an icon of popular culture, casually mentioning that, yes, in the future, free-market capitalism and its hallmark, money, have been discarded and consigned to the history books as bizarre and somewhat retrograde customs.

It was not always so. *The Original Series* is rife with allusions to currency and currency-based dealings. The original *Enterprise* crew members are paid their monthly salaries in Federation credits and have the opportunity to spend their pay at various ports of call and star bases. They can buy Romulan ale at bars across the galaxy, and even, sometimes, troublesome furry little pets called Tribbles.

This rather inconvenient inconsistency in the *Star Trek* canon remained unresolved until a short acerbic scene in the sixth season of *Deep Space Nine*. Jake Sisko, the son of the station's commander, announces that he just sold his first book to the Federation News Service. Quark, the genial Ferengi bar owner and businessman, inquires how much Jake is getting paid. Jake replies that "it's just a figure of speech."[5] This is the mother of all "retcons" for the *Star Trek* universe—nerd speak for the act of retroactively restoring the continuity between pre- and post-*ST IV: The Voyage Home*. That benign piece of dialogue turns into "figures of speech" all prior mentions of finances, crew wages, currency, and Federation credits in the movies and *The Original Series*.

If "Federation credits" sounds like a fairly generic term for an interstellar currency unit, that's because it is. It appears to be the coinage of choice in the various *Star Wars* movies—in the cantina, Luke and Obi-Wan Kenobi offer Han Solo "credits" for smuggling them

5.   *ST:DS9*, 6x07: "You Are Cordially Invited."

onto the *Millennium Falcon.* "Credits" are similarly used by Arnold Schwarzenegger in *Total Recall.* Business on J. Michael Straczynski's *Babylon 5* is conducted in Earth Alliance Credits. Credits feature prominently in many of Isaac Asimov's novels, including the Foundation trilogy (whose main protagonist, fortuitously, is none other than galaxy-wide economics). The term itself suggests united political entities: the Federation, the Earth Alliance, this or that galactic Empire. At the same time it has an almost placeholder-like quality, as if nobody had really bothered to give it enough thought, even though real-world currency designations are loaded with deep historical and economic meaning. A good chunk of the origins and transformations of the United States are encapsulated in the word *dollar* itself. The word comes from the Spanish word for *Thaler,* the silver currency of Germany from the Renaissance all the way to World War I, by way of the Czech *Tolar* and the Dutch *Daalder.* In light of the painstaking detail work that goes into creating speculative civilizations, calling their currencies "credit" is rather anticlimactic. All these intricate technologies, these swashbuckling heroes, these elaborate political intrigues and operatic confrontations, and the only name one finds for money is the good old run-of-the-mill "credit"? If anything, it betrays a distinct lack of inquisitiveness about how economic forces shape these hypothetical civilizations.

The widespread use of the term *credit* in classic science fiction acts as a useful reminder of *Star Trek's* extraordinary boldness, especially given its unique status in popular culture. Money in science fiction is truly everywhere, just like in the real world. Its existence is seldom questioned or put in play as it is by *Star Trek* after *ST IV: The Voyage Home.*

NO MONEY, NO PROBLEM

The Next Generation fully embraced and even doubled down on what seemed like a few funny scenes and throwaway quips in *ST IV: The Voyage Home*. In the last episode of *The Next Generation*'s inaugural season, the *Enterprise* chances upon a ship adrift in deep space that carries people from the late twentieth century. They were put in cryogenic suspension at the time of their deaths, in the hope that future medicine could cure them of their ailments. Among them we meet a certain Ralph Offenhouse. Maurice Hurley's shooting script sums him up tersely as "a power broker on both coasts."[6] The episode aired in March 1988, a few short months after the release of Oliver Stone's *Wall Street* and the stock market crash of October 1987. Offenhouse is *Star Trek*'s take on Gordon Gekko and all that he stands for. Offenhouse immediately inquires about how to contact his law firm and blusters about the size of his portfolio, which must have grown to even grander proportions during the time he spent frozen in space. Greed is good, indeed.

Toward the end of the show, Picard gives the blowhard the dressing-down he so richly deserves. The captain's retort would have sounded stilted and self-righteous if not for Patrick Stewart's haunting performance. He manages to pack his lines with both spite and compassion in a riveting, devastating scene: "People are no longer obsessed with the accumulation of things. We've eliminated hunger, want, the need for possessions. We've grown out of our infancy."[7] Later in the episode, a chastened Gordon Gekko / Offenhouse says to the captain: "There

---

6. Maurice Hurley, "The Neutral Zone" (unpublished script, 2nd rev. final draft, March 17, 1988), Text file, accessed March 2, 2016, p. 19.

7. *ST:TNG*, 1x26: "The Neutral Zone."

is no trace of my money. My office is gone. What will I do? How will I live?"

> PICARD: This is the twenty-fourth century. Material needs no longer exist.
> OFFENHOUSE: Then what's the challenge?
> PICARD: The challenge, Mr. Offenhouse, is to improve yourself. To enrich yourself. Enjoy it.

Picard reiterated the notion even more forcefully several years later, in *ST: First Contact* (which, like *ST IV: The Voyage Home*, is an excellent time-travel romp). Lily Sloane, the twenty-first-century engineer who helped Zefram Cochrane build the first warp-capable ship, is stranded with Picard on the Borg-infested *Enterprise*. She marvels at the *Galaxy*-class ship's size: "How much does this cost?"

> PICARD: The economics of the future is somewhat different. You see, money doesn't exist in the twenty-fourth century.
> LILY: No money? You mean you don't get paid?
> PICARD: The acquisition of wealth is no longer the driving force in our lives. We work to better ourselves and the rest of humanity.[8]

The pithy dialogue, penned by *Next Generation* regulars Brannon Braga and Ron Moore, is one of the most direct and cogent articulations of trekonomics I can think of. In a few short sentences, money, markets, and the profit motive—basically, the building blocks of our everyday lives—are thrown out the air lock. It falls on Patrick Stewart's acting witchcraft to make it all true.

---

8.   *Star Trek: First Contact.*

Make no mistake. To forgo money is no small feat. It means for-going one of the single most useful instruments of civilization. The substitute should not only be worth it, but orders of magnitude better.

Money is the universal translator for things. Money acts as a medium: it allows us to exchange goods that are not commensurate; that is, it puts a numerical value on objects that would otherwise be very difficult to trade in a fair and predictable fashion. Money is also the instrument of choice for setting prices: a universal mathematical tool to express and resolve imbalances between supply and demand. If there is not enough dilithium—the exotic material that helps power *Star Trek*'s warp engines—and too many apples, purchasing dilithium will require considerably more apples (as expressed in currency).

Money's defining advantage is to free us from the inefficiency of bartering. Try to exchange your shipment of apples for a pound of dilithium crystals. It won't work. Your dilithium dealer does not have a use for all your apples, and besides, you can't harvest and deliver that many apples anyway. On top of that, you're stuck if apples are the only thing you have to barter. And what if you have too many? What do you do with the leftovers?

Now consider selling all your apples for cash. Better still: consider selling your five future harvests in advance, even at a discount, to a galactic apple distributor. You end up with a large sum in hand: you can use a portion of that sum to purchase dilithium, and you can spend the rest on some well-deserved Klingon bloodwine or Romulan ale.

In a way, money is the only proven method to transmute apples into dilithium and lead into gold, and back. Why bother with alchemy when you have coinage? In fact, money is so useful that it is not a stretch to hail it as one of humanity's most fundamental technological breakthroughs. No wonder it arose in the first great trading empires of the Fertile Crescent, alongside writing and mathematics. To wit: the oldest cuneiform clay tablets are mostly accounting records.

That being said, money, like any other technology, is not exempt from shortcomings or the occasional massive failure. In the most extreme cases, it has been known to provoke society-wide collapses through hyperinflation and financial bubbles. Under more quotidian conditions, money tends to foster a whole range of irrational, vulgar, and unpalatable behaviors among our fellow humans. Until further notice, these inconveniences seem like an acceptable trade-off because money excels at one crucial function. Through the market-pricing mechanism, money provides an adequate solution to the distribution and allocation of scarce goods.

The *Star Trek* canon makes it clear that scarcity is no longer an issue in the twenty-fourth century. The Federation does not need money. It is an a-numismatic society (to coin a neologism), because everything is so plentiful that nobody has to pay for anything. In the Federation, goods, food, labor, medical care, education, entertainment, space travel, and whatever else you can think of are like MasterCard: priceless.

How does this actually work?

First, save for the alien Ferengi Alliance, money and wealth are not prominent preoccupations of other notable *Star Trek* civilizations of the Alpha Quadrant. Klingons seem to use it,[9] but it is undeniable that their value system revolves around very abstract norms. Cardassia is a bureaucratic dictatorship not dissimilar to Soviet Russia, and the Romulan Star Empire is an enigma. As for the major villains, the Dominion and the Borg, it is pretty obvious that they are not animated by the advancement of their mercantile interests.

The allocation of goods is never really addressed in the series or the movies. It seems that sheer abundance resolves most potential

---

9.   See Quark's marriage to a Klingon aristocrat in *ST:DS9*, 3x03: "The House of Quark."

distributive problems. There is so much of everything in the Federation that, in the unlikely event that the supply of goods or a commodity runs low, there will always be plenty of substitutes available. As a result, you're just not as hung up on getting what you want right now, at the best price possible. As a system, trekonomics is predicated on near-absolute abundance, which in turn negates the need for money or market-pricing mechanisms to allocate scarce goods. Nothing—or almost nothing—is scarce.

AIN'T NOTHING LIKE THE REAL THING

Near-absolute abundance leaves a few scarce items to deal with at the margins. What are they, and how are they allocated?

The *Star Trek* canon allows us to infer that there are two types of scarce goods in the Federation. In classical economic terms, their supply is deemed inelastic—their availability is largely unresponsive to changes in price. On the one hand, there are what could be termed strategic goods, those few resources that are essential to maintaining the Federation's polity and way of life: dilithium crystals, starships, and people. On the other hand, there is a broad category of one-of-a-kind, custom-made, unique goods: mostly experiential goods and services, such as the Picard family's Bordeaux wine, the pleasure planet Risa,[10] and Sisko's restaurant in New Orleans.

In the absence of money, and therefore market and price, how do you get a highly coveted spot for a stay on Risa? Or how do you secure a few bottles of Château Picard? Is it first come, first served? Do

---

10. Risa is the backdrop of several episodes in the franchise. These consist of *ST:TNG*, 3x19: "Captain's Holiday"; *ST:DS9*, 5x07: "Let He Who Is Without Sin . . ."; and *ST:ENT*, 1x25: "Two Days and Two Nights."

family connections and social networks, such as *blat* in the old Soviet Union, or *guanxi* in China, have a place in the twenty-fourth century? Do Starfleet officers get to jump in front of the line for *jamaharon*? In other words, how does society manage the allocation of those few marginally scarce goods?

The canon is rather vague on that specific topic. You never see people fighting each other over the last bottle of Château Picard. These kinds of petty conflicts are never shown—not just because petty conflicts among Federation members are never, ever shown in *Star Trek*, but also because luxury shoppers' angst is not good TV (*Keeping Up with Lwaxana Troi*, or *Real Housewives of Risa*—that ain't happening). One must assume that the scarcity of some unique goods never leads to conflict or competition. The motivation for acquiring them—showing off social status through the ownership of objects—has long been excised from the Federation.

In our less advanced society, we mainly acquire and consume luxuries to display status and wealth: this is what sociologist Thorstein Veblen described as "conspicuous consumption."[11] Consider the car. Not everyone can afford a BMW, and nobody would bother to try, if it were not for the purpose of showing off.

All indications are that trekonomics has successfully done away with conspicuous consumption. High-minded and altruistic Federation citizens could not care less about signaling their status through the consumption of luxuries. In the Federation, nobody cares about your Louis Vuitton bag or your Beamer. And nobody would really bother keeping up with you. In that sense, the relative absence of scarcity is also a function of individuals' choices and overall ethics. If you can't get that last bottle of Château Picard 2378, so be it, no big deal. It's almost

---

11. Thorstein Veblen, *The Theory of the Leisure Class* (New York: B.W. Huebsch, 1924).

as if the absence of money leads to the absence of scarcity in the case of nonessential, nonstrategic items.

For these goods that are unique and scarce by nature (Château Picard, seats at Sisko's restaurant), people are just not keyed up at the prospect of showing off—nobody gives a crap, and therefore these unique goods lose their appeal as positional status symbols. One could say that even in the case of supply constraints, demand is simply not there. It's just not that big of a deal. Furthermore, and lastly, there is an infinite supply of potential substitutes at the same price—that is, zero. This is what economists describe as "local nonsatiation." Can't get this year's vintage of Château Picard for your cellar? Just go crazy and get some of that fine Klingon bloodwine from Lieutenant Worf's family estates instead.

In trekonomics, the absence of money implies that status is not tied to economic wealth and discretionary spending. Conspicuous consumption and luxury have lost their grip on people's imaginations. The opposition between plenty and scarcity, which under our current conditions determines a large cross section of prices and purchasing behaviors, is no longer relevant.

For Federation citizens, the notion of luxury itself has evolved to encompass the full range of experiences available to humanoids. It is possible to envision that people seek the unique and the memorable in personal relationships and in fleeting moments of satori, rather than in the acquisition of things. Looking for and collecting artful artifacts, ancient or otherwise, seems to be among the few areas where one can exert her erudition and flaunt her good taste.

EVERYONE'S LOT HAS BEEN TERMINALLY IMPROVED

What of strategic, nonreplicable goods? The main thing here is dilithium crystals—although the model could apply to other similar items. While supply is constrained, it is not nearly as constrained as one might think. It bears repeating that labor, prospecting, and extraction technologies are close to free. As a result, even the most marginal and hard-to-reach deposits become available because the cost of exploiting them stays very close to the baseline, zero.

So what if there are not enough people willing to spend some quality time on a mining asteroid? This is where ethics comes into play. The deeply ingrained civic sense of every Federation member leads enough of them to respond to the call of duty. As Spock would say: "The needs of the many outweigh the needs of the few."[12] These are not idle words. People are ready to die for this noble principle. And if push comes to shove, the 675 discarded Emergency Medical Hologram Mark 1s will do the trick.[13]

Ultimately, the galaxy is so vast that there is no chance of peak dilithium. The only limit to dilithium mining is political (those rogue, disputed planetoids in the Cardassian badlands). On top of that, given the Federation's highly advanced scientific community, it is not inconceivable that the Daystrom Institute's staff would come up with a substitute at some point.

No scarcity means no money, no price, and no markets. This also implies that in trekonomics' society, the profit motive does not exist. This is particularly galling. How do things get done in most situations, when urgent appeals to civic duty are not required? Why would people invent and invest without the expectation of a material reward? And,

---

12. *Star Trek II: The Wrath of Khan.*

13. *ST:VOY*, 7x20: "Author, Author."

more fundamentally, how do people make decisions about their lives, either present or future, in the absence of money? How do they assess their options and measure the outcome of their decisions without an objective and quantifiable unit of account? It takes a real leap of the imagination, even for the early twenty-first-century die-hard *Star Trek* fan, to conceive of such a world, consumed as we all are by the pursuit of our own self-interest.

Logic would dictate that near-absolute abundance has driven prices to zero on all but a few strategic goods. These strategic goods are of limited use for most people anyway. I do not need a big chunk of dilithium crystals in the course of my everyday life. Matter-antimatter power plants require it, whether on board starships or on the ground, but not me. I am not in the market for it, society as a whole is.

For the rest of the stuff, the overwhelming majority of goods and services, any improvement or invention I may come up with will cost essentially nothing to produce and distribute. And even if it does, since the price of everything else is zero, chances are I will not be able to extract much for my new gizmo until its price is competitive with the rest of the marketplace, i.e., zero. A final price equal to zero considerably curtails the reward expectations for the risk I took and my opportunity cost for focusing on making that particular gizmo, instead of going with the flow and enjoying my life.

It goes even further than that: economics tells us that the aggregation of all the actors' self-interested actions in the marketplace leads to growth and material improvement for all. Individuals and firms, by constantly seeking profits, tend to lower prices to gain market share. Competition leads to innovation, and innovation leads to substitution. Better and more things at a lower price. Of course, a strong legal framework is necessary to thwart those who try to bend the rules to their advantage. For example, laws exist to hinder monopolists, firms that have achieved such market dominance that they are no longer forced to lower their final prices, because of the lack of competing alternatives.

The sum of all the greed and self-interest in the world is supposed to turn positive, not just because it is ultimately a benefit to all but also because it keeps the system in a state of dynamic equilibrium. It is akin to a person walking: each step requires one to lose balance temporarily, but the overall result is upright and steady forward movement.

According to the optimistic philosophy of Adam Smith and his successors, competition in the marketplace turns private vice into a public virtue. A competitive market tends to allocate goods, resources, and labor efficiently. It may not seem like it—that's the whole point— but greed is indeed good. This is the ideal theory. In practice, that ideal conceals a potentially fatal flaw that we will explore later. For now, we will just notice that the ideal world of economics is not that far apart from the ideal world of trekonomics. Economics assumes that left to their own devices (and with a sprinkling of legal boundaries and tax incentives here and there), individuals and firms will make decisions based on their perceived optimal self-interest. These individuals and firms, by virtue of competing and conflicting with each other, will make more things available at a constantly declining price, thus improving the lot of everyone on average.

Trekonomics, for its part, assumes that the lot of everyone, on average, has been terminally improved. There is nothing left to optimize, economically speaking, when everything is available at zero cost. Self-interest, conflict, and competition may certainly exist, but the reward for winning in the marketplace cannot be monetary because there is no excess return to expect or gain. The reward is of an intangible but no less real nature: glory.

REPUTATION AS CURRENCY

If the reward for winning in the marketplace consists of merit, prestige, and recognition, then self-interest will drive at least some individuals to excel at their trade and to shoot for the moon in their endeavors. The product of their combined labor will be available to all at no cost. The benefits of countless strokes of genius will freely accrue to society. Think for a minute of Dr. Lewis Zimmerman, the inventor of the Emergency Medical Hologram. He is the epitome of the insufferable pompous ass, even more so because his contribution to the world is very real—tangible and useful in the extreme. His EMH programs, made in his likeness, can bring a physician into every home, however remote. The EMH already delivers babies, saves lives, and annoys the crew on *Voyager* week in and week out. Dr. Zimmerman has certainly earned the right to be prickly. He also sought it with all his talent and energy. Do not underestimate the power of vanity.

In the Federation, type A scientists, engineers, artists, and Starfleet officers compete for excellence. Prestige and awards are a form of social currency. They are pursued and accumulated over a lifetime, just like savings. They even get passed on to children in the form of societal pressure to live up to their famous parents' achievements. Just like his father, young Wesley Crusher is expected to become an amazing starship captain himself. Your currency is your good name, and what is attached to it gets passed down to your offspring.

The main advantage of a reputational currency is that even if you trade it for favors, the total amount you control rarely decreases (unless you abuse your position and the goodwill it commands by requesting too much *jamaharon*). You can never go broke or even get into too much debt. You retain all your earnings. If you are a scientist, there is a strong disincentive to lose it all by turning into a global-warming denier or an antivaccine crusader. There is nobody with ulterior motives to subsidize your fake science. And the institutions of science themselves are very good at adjudicating the validity of a theory or the effectiveness of an invention. Science, as a collective enterprise, certainly makes a lot of mistakes. However, over time it has developed much better procedures than most other institutions to investigate and correct these mistakes. As a Federation scientist, the value of your reputation is backed by the full faith and credit of the scientific community.

Dr. Noonien Soong, Data's creator, is a good example. He worked for decades in the secrecy of his faraway outpost to build the most perfect android. He did not plan to release a half-baked prototype product and to "iterate" it (as people say in Silicon Valley). He did not seek patents or royalties or to turn his invention into a mass-market protocol droid. The glory of being the greatest roboticist that ever lived and humiliating all his colleagues and competitors is the highest possible reward for his work, besides Data's existence and shining personality. His enduring fame is all his.

It is very likely that science serves as a model for most other domains of activity in the Federation—but with varying degrees and standards for objective judgment. Starfleet may apply a very different logic to bestowing reputational currency upon its members than the Vulcan Science Academy or the Aldebaran Music Academy. In the same vein, restaurants and wine are deadly serious matters, but cannot be rated according to the same objective criteria as warp-field theory applications or positronic architecture. In the arts, culinary or otherwise, reputation is built on the subjective judgment of the public and of the other specialist-practitioners, since there are no aristocratic patrons or wealthy collectors to cultivate.

There are no starving poets in the Federation. With self-expression being highly valued and respected, anybody can write and publish a holonovel. Even a self-aware holographic program can be an author! There is very minimal gatekeeping since publishers themselves do not have to make decisions based on the purported commercial viability of any work of the imagination. Distribution and production costs are nil. Public response from the masses and from the specialist community is ultimately what will earn you your reputation as an artist. You know you've got it made if your holonovel goes viral, even if it's for all the wrong reasons.

The competition between all these high achievers is never petty nor impolite. But that does not mean that it is not merciless. Your rivals are always on the prowl, ready to pounce at the first misstep. Each challenge successfully repelled earns you more reputation, until you fail and stall. This Darwinian honing and pruning of talent is both thankless and extremely productive. It is the engine for the Federation's growth and power. It is the reason why the Federation produces the best scientists and engineers and doctors and artists in the galaxy. Yet there can be only one number one roboticist or warp-field theorist in the whole Federation. That is the greatest of all prizes. And the odds are overwhelmingly stacked against you becoming that person. Being Vulcan might marginally improve your chances, but not by much. If, by an extraordinary set of coincidences, you still end up at the pinnacle of the apex of your chosen field, don't worry. It won't last. There are too many talented kids out there looking to maul you and sweep you from your throne.

This picture of the Federation reminds me of an old friend, himself a Trekker. He graduated from the best math program in the world at age eighteen, earned a doctorate from the other best math program in the world four short years later. If I ever met someone who fit the definition of genius, that is him. He explained to me very matter-of-factly that, like the Beatles, mathematicians usually do their greatest work by the time they reach thirty. As brilliant and precocious as he was, he would never come close to the top of his profession. He was neither sad nor angry about it. It was just the cold, hard, objective truth. Equality in law and in opportunity seldom results in equality in fact. Mathematics is believed to be the most meritocratic of all scientific disciplines. No gimmicks, no machines, no labs, no outside funding, very little politics. It's just you and a blackboard. Diplomas, academic position, and fame do not matter. Either you prove Fermat's theorem or Poincaré's conjecture, or you don't. Pure meritocracy can be very cruel.

THE BURDEN OF PRIVATE OWNERSHIP

Even though there is no currency in the Federation, it does not mean that there is no capital per se. Capital exists independently of mere accounting units. This may sound somewhat paradoxical, but it is in fact obvious. Think of it as matter: whether in solid phase or liquid or gaseous, matter exists independently of the units we use to measure it.

Capital is one of the inputs of economic production. Combine raw materials with labor, and you'll get nothing without tools, accumulated knowledge, and sometimes money. At a very basic level, capital is just that, the productive assets, material and immaterial, that allow labor to transform natural resources into finished products. For instance, a caveman must use a hard rock and his experience to shape a biface. The rock and his knowledge constitute the capital stock he uses to make the stone blade. The value of his knowledge and his tools is probably measured in the woolly mammoth meat he can obtain in exchange for his labor and craft. His capital does not have a numerical or nummary value, but it nonetheless has a value, if only in the sustenance he gets out of putting it to productive use. Yet this is another case where money proves superior: it protects the blade carver from the whims of the mammoth hunters, it allows him to say, "This my price, I won't accept any less meat in exchange for the product of my work."

Part of the confusion between money and capital probably stems from the fact that we have become accustomed to quantifying capital in monetary units. It is incredibly useful: the reduction into numbers allows for all sorts of mathematical measurements and calculations, which in turn enable better, more optimal decisions. But it tends to obscure the fact that capital does not consist exclusively of monetary inputs.

If you remove money from the equation, you still have tools, machines, and knowledge. These are all products of human ingenuity and work, culled from nature and shaped by humans. Money is but one form of capital, there to ease exchange, credit, accounting, and occasionally the payment of wages (in the case of a wage-based economy).

The other source of confusion is ownership. In the case of the Federation, ownership takes on a slightly different meaning than in today's world. It is not because the Federation does not use money as an input or as a unit of account, but because capital, whether in the form of tools or machines or in the form of education and talent, does not yield any exchangeable value. You may own a replicator unit in your home, but you did not purchase it and you do not use it to make gizmos that you will sell to other folks at a premium on the interstellar version of Etsy. The replicator does not save you money nor does it make you money. You do not derive any excess wealth from the ownership of your home replicator.

Conversely, suppose you are the only person to own and operate an industrial replicator on your faraway outpost. There is no point in charging other people money for its usage, because there is no money. You may decide to restrict access to your replicator unless you get paid in kind. Well, first of all, why would you do that? It's just not really how we roll in the Federation. You would probably lose your replicator by court order.

Since there is no way to benefit from your replicator, chances are you don't really want to own it in the first place. Your ownership means in fact that you are responsible for its operation and maintenance. It is a burden to you and a service to the community. In addition, you must use your knowledge, your capital, to maintain the contraption. In that specific case, private ownership of capital (the replicator) implies service more than anything else. It is a cost to you, if only in time. It may provide you with marginal reputational gains, but it might not seem like an optimal way to allocate your capital. You probably have better things to do than trying to corner the market on industrial replication. In trekonomics, market dominance or monopoly over a given good or service cannot translate into pricing power and outsized returns. Abundance has replaced scarcity as the baseline. Procuring consumer staples is a trivial matter. That is why, in many instances, it may seem rather illogical and inefficient to take the weight of property on your sole shoulders.

It seems that private property in *Star Trek* is above all sentimental. The Picards' family home in the picturesque French countryside offers a good example of what ownership can mean in trekonomics.[14] Jean-Luc Picard's older brother Robert continues the family legacy of wine making. The house and the vineyard are not objects of speculation or repositories for wealth. They are heirlooms to be carefully tended. Their value is subjective and symbolic.

---

14. See *ST:TNG*, 4x02: "Family."

Economics, the science and the everyday behaviors, is all about choices. How do we make choices as individuals and as groups, as populations, as societies? And, even more pointedly, how do we make the best choices? More specifically, how do we get the most pleasurable outcome from a situation where scarcity, other people, and incomplete information limit our choices? It is a refinement of Jeremy Bentham's formulation of utilitarianism, the idea that all humans tend to gravitate toward what makes them happy, and to stay away from what hurts them.

On that account, trekonomics could be seen as the highest form of utilitarianism. The Federation is organized in such a way that every one of its citizens gets a chance to maximize his or her own utility. Since almost nothing is scarce, the necessity to make choices on budgeting and spending is removed from everyday life. The only thing that one really needs to decide upon is how to balance the goal of bettering oneself vis-à-vis the injunction to better humanity. In other words, the biggest challenge for every Federation citizen resides in how to allocate his or her talents, time, and capacity for empathy, and how to best contribute to the common wealth.

CHAPTER 2

"...WHY IS EVERYONE SO WORRIED ABOUT HOLOGRAMS TAKING OVER THE UNIVERSE?"[15]

THE MEANING OF WORK IN STAR TREK'S SOCIETY

Nog, the nephew of Quark, the Ferengi bar owner on Deep Space Nine, has decided to join Starfleet. No Ferengi has ever been admitted to Starfleet Academy. He goes to Captain Sisko to request a letter of recommendation. At first, the captain is taken aback. He is highly suspicious of the young Ferengi's motives. His species is feared and loathed around the galaxy for its ruthless entrepreneurial drive and shady business practices. Heroism, enlightened ethics, and self-sacrifice are not the first things that come to mind when thinking of the Ferengis. Besides, Nog is the space station's resident juvenile delinquent. He is not an assiduous student at school, and he has had several run-ins with

15. *ST:DS9*, 5x16: "Doctor Bashir, I Presume."

the law. The captain would know, as Nog and his own son Jake are best friends. Nog does not help his case by presenting Sisko with a hefty bag of gold-pressed latinum "as a token of [his] appreciation."[16] The faux pas is a tragic cultural misunderstanding. When young Ferengis come of age, they are supposed to purchase an apprenticeship from a weathered elder who will teach them the ropes and initiate them in the ways of the Great Material Continuum, while duly exploiting them as a matter of course. To all but a Ferengi, Nog's offering of his lifetime savings comes across as an undisguised bribe.

Despite the ill-advised attempt at a *bakchich*, Sisko is intrigued by Nog's request. With the help of Jadzia Dax, his trusted science officer, he decides to test the kid's resolve. They instruct Nog to take inventory of Cargo Bay 12, where Starfleet stores a lot of "very valuable" supplies.

Nog passes with flying colors. He completes his assignment in record time. To Sisko's relief, it appears that Nog has not stolen anything. On the contrary, he managed to locate items that had escaped the scrutiny of Starfleet officers during previous inspections. Nog has not only demonstrated his work ethic to Sisko and Dax, but also his honesty.

"He is a hard worker," concludes Sisko. But what of his true reasons? Why Starfleet? After all, nothing could be further from the Federation's ideals than the Ferengi way of life, enshrined in the almost three hundred Rules of Acquisition. Sisko confronts Nog. He announces to him that he will not write the recommendation because it looks like "another one of [Nog's] schemes."

Angry and crestfallen, Nog finally gives away the truth in an impassioned plea that, in turn, reveals considerably more about both his character and the circumstances he finds himself in. It is one of these perfect *Star Trek* moments where the writing and the acting coalesce

---

16. *ST:DS9*, 3x14: "Heart of Stone."

into a scene much greater in emotion and significance than the sum of its parts.

"I don't want to end up like my father! My father is a mechanical genius. He could've been the chief engineer of a starship if he'd had the opportunity. But he went into business like a good Ferengi. The only thing is, he's not a good Ferengi . . . not when it comes to acquiring profit. So now all he has to live for is the slim chance that someday, somehow, he might be able to take over my uncle's bar. Well, I'm not going to make the same mistake. I want to do something with my life . . . something worthwhile."[17]

The cultural norms of Ferengi society impose terrible constraints. Ferengi males (and males only) are expected to go into business and to seek profits all their lives, whether or not they like it or "have the lobes" for it, an innate talent for the acquisition of wealth. Those who don't, like Nog's father, Rom, are relegated to working in meaningless obscurity, enriching their bosses under the comically exploitative terms of Ferengi employment contracts.[18] Besides the soul-crushing toll it exacts on individuals, such blind deference to Ferengi tradition amounts to gross economic malpractice.

Nog is right about his father. The "idiot brother," as Quark affectionately calls his sibling, truly *is* an engineering genius. He single-handedly invents the self-replicating cloaked minefield that delays the Dominion's invasion of the Alpha Quadrant.[19] Ferengi society, because of its strictures and its obsession with profits, cannot recognize nor make any use of Rom's genius. This complete waste of talent is also a waste of opportunity. One would expect better in the way of humanoid

17. Ibid.

18. For more on that, see *ST:DS9*, 4x16: "The Bar Association."

19. *ST:DS9*, 5x26: "A Call to Arms."

resources management from a species that prides itself on its business acumen.

THE MEANING OF WORK

By contrast, the Federation offers the promise of finding one's true calling, free of the shackles of tradition and economic necessity. A "mechanical genius," a mad scientist, a cook, a writer, even a young Ferengi ne'er-do-well—all will get a chance to find a role commensurate with their talents, if not their hopes. The Federation does not require anyone to twist themselves into knots, to become someone that they are not, in the pursuit of material wealth. Work in the Federation is not a matter of compulsion or survival. Federation citizens need not perform tasks or exercise professions that do not suit their inclinations just so that they can afford to put food on the table and enjoy the respect of their peers.

Technology alone does not make the Federation what it is. Free and plentiful energy, pervasive automation, artificial intelligence, and replicators certainly help. They are superb engineering solutions to a vast engineering problem: the supply of the basic necessities of life. The benefits they accrue depend entirely on value systems and social organization. Case in point: Quark makes extensive use of all these incredibly advanced technologies in the operation of his dining and gambling establishment. The replicators must really cut down on his food preparation costs. He just happens to keep all the profits to himself.

What makes the Federation so appealing to Nog is not the technology-driven cornucopia or the absence of money (in fact, he harbors a dim view of that particular aspect of the Federation's economic system). It is the nature and meaning of work. It is almost a paradox to state it this way, but in a society where nothing is scarce and consequently where work is no longer a prerequisite for survival, finding good reasons to work becomes paramount, the defining existential question that everyone has to ask themselves. Why work at all if it's not necessary? Because learning, making, and sharing is what makes life in the Federation worth living. Work, no longer a necessary burden, is the glue that holds the Federation together. It is the social bond and the social contract that impart substance and significance to life. Work, its life-affirming power, is why aliens and artificial life-forms are so eager to join the Federation.

In *Star Trek*'s twenty-fourth century, you don't work for money— because you can't work for money. There is no money, and therefore no salary work and no profit motive. Starfleet officers do not get monthly pay or bonuses for re-upping, and neither does Ben, the jovial civilian waiter from the Ten-Forward lounge who hustles Starfleet officers at poker.[20] Poker chips have no monetary value, by the way. Ben's employer, Guinan, the mysterious El-Aurian bartender, does not really run a synthehol concession business on a starship, because her bar, Ten-Forward, does not charge for drinks. Risa's *jamaharon* attendants cannot be qualified as sex workers, since they do not require pay for their services and even make it a point to dispense their favors freely to any off-world visitor. Dr. Zimmerman does not earn royalties for his invention of the Emergency Medical Hologram, as there are seemingly no patents in the Federation. And the Federation News Service does not pay per word to publish Jake Sisko's stories from the front lines of the Dominion War.

In short, everyone in the Federation seems very busy and hard at work, yet nobody gets paid. It sounds like a rotten deal. What could be so enticing to a young, wayward Ferengi? What gives?

---

20. He appears in *ST:TNG*, 7x15: "Lower Decks."

WORK AND GIFT-GIVING

The most striking aspect of work in the Federation is not so much that nobody gets paid for their toil, but rather that anybody would even toil at all. There is no material, objective rationale for anyone to do anything. All the basic necessities of a good life are free and available at the cost of zero. Replicators harness the quasi-unlimited power of the matter-antimatter reactor to convert energy into any type of finished goods, from Captain Picard's "tea, Earl Grey, hot" to cheesy wedding presents to weapons.

Furthermore, if you want to spend your entire life bumming around the beaches of Risa, you are most welcome to, and you probably should if you ask me. Nothing and nobody will prevent you from wallowing in the most abject and satisfying sloth. Considering that there does not seem to be any disincentive to slouching your life away, it is amazing that starships are being built in such great numbers, that cities are bustling with activity, that planets are being settled, and that scientific labs and facilities are pumping out research papers and inventions at a brisk pace. On all accounts, the Federation is a thriving society, made of a small cohort of extraordinarily creative individuals on the one hand, the proverbial 1 percent, and of an overwhelming number of very industrious regular folks, human as well as nonhuman, on the other hand. The Federation's 99 percent, in the parlance of our times, is surprisingly bereft of free riders.

There is nothing particularly odd in choosing to work for free (by "free" I do not mean coercion or slavery, of course). Even today, we often get to practice our skills and share their fruits freely. We volunteer to clean up beaches or to chaperon kids at school, we help out friends and neighbors, we share our experiences and knowledge online. We already make a ton of things out of passion, that is, without expectation of a financial reward (this little book being a good example).

We even have the opportunity to contribute these labors of love to the greatest common pot that has ever been invented: the Internet.

Some economists have attempted to determine the value provided by communally built and shared resources such as Wikipedia. If included in official statistics, they would add a couple points to the US GDP. For instance, Hal Varian, from Google, estimates that search engine use adds $500 per user, per year, of consumer surplus in time saved. MIT professor Erik Brynjolfsson, for his part, pegs the value of free Internet information at $300 billion annually.

Official GDP calculations and the so-called leading indicators were not geared to account for the value of freely exchanged goods and services. There is a large and growing part of the economy that escapes the accountants' and statisticians' fastidious gaze.

Yet, from the gifting rituals of the Pacific Northwest's First Peoples (the Kwakiutls' potlatch) to food banks and philanthropy, gifting goods, services, and time has always been an integral part of civilization. Altruistic collaboration counts as a uniquely human trait. A powerful adjuvant to social relations, it has given our species a critical evolutionary advantage. The advent of the Internet has enabled us to intensify and expand our deep-seated habit of sharing, giving, and collaborating. Ugly and buzzy Silicon Valley words such as "crowdsourcing" and "sharing economy" fail to obscure the undeniable fact that thanks to the Internet I can have free, unlimited, and immediate access not only to craigslist but also to the accumulated wisdom of almost all of humanity, present and past. One can debate at great lengths about the very nature and definition of progress, but sometimes progress is just like porn, you know it when you see it. And in this case, it is glaringly obvious.

In the Federation, work is not essential to maintaining the physical well-being of people. The basic reason for working—survival—no longer applies. Work is still essential to trekonomics, but for purposes of a higher order: increasing knowledge, perfecting technology, and promoting individual and collective self-improvement. The objective necessity to transform raw materials into consumable goods has not magically disappeared. But, for the most part, it has been offloaded to replicators.

CITIZEN ROBOTS

Replicators seem to make robotic labor largely redundant in the daily operations of trekonomics. Besides Data and his brother Lore, one hardly ever sees robots in action, whether android or specialized. Ships are manned by multispecies crews, asteroids are mined by workers, restaurants and bars are staffed by flesh-and-blood waiters. Artificial intelligence seems to reside only in ships' computers, which can respond to queries and orders in natural language. That, however, is hardly a sign of self-awareness, just raw processing power and very good programming. When the occasional holodeck program becomes self-aware, such as in the case of Sherlock Holmes's nemesis Professor James Moriarty, it is chalked up as a freak occurrence of emergent properties rather than a deliberate creation.[21]

One notable exception to the paucity of robotic workers is the assignment of the entire complement of the first version of the Emergency Medical Hologram, all 675 of them, to waste-transfer barges and dilithium mining.[22] This is the only example in the canon of large-scale use of nonspecialized, self-aware mechanical labor (if indeed a collection of photons generated by a holomatrix can be counted as mechanical). And then again, this happened because the

---

21. *ST:TNG*, 2x03: "Elementary, Dear Data," and *ST:TNG*, 6x12: "Ship in a Bottle."
22. *ST:VOY*, 6x24: "Life Line," and *ST:VOY*, 7x20: "Author, Author."

EMH Mark 1 was deemed defective, to the great humiliation of Dr. Zimmerman, its creator and model.

There is some logic to not using robots or holographic beings in production: in trekonomics replicators handle the bulk of commodity-manufacturing duties, while handmade products have outsized perceived value. There is almost no automation in agriculture because that is the whole point: everyday food is replicated while "real" food, grown with great love and an intense care for tradition, is very special indeed. Upon being presented with the airline-meal-sounding "entrée number one-oh-three: curried chicken and rice, with a side order of carrots," a dejected Commander Eddington remarks: "It may look like chicken, but it still tastes like replicated protein molecules to me."[23] General-purpose robotic labor is squeezed between the ubiquity and convenience of replicators and the output of countless artisan masters.

Another possible explanation for the apparent lack of robotic labor in the *Star Trek* canon is citizenship. It may be found in two of the most extraordinary episodes of the TV run, written and broadcast ten years apart: "The Measure of a Man" from *The Next Generation* and *Voyager*'s "Author, Author." Both of these episodes deal with the issue of the rights, under human law, of self-aware artificial intelligence. In other words, what constitutes sentience and personhood in the age of general, programmatic artificial intelligence? And if sentient machines exist, how can they be put to work and treated as mere servants or slaves when they are seemingly endowed with free will and aspirations of their own?

Both episodes expand on Isaac Asimov's pioneering work in *Bicentennial Man*, where Andrew Martin, the robot protagonist, gains the right to be declared human by having his positronic brain programmed to die after two hundred years of existence. It is one of

---

23. *ST:DS9*, 5x21: "Blaze of Glory."

Asimov's most striking stories because of its singular depth of psychological development (Asimov was notorious for his cardboard approach to human characterization).

"The Measure of a Man" is one of the high points of *Next Generation*'s entire seven seasons.[24] It is essentially a legal drama. On layover at a star base, the *Enterprise* welcomes Commander Bruce Maddox onboard. A noted Starfleet roboticist, Maddox has come all this way to order Data to report to his lab so that he can study the android's programming and positronic brain. His objective is to reverse engineer Dr. Soong's creation to provide Starfleet with a multitude of androids.

Maddox's plan to disassemble Data may put his subject's life in jeopardy. Except that, as Maddox argues, Data is neither a life-form nor a subject, but merely the property of Starfleet. As his superior officer, Maddox can therefore order him to submit to the cybernetic equivalent of a dissection—without impinging on his fundamental rights or breaking any established law. Upon Data's adamant refusal, a hearing is convened. Due to staff shortages at the star base, Will Riker is summoned by Captain Philippa Louvois, the base commander who presides over the proceedings, to prosecute Maddox's case against his *Enterprise* brother-in-arms. Captain Picard will act as Data's advocate.

Riker convincingly demonstrates Data's artificial nature to the court: he makes him bend a steel rod, and asks him to remove his mechanical arm. He then turns off the android by dramatically pushing a switch hidden beneath his rib cage. "Pinocchio is broken, its strings have been cut!"[25] Riker exclaims, devastated rather than triumphant. The prosecution rests.

A dispirited Picard mulls his defense with Guinan. The wise bartender remarks with gravity: "Consider that in the history of many

---

24. *ST:TNG*, 2x09: "The Measure of a Man."

25. Ibid.

worlds there have always been disposable creatures. They do the dirty work. They do the work that no one else wants to do, because it's too difficult or too hazardous. And an army of Datas, all disposable? You don't have to think about their welfare; you don't think about how they feel. Whole generations of disposable people."[26]

After proving to the court that Data meets Maddox's own criteria for sentience, Picard passionately argues that according to the ideals of the Federation a sentient being cannot be treated as property. Patrick Stewart, the consummate thespian, hits all the right notes of a very challenging legal monologue: "Sooner or later, this man [Maddox]— or others like him—will succeed in replicating Commander Data. The decision you reach here today will determine how we will regard this creation of our genius. It will reveal the kind of people we are; what he is destined to be. It will reach far beyond this courtroom and this one android. It could significantly redefine the boundaries of personal liberty and freedom: expanding them for some, savagely curtailing them for others. Are you prepared to condemn [Commander Data]—and all who will come after him—to servitude and slavery? Your Honor, Starfleet was founded to seek out new life: well, there it sits! Waiting."[27]

The court rules in favor of Data. Sentience is sentience, whether biological or cybernetic. Data cannot be treated as property. He is an autonomous, self-aware, sentient being. He is a subject in every sense. Therefore, he cannot be denied the same rights and protections enjoyed by every other Federation citizen.

The ruling helps cement the notion that self-aware android robots cannot be used as the "reserve army of capital," to quote Marx's famous broadside on industrialists' use of cheap labor. It also precludes any chance that the Federation would evolve into a version of Isaac

---

26. Ibid.

27. Ibid.

Asimov's Spacers' Worlds, where the robot-to-human ratio can rise up to ten thousand to one. When more Datas are finally built, they will be citizens. They will freely choose their paths in life and will not serve anyone but society as a whole, like everybody else.

It remains to be seen how their unlimited lifespan and superior cognitive abilities will affect the society-wide reputational sweepstakes. The institutions of the Federation already have many procedures in place to accommodate interspecies variations and division of labor. For instance, the Vulcans' well-known affinity for logical reasoning may make them prominent scientists but certainly not the dominant ones. All in all, there seems to be a place in the Federation for many more of Data's kind. Like Data, they will become great scientists, Starfleet officers, stage actors, engineers, and artisans. They will be encouraged to experience humanity's journey to its fullest, and their achievements and contributions will be warmly welcomed.

PHOTONS BE FREE

The situation is somewhat more complex in the case of holographic beings. *Voyager's* "Doctor" presents a whole different set of challenges to trekonomics. Unlike Data, whose parts and programming are very hard to copy even for Starfleet's foremost roboticists, the doctor is exactly the same thing as a replicator pattern, infinitely reproducible because he is purely software. As I mentioned above, this particular feature allows for a relatively hassle-free deployment of the EMH for a wide range of missions, medical or not. In addition, upgrading software is much less taxing than building positronic brains and limbs from scratch. Forking and adapting the basic software into new instances and thus new holographic beings is entirely manageable by one person. We discover that the irascible Doctor Zimmerman, the original, has populated his lab with holographic animals and even a young human female assistant.[28] Not to mention that the holographic doctor, throughout the course of *Voyager*'s seven seasons, has constantly added to his programming in his spare time. He even chose to leave untouched the original behavioral subroutines written by his creator. The doctor has a horrible bedside manner, to unending comical effect.

While the doctor exhibits all the usual traits of a person, including an overinflated and mildly delusional sense of self-worth, he is not considered an individual subject under Federation law. And neither are his "brothers" as he calls the other "photonics."[29]

The show starts as a farce. The doctor has become a published author, to his great satisfaction. And who would not be? His first novel, *Photons Be Free*, allows the reader/player to be the holographic doctor's character in a dramatized version of *Voyager*'s adventures in the Delta Quadrant. A reputable publisher, Broht & Forrester, has agreed to distribute the doctor's work throughout the Federation.

As its title suggests, *Photons Be Free* is not a particularly subtle piece. The protagonist, in effect a human simulacrum of a real-life hologram, must endure terrible torments at the hands of brutish, violent, and bigoted fictional crew members, precisely because she is a hologram. While the caricatures of *Voyager*'s ensemble are hilarious and offer a parody of the whole show, the author's intent is very serious. The doctor wants to raise awareness of the plight of photonic beings and to turn his advocacy for his rights as an individual into a movement. It works almost too well. So much so that the doctor reluctantly agrees to tone down his opus, out of consideration for his fellow crewmates and friends. Meanwhile, unbeknownst to him, Broht & Forrester has begun to distribute his garish original draft to great acclaim.

---

28. *ST:VOY*, 6x24: "Life Line."

29. *ST:VOY*, 7x20: "Author, Author."

The doctor wants it recalled immediately, but the publisher refuses on the ironic grounds that the author, not being a person, does not have rights over his own creation. A hearing is convened to settle the matter.

Voyager's senior staff give heartfelt testimonials of the doctor's humanity. As proof of his agency and personhood, Captain Janeway recounts how the doctor once disobeyed her orders so as not to break the Hippocratic oath. Yet, all that is not enough to sway the arbitrator. In the end the doctor is granted limited rights as an author but not his full rights as a person.

In the show's last scene, we see several copies of the doctor mindlessly working underground in a dilithium-processing facility. One of them recommends to a fellow worker that he check out this new holonovel called *Photons Be Free* on his next diagnostic and maintenance break. And thus, on a forlorn mining asteroid, begins the holograms' liberation movement.

Lewis Zimmerman's quip about people's fear that holograms may someday take over the galaxy should be taken very seriously.[30] His holographic "Doctor" is indeed a person, and an extraordinary one at that. By his own efforts, he has grown far beyond his original programming. He has even become a popular holonovelist! It is only a matter of time before he and his brethren rise up from their position as exploited laborers and claim their full civil rights.

Zimmerman does not regard this as a threat. He believes that holographic beings will not suddenly throw good people out of work. Their integration into the Federation's economy will be no different than normal demographic growth or inducting another star system as a member. Once integrated, "photonics" will show the same dedication and love for creative activities as "organics." They will join the frantic

---

30. *ST:DS9*, 5x16: "Dr. Bashir, I Presume."

competition for reputation, and their contributions to sciences and arts will add to the Federation's overall wealth.

THE ZEN OF FLIPPING BURGERS

To get a better sense of the emotional aspect of work in trekonomics, we should set aside holograms, androids, and replicators and focus on low-tech flesh-and-blood people for a moment. Let's take a look at a typical Federation small business that eschews automation and relies on human craft for its fame: Captain Sisko's father's famous restaurant in New Orleans's French Quarter, Sisko's Creole Kitchen.[31]

Every business owner can appreciate that controlling labor costs is critical to her company's survival. The good news is that in trekonomics labor costs are nonexistent. There is a trade-off, however: business owners will not generate any cash flow or profits because money does not exist either.

Sisko's Creole Kitchen's success is gauged in reputation and popularity. It is highly dependent on maintaining the highest standards of quality and service. It must keep its five-star rating on the galactic version of Yelp at any cost (and unfortunately, there is no easy way, monetary or otherwise, to make bad reviews disappear).

Like today, Sisko's Creole Kitchen's business hinges as much on the owner's managerial abilities as on the employees' involvement. One could argue that because employees are free from the necessity to take on a job, any job, they are self-selected for passion and natural inclination for the tasks at hand. They also participate in the company's reputational gains (or the opprobrium!) so that they are highly motivated to deliver outstanding products to customers. For Nathan, Sisko's Creole

---

31. First seen in *ST:DS9*, 4x11: "Homefront."

Kitchen's executive chef, cooking is much more than just a job. It is an opportunity to shine, to build credibility, to make a name for himself, however trivial or menial the assignment.

In that sense, the organization of work in the Federation resembles older, preindustrial forms of arrangements. Working as a chef at Sisko's restaurant must hold a deeper and more personal meaning to Nathan than merely flipping burgers in order to make the rent. It is more akin to an apprenticeship with a master of the trade. It requires great passion and dedication. The potential rewards for the apprentice are proportional to his or her commitment.

Nathan seems to have spent his entire life honing his craft at Sisko's in the way of a great Japanese sushi master. But other people may choose more eclectic paths in their career explorations. Both options are readily accepted. The only real limits are one's imagination and job availability. Not all jobs or positions are open at all times. The kitchen at Sisko's can only accommodate so many interested job seekers. To a certain extent, intriguing jobs and careers, whatever their duration, belong in the same category as experiential, one-of-a-kind goods, such as Château Picard. They are rivalrous. Your getting the line cook job at Sisko's prevents somebody else from getting it.

PEOPLE WHO ARE NOT GOING TO MAKE IT

In the Federation, work exists to make you happy. This is reminiscent of many nineteenth-century utopian works, which all tried to imagine worlds where labor, leisure, and art would merge into a single activity. As a literary idea, the dissolution of work into leisure and passion arose in reaction to the industrial rationalization of production. *Star Trek* draws directly from that tradition and updates it for late twentieth-century postmodern audiences. By creating excitement and a larger meaning to life, work in the Federation fulfills the deep human need for belonging and recognition. Work is another way to love and be loved and to express one's unique sensibility.

Some never quite succeed at this. The constant striving for recognition and social currency has a darker side. One has to work without respite. It is easy to lose yourself in dead-end projects, and the ladder is crowded and seemingly has no end. Society demands that you try your very best, and at the same time evaluates your progress and judges your achievements. Performance anxiety is a common mental illness. Lieutenant Reginald Barclay's recurring holodeck addiction is a testament to the inherent challenges of adjusting to an economy of reputation, especially if you tend to be a bit shy and clumsy instead of a take-charge Starfleet command-level officer.[32]

Dr. Bashir's father presents an even more poignant instance of that type of maladaptation.[33] Richard Bashir and his wife, Amsha, are summoned to Deep Space Nine by Dr. Lewis Zimmerman, in order for the doctor to conduct background interviews about their son Julian's psychological profile. He needs their insights to create a more life-like holographic model of the doctor. Richard, Amsha, and Julian are deeply worried about Dr. Zimmerman's curiosity. They share a dark secret that could tarnish the good doctor's spotless record and indeed derail his whole career at Starfleet Medical. Richard Bashir introduces himself to Captain Sisko and Lieutenant Dax in a boastful and slightly flippant fashion: "Oh, I've done many things. At the moment, I'm involved in landscape architecture—designing parks and public spaces mostly. I love working on projects that will be enjoyed by thousands of people long after I'm gone."

---

32. *ST:TNG*, 3x21: "Hollow Pursuits"; *ST:VOY*, 6x10: "Pathfinder."

33. *ST:DS9*, 5x16: "Dr. Bashir, I Presume."

Later, in the privacy of their quarters, Julian confronts his father: "So you're doing landscape architecture now . . ."

Richard replies: "Some very important people have expressed interest in my park designs. I have several good prospects on the horizon."

Julian retorts bitingly: "You always have 'good prospects.' But they always seem to stay just over that horizon."

In fact, Richard has held many jobs, including third-class steward on a spaceship, but could never quite hold on to any of them. His restlessness and feelings of inadequacy must have been compounded by the fact that his young son showed all the early signs of a serious learning disability. Ron Moore, who wrote the episode, describes Richard's anguish as an illustration of all those who have a hard time coping with the demands of the Federation's reputational economy: "The-Federation-is-a-very-nice-place-to-live [sic] . . . But that doesn't mean you can't be a loser and you can't screw up. In the twenty-fourth century, everybody seems to have a job, and everybody's taken care of and everybody has food. But there are people who are just not going to make it. And Bashir's dad is like that, the kind of guy who's always posturing himself as a success, but never has succeeded at anything."[34] Meritocracy does not mean that everyone is a winner. For those who can't swing it, the imperative to build a meaningful life through work becomes a source of unbearable anxiety.

Some are tempted to find a quick fix, to cheat. In a meritocracy such as the Federation, cheating is the highest crime. Richard is painfully aware of his existential difficulties in a society that thrives on achievement and recognition. He does not want his son to endure the same problems, to aimlessly bounce from job to job in search of a way to contribute his meager talents, to be acknowledged. This leads him

---

34. Terry J. Erdmann, *The Star Trek: Deep Space 9 Companion*, with Paula M. Block (New York: Pocket Books/Star Trek, 2000), p. 431.

and his wife to seek a medical solution to Julian's disability so that he may have a chance to compete at the highest level. They break the cardinal law of the Federation, and take little Julian to Adigeon Prime, a nonaligned world, to undergo genetic enhancement. As Julian reveals to his friend Chief O'Brien, "The technical term is 'accelerated critical neural pathway formation' . . . in the end everything but my name was altered in some way." Afterward, Julian thrived. Nobody ever knew, because in the Federation "there is no stigma attached to success."[35]

The Federation has two absolute prohibitions. The Prime Directive, which forbids interference with other cultures, is directed outward, so to speak. Meanwhile, the other absolute prohibition, genetic enhancement, fulfills an internal purpose. It aims to maintain the balance of Federation society. It enforces the Federation's commitment to equality of opportunity. By having his son's abilities genetically augmented, Richard Bashir deliberately subverted the meritocratic ethos that enables trekonomics to exist. Any person who seeks an unfair advantage, however heartfelt their motives, only creates incentives for others to seek the same unfair advantage. As Worf dryly observes about the likes of Dr. Bashir: "If people like them are allowed to compete freely, then parents would feel pressure to have their children enhanced so they could keep up."[36] Soon it's an arms race among parents, everybody's doping, and the process by which reputation is acquired is forever tainted. Trekonomics no longer functions.

As we have seen, in trekonomics, economic capital and reputational capital are very different things. While one may inherit his or her

35. *ST:DS9*, 5x16: "Dr. Bashir, I Presume."

36. *ST:DS9*, 6x09: "Statistical Probabilities."

parents' names (and some of their reputation), there are no privileges afforded by economic capital, because there is no economic capital to be had and therefore none to inherit and pass on to the next generation. There is no lottery of birth. Anyone can become captain, provided hard work, dedication, and a few lucky breaks. You rise on your own merits. Everybody gets a fair shake. The system is not rigged.

An economic system where work is entirely decoupled from biophysical necessity and survival has its pitfalls and its dark corners. Utopia only works so long as everybody plays by the same rules. And even then it might not be a perfect fit for all. There are several instances of Federation natives who choose to leave it for good. Some may elect to live on nonaligned worlds, while others end up working for the Orion Syndicate, the criminal organization that even Ferengis fear.[37]

Of all the misfits, the strangest and the scariest are those who ply their trade in Section 31. The secret agency, whose existence is not acknowledged by Starfleet, is in charge of protecting the Federation by any means necessary. Ira Behr, *Deep Space Nine*'s showrunner and inventor of Section 31 (among other very twisted and fascinating additions to the *Star Trek* universe), describes its members as the ones "doing the nasty stuff that no one wants to think about."[38] Section 31 operatives seem to be able to set aside any ethical qualms in the pursuit of their mission. Luther Sloan, who appears in several episodes of *Deep Space Nine*, is a certified sociopath by the Federation's standards. In lieu of seeking fulfillment in scientific endeavors or in the mindful practice of an art, he finds meaning in deceit, manipulation, and covert violence. He rationalizes the amorality of his actions by invoking the superior interests of the Federation.[39] Sloan and his colleagues are relics

---

37. *ST:DS9*, 5x09: "The Ascent"; *ST:DS9*, 6x15: "Honor among Thieves."

38. Erdmann, *The Star Trek: Deep Space 9 Companion*, p. 551.

39. *ST:DS9*, 6x18: "Inquisition."

of a distant past, our less-than-idyllic present, where the ends seem to almost always justify the means. Section 31's existence calls into question the utopian romance of *Star Trek* by introducing an alternative, and deeply disquieting, explanation of the Federation's socioeconomic stability and endurance as a polity. As if, at every turn, paradise had been buttressed by a cabal of trained spies and professional assassins.

HUMANOID CAPITAL

All these characters, from Data and Dr. Bashir to holographic beings and Section 31, are extreme cases. They exist at the edges of what is considered normal in the Federation. They help us grok what lies within the limits they outline, mostly comfortable and happy places, such as the Picard family Bordeaux estate, the pleasure planet Risa, or Sisko's Creole Kitchen. Which begs the question: How does normal productive activity in the Federation, organized as it is around the fulfillment of human pursuits, allow for overall progress and economic growth?

The rate of technological progress and productivity growth is likely much higher in trekonomics than in any other type of society, even without the profit motive. The proportion of people who devote their time and talents to scientific research is considerably higher than under classic economic conditions. Between those who make it into the 1 percent and those who are actively trying, the Federation can cultivate and mobilize a staggering amount of human(oid) capital. This is a direct result of low-skill labor replacement. Guaranteed abundance and reputational incentives create very significant efficiencies in humanoid capital allocation. Creative minds and scientific aptitudes are no longer wasted due to accidents of birthplace, the bad luck of challenging circumstances, or the necessity to survive. In that sense, the absence of poverty has a very high multiplier effect on both productivity and innovation.

Further, the absence of a profit motive in the invention process itself radically broadens the scope and the outcomes of research programs. While profit-driven product development has undoubtedly made enormous contributions to our world, it has had the unintended consequence of summarily leaving fallow entire avenues of potentially fruitful research. Consider genetically modified crops: most of those in use are designed to resist just one particular brand of pesticide. Who knows what GMO could do if the same amount of intellectual firepower were trained on less narrow, less exclusively profit-driven aims? The same goes for so-called orphan diseases or new classes of antibiotics: pharmaceutical companies tend to orient their efforts toward fairly trivial and barely effective psychoactive and erectile dysfunction drugs because this is where the profits are. No one can fault agrochemical or pharmaceutical companies for acting as competitive businesses rather than humanitarian organizations. Within the confines of a suboptimal set of incentives, their behavior is perfectly rational.

The benefits of reputation-driven, open-source innovation cannot be overstated. There are many instances of this in the past century. The Green Revolution spurred by the work of agronomist Norman Borlaug in Mexico and South Asia, the Homebrew Computer Club at Stanford University, and the cosmopolitan particle-physics community around Niels Bohr and Albert Einstein are but the most famous. In that respect, very little should be expected from profit-oriented attempts at duplicating these models of communal creativity. The quality of the people involved in such endeavors is not in question. However, the imperative to develop and accumulate patents for the mere purpose of private gains tends to constrain genius in unexpected ways, and to funnel outsized rewards to much less deserving intellectual-property litigation specialists. Humanity celebrates genius. It seldom remembers lawyers.

Trekonomics' premium on ingenuity and reputation acts upon people as an overwhelming incentive. This inevitably results in an anarchical profusion of inventions, and provides a fertile ground for social disruption. In a society where human(oid) work has massively migrated toward research, invention, and art, and where the rate of technological progress is extremely high, the specter of creative destruction is an ever-present concern. One would have to assume that a lot of Federation policies revolve around channeling and marshaling that overflow of creative chaos. Yet, like riding a tiger, the march of technology is difficult to stop.

In trekonomics, tens of billions of tinkerers and amateur scientists are constantly hacking away at intractable conundrums, either in their garages or in more formal settings. Because demand does not condition research paths or adoption, the range and depth of products is not nearly as restricted as in our world. When Starfleet or the Vulcan Science Academy needs a nagging engineering problem solved, they can readily tap legions of inquiring minds all over the Federation, as well as an enormous library of preexisting open-source technologies. Volume, unrestricted access, and wild creativity are decisive advantages over all the other civilizations of the galaxy, Borg and Dominion included. In the final analysis, people are the true wealth of the Federation, and the source of its tremendous power.

In *Star Trek*, automation provides the material basis for free work—it makes it possible. But wondrous machines are not sufficient. Shared values—the power of community norms—is what brings trekonomics alive. If making money and owning a big car and a big house are the universally agreed-upon ways to achieve status in your community, it is very likely that you will try your best to rise to these expectations. First and foremost, humans are social animals. The rewards for not conforming to society's standards are at best uncertain. You always run the risk of being cast out of the group, thus drastically reducing your chances to reproduce and pass on your genes. Similarly, if a society's prevailing norm is to accumulate reputation through the free exercise and sharing of one's talents, chances are most people will adhere to this convention.

CHAPTER 3

"TEA, EARL GREY, HOT"[40]

THE REPLICATOR

Early on in *Voyager*, one of the strange alien species from the Delta Quadrant obtains replicating technology from the stranded Federation ship through subterfuge and treachery.[41] However, the aliens are not able to make the machine work properly. Their ship's crew gets contaminated by radiation leakage. When Lieutenant Torres discovers the nature of the robbery, Captain Janeway remarks of the aliens' motivations: "We may take replicators for granted, but imagine what it would mean to a culture that doesn't have this technology?"

Indeed. Imagine for a minute, because in more ways than one we are that alien culture. What makes the replicator, an automaton that

---

40. *ST:TNG*, 2x11: "Contagion."
41. *ST:VOY*, 1x11: "State of Flux."

produces everyday things on demand so menacing? That seemingly benign machine and the questions it raises are the heart of *Star Trek*'s speculative economics.

Replicators are perhaps the most significant of all of *Star Trek*'s inventions. The warp engine, transporters, and tricorders cannot hold a candle to the replicator. It is the technological foundation of trekonomics, the keystone of the Federation's prosperity, the device that really sets it apart and makes it so intriguing and pregnant with possibilities. After the absence of money and the abolition of human labor, we now turn to the replicator.

LIVE BETTER ELECTRICALLY

Captain Jean-Luc Picard is the replicator's most famous and iconic user. Even though he is the scion of an esteemed family of French vintners, Captain Picard is forever associated in fans' imaginations with the more gentlemanly, more British, more bergamot-scented mannerism: afternoon tea. His instruction sequence, "tea, Earl Grey, hot," is the equivalent of Kirk's earlier "Beam me up, Scotty." I suppose this Briticism was meant to impart an aura of aristocratic refinement to the character. That is what old England means to American audiences, and therefore it fits well with Patrick Stewart's Shakespearean roots. In real life, Sir Patrick himself is a proud workingman, and has been a vocal advocate for England's Labour Party: he does not fool the class-conscious Brits, and probably would not wish to. But this is Hollywood. Impeccable Oxford accent plus Earl Grey tea means gentility and sophistication.

Despite its role in fleshing out the character, the captain's fondness for the beverage is revealed somewhat late in the series. The concoction's first mention occurs around the midpoint of *The Next*

Generation's second season.[42] And like most first times, it is rather inauspicious. The *Enterprise* finds itself under attack by a computer virus, and as a result all its highly integrated systems are experiencing a cascade of malfunctions. This includes the replicator in the captain's ready room. Its ability to process natural-language commands has been compromised. The machine screws up the captain's request and serves him a potted plant. At least it got the pot right.

That scene does not hold the title for the first-ever appearance of the replicator in all of *Star Trek*. It happens much earlier in *The Next Generation*'s run. Stardate 41235.25, per the captain's log (or year 2364, in the old Human calendar), during the third episode of the first season, which aired on October 12, 1987.[43]

In all fairness, it should be noted that *The Original Series* had featured a similar device, the food synthesizer. That appliance delivered what looked like spiffed-up TV dinners and would not have been out of place in Ronald Reagan's GE House of the Future (*Live Better Electrically*: look it up on YouTube; it is an American monument, the best work the Gipper ever did). On the other hand, the *Enterprise* in director Nicholas Meyer's *ST VI: The Undiscovered Country* still featured a galley kitchen. The crew prepared and served *Gagh* to their Klingon guests, and the live worms were definitely not replicated. Just ask the actors. We even get to visit that space kitchen in the scene where Lieutenant Valeris, Spock's Vulcan protégée, vaporizes a simmering Crock-Pot to demonstrate to Chekov that shooting a phaser anywhere on the *Enterprise* would trigger all sorts of loud alarms.

The Undiscovered Country was released in 1991, at the peak of *Next Generation*'s popularity. This proves that not only was the replicator a

---

42. *ST:TNG*, 2x11: "Contagion."

43. *ST:TNG*, 1x04: "Code of Honor"; the pilot, "Encounter at Farpoint," counts for two episodes (*ST:TNG*, 1x01 and 1x02).

genuine invention of *The Next Generation* but also that it had been enshrined as canon, a bona fide part of the *Star Trek* timeline. This was later confirmed by the prequel show, *Enterprise*, where much like in today's submarines, chow played an outsized role in keeping the scrappy explorers' spirits high. Replicators did not exist in the *Star Trek* universe before their introduction on Captain Picard's *Enterprise*. Believe it or not, but between the twenty-third and the twenty-fourth centuries, things had managed to get even better.

The replicator does not make a grand entrance in "Code of Honor." It is quick and dirty, as if it were completely pedestrian. Dr. Crusher complains in passing of her inability to replicate batches of live vaccine from planet Ligon II. If you do not pay attention, you might not notice it, and even more so if you are not watching (or rewatching) the series in its original order.

From a narrative standpoint, replicators are utterly superfluous. They pass as background color, everyday technology, the boring pieces of furniture in the corner that supply tea to the captain. They rarely, if ever, move the stories forward. Think about it: the captain could drink his Earl Grey tea out of a thermos or have a pot prepared by a lowly ensign, and it would not make the slightest bit of difference in the way he and his crew save the day, and the galaxy, time and time again.

I can think of only one episode that touches upon the technology's revolutionary potential: "The Quality of Life."[44] Commander Data discovers that maintenance robots, equipped with miniature replicators that can synthesize tools on demand, have become sentient. The episode is yet another twist on the status of self-aware machines in the *Trek* universe, rather than a detailed examination of replicating technology.

---

44. *ST:TNG*, 6x09.

Even the shows' writers seemed blissfully unconcerned by the awesome powers of the replicator. As *Enterprise* writer and coexecutive producer Chris Black retells it, in the writers' room such technology "was generally addressed with a shrug and the attitude 'Hey, it's the future.'"[45] And yet, they did put them in there, didn't they? They could have used extras at a marginal cost to the production, they could have had a galley kitchen on the *Enterprise-D*. But had they done so, they would have missed their chance to change the world (at least in fiction).

So what does the replicator do that is so unique and so portentous? The name says it all: the replicator is a machine that replicates stuff. Almost any stuff. You ask it for stuff, and the stuff you just asked for instantly materializes before your eyes on the device's softly lit plate. Add the signature twinkling visual effect, and the whole gadget looks and feels like a one-way transporter.

There are some limits and safeguards to what a replicator will make. For instance, Starfleet regulations put a software lock on the replication of weapons aboard a ship. Also, replicators do not have the ability to make living tissues or organisms because of the exponentially higher complexity of life compared to inanimate objects. Thus replicators can produce nutritious meals and savory beverages, but not Kumamoto oysters on the half shell.

So here is a futuristic contraption that can scramble eggs and unscramble them. Fine. What is the big deal? The big deal is this: because of the replicator, nobody in the Federation has to work ever again. Nobody. Ever. The compulsion to work in order to survive has vanished. And furthermore, because of the replicators' ubiquity, the

---

45. Chris Black, interview with the author, May 4, 2015.

necessity for markets has vaporized as well. Imbalances in supply and demand have largely become moot. The entire edifice of society as we know it has been upended. The old world, our world, is gone, and all it took was a cup of Earl Grey tea.

THE GREAT DEPARTMENT STORE IN THE SKY

The Next Generation and the subsequent shows give many examples of replicators' usage. In the twenty-fourth-century Federation, replicators are indeed everywhere. One can find them on Deep Space Nine's promenade, at Quark's as well as at the Replimat, where Dr. Bashir and Elim Garak, the spy, have their periodic lunches. The Federation also gives away industrial replicators as humanitarian aid.[46]

In *Next Generation*'s wistful and extraordinary episode "Family,"[47] Picard's sister-in-law discusses her family's hesitations to acquire a replicator for their traditional French wine-country household. The tension between technological convenience and the attachment to manual work and ancestral ways is never fully resolved. Or rather it is, but not by the quarrelsome older folks. The show closes on Picard's young nephew, René, dreaming of starships under the night sky, like many of us still do. No doubt, like many of us, he will wholeheartedly embrace the replicators, and all that comes along with them.

In "Data's Day," Worf and Geordi La Forge are going to the *Enterprise*'s replicating center to fetch wedding presents for Chief Miles O'Brien and Keiko Ishikawa.[48] We see them scanning through set after set of wineglasses and various knickknacks on the replicator unit's

---

46. As in *ST:DS9*, 4x22: "For the Cause."

47. *ST:TNG*, 4x02.

48. *ST:TNG*, 4x11.

touch screen. If you notice, in the background a couple of Starfleet parents are busy choosing something with their young kid. While Worf and Geordi are comparing hapless notes about the meaning of wedding rituals, the family leaves the room with a stuffed animal. This is how you shop in the twenty-fourth century. Think about the consequences of the replicator. A whole new level of instant gratification: no more trips to the big-box retail store, no overbearing sales clerk asking you how you are doing, no global supply chain and logistics, and no unsold inventory. The labor involved is minimal, mostly consisting of designing and updating the objects' software models and loading them into the replicator's memory banks. The craft, the talent, the art are all concentrated at the design stage.

This strongly suggests that all that is handmade, all that is infused with human intervention, the touch of a single unique person, must hold special value to Federation citizens. This must even be true of infinitely reproducible designs stored in a replicator's pattern buffers, exactly like how the Beatles' *Abbey Road* is absolutely unique and can be on everyone's music player at the same time. In trekonomics, the designers' or the artists' craft fills many utilitarian objects with affects, the tangible traces of their singular sensibility or vision. Like some people today, this is what Federation consumers seek and respond to in a product, replicated or not. The main determinants of value are not utility or scarcity, but affects, sentimental taste, personal idiosyncrasies, love.

In that sense, the replicator is not fundamentally different from today's mass production of goods. It just behaves more like the Internet does with information: it makes everything widely and instantly available, every recipe, every piece of clothing, every object ever dreamed up, and at very little to no cost to the end user.

ZILLIONS OF PETABYTES

The way replicators perform their task is a bit of a stretch. Keep in mind this is science fiction, not Electrical Engineering 101. Again, Chris Black: "The replicator works like the transporter. It doesn't turn energy into matter, so it doesn't technically violate any laws of thermodynamics. It reconstitutes a supply of matter stored somewhere on the ship into Earl Grey tea or whatever. And any waste material is recycled through the system (and periodically the tank of building material would need to be 'topped off'). The real problem . . . is processing the data and the amount of energy required. Both issues are sort of 'gimmes' of *Star Trek*—we just assume that they have incredible sci-fi supercomputers of unimaginable speed and power that can process the data required. And that via dilithium and antimatter we can provide the impossible amounts of power needed for warp drive, transporters, and so on. Honestly, it's not anything any of the writers I worked with on the show concerned themselves with."[49]

Chris points here to the main real-world problem behind the transporter concept: the hypothetical amount of data it must process and transfer from one point to the next is at least as huge as the amount of matter. While the replicator does not need to decompile and disassemble matter on the spot and send it over long distances, it still needs to store the information about each product or object, down to molecular resolution. On top of that, it has to shuffle matter around from its tanks, through the pattern buffers (whatever those are) and finally onto the plate, in a coherent, finished form. The energy required to rearrange atoms into molecules, and then molecules into liquids, complex organic compounds, or crystalline structures (for the tea mug) adds to

---

49. Black, interview.

the challenge of storing an almost unlimited amount of data. Gigantic databases of entire genomes are fairly commonplace nowadays. Scientists routinely consult them and run statistical analyses on them. This simply was not a workable notion when *The Next Generation* first came on the air, which makes you appreciate *Star Trek*'s foresight. Still, in terms of structured data, there is probably a quadrillion petabytes of difference between a genome and the full atomic structure of a glass mug of Earl Grey tea.

The other nifty function of the replicator is recycling. Once you are done with your tea, you place the mug on the plate, and it beams it away just like a transporter. The matter is disassembled and stored again in the machine's innards for reuse. Some of the atoms are consumed by people as tea or as food, and thus not all the original matter is returned and recycled into the replicator. This makes you wonder if waste extraction units on the *Enterprise* are in fact one-way recycling replicators. There are a few tangential discussions of reclamation systems, especially in *Deep Space Nine*, where Rom's first engineering job upon quitting his brother Quark's bar is working the nightshift on the station's waste reclamation.[50] It is never quite clear whether these are still made of good old plumbing or if they have been upgraded. At the very least, this implies that with or without advanced toilets, the replicators' tanks still need the occasional topping off.

In *Star Trek*'s own chronology, the replicator is explained as an outgrowth of the transporter. The story behind the transporter is well known to fans: Gene Roddenberry had come up with it as both a narrative shortcut and a money-saving scheme. Thanks to the transporter, the crew of *The Original Series* did not have to waste valuable screen time shuttling back and forth between the *Enterprise* and the surface of the various planets they visited on their five-year mission.

---

50. *ST:DS9*, 5x05: "The Assignment."

Consequently, the production did not have to build another set and another ship model, and it could get around ordering additional special effects for takeoff, landing, and atmospheric braking. Kirk could go down in a snap to the desert planet to fight the Gorn.[51] The transporter was a cheap trick, born out of bean counting. While it was expedient, it was also a stroke of genius, an immense triumph of storytelling and imagination, physics be damned. There was nothing like it anywhere, and especially not on prime-time network TV. Along with Mr. Spock, it quickly became an emblem of *Star Trek*, and perhaps its greatest claim to fame.

VON NEUMANN AND THE ENGINES OF CREATION

Contrary to the transporter, the replicator was not created as a way around tight production budgets. As it turns out, it draws widely from sources outside of the *Star Trek* universe. Its origins can be located in both science-fiction literature and in real life. Since the early fifties and the rise of cybernetics, scientists and engineers have been obsessed with the concept of the so-called Santa Claus machine, which could make anything on the spot.

As with a lot of famous sci-fi ideas, such as Asimov's Psychohistory or Three Laws of Robotics, the replicator can be traced back to the pages of *Astounding Science Fiction*. From the late 1930s to the early 1950s, the monthly pulp, under the guidance of its legendary editor John W. Campbell, was the undisputed center of what became known as the golden age of science fiction. Campbell groomed many of the early masters of the genre, from Isaac Asimov and Robert Heinlein to

---

51. *ST:TOS*, 1x18: "Arena." I know, I know, technically it was not the *Enterprise*'s transporter that beamed Kirk to the surface.

Ray Bradbury and Lafayette Ron Hubbard. *Astounding* set the agenda and the format: rigorous and vigorous scientific and social speculation, packaged as entertainment for teenagers.

The first iteration of the replicator I could find surfaced in the March 1945 issue of *Astounding*, in a story written by George O. Smith titled "Special Delivery." The story is part of a longer series set on a communication relay station in space, later collected as a book, *Venus Equilateral*.[52] In the installment, the machine is called a "matter duplicator," and can replicate anything. The owners of the relay station sue the inventor to gain control of the device, arguing that it is a transmitter and therefore falls under their operating license. Wes Farrell, the inventor, wins the case by replicating the judge's antique watch, thus proving that the machine is primarily a matter duplicator instead of a transmitter. In the continuation, "Pandora's Millions," published in the June 1945 issue, matter duplicators, now sold everywhere in the solar system, cause an economic collapse. The market is suddenly flooded with objects and precious metals of all sorts. People who can't afford to buy a duplicator end up destitute, while everyone else has to resort to barter since money has no value anymore. The Venus Equilateral station scientists save the day by inventing a substance that cannot be duplicated. Needless to say, this is not uncharted territory both in terms of settings (like in *Deep Space Nine*, social life on the Venus Equilateral station revolves around a bar) and in terms of theme (the economic impact of automation).

In real life, the theoretical groundwork for the replicator should be attributed to mathematician John von Neumann, arguably the greatest scientific mind of the twentieth century. Von Neumann's achievements

---

52. George O. Smith, *Venus Equilateral* (New York: Prime Press, 1947). The book's original cover art is strongly reminiscent of *Deep Space Nine*. The book is available in paperback from Del Rey.

are too numerous to list here. Suffice it to say that he was instrumental in the success of the Manhattan Project, and invented modern computer science and game theory in his spare time. In the late 1940s, von Neumann first sketched out the theoretical requirements and the mathematical proof that, given the right conditions, discrete systems from simple cells to complex machines could self-replicate. He called the smallest possible of such systems a cellular automaton. Fast-forward four decades to just a year before *The Next Generation* went on the air. MIT engineer K. Eric Drexler built upon von Neumann's seminal work to popularize the concept of molecular nanotechnology. His 1986 book *Engines of Creation*[53] foresaw a future where molecule-size programmable machines would be able to assemble any object on demand. By the time of *Star Trek: The Next Generation*, the twin concepts of replicators and machines making machines had moved from down-market pulp hypothesis to mainstream scientific publications and the *New York Times'* bestsellers list.

ADDITIVE MANUFACTURING

The replicator represents a signal improvement over transporter technology. For all its genius and iconic status, the transporter holds considerably less economic promise than the replicator. It does one thing, and it does it very well, at least in the realm of fiction, far beyond the present possibilities of science. It is a godlike machine that confirms

---

53. K. Eric Drexler, *Engines of Creation: The Coming Era of Nanotechnology* (New York: Doubleday, 1986); for an exhaustive discussion of Drexler's book's genesis and impact, see W. Patrick McCray's excellent *The Visioneers: How a Group of Elite Scientists Pursued Space Colonies, Nanotechnologies, and a Limitless Future* (Princeton: Princeton University Press, 2012).

sci-fi master Arthur C. Clarke's principle that any sufficiently advanced technology is indistinguishable from magic.

The replicator is a different animal altogether. It is much less impractical than it would seem at first sight, and in its broad outline, it is grounded in academic research and industry innovation. It is the ultimate and idealized application of what is known as additive manufacturing, 3-D printing for short. Additive manufacturing is the process by which objects are built automatically bit by bit using preexisting schematics stored as data. These 3-D printers are a specialized type of a much older technology: computerized numerical control (or CNC) machines. CNC machines carve objects out of solid blocks of material (from wood to metal) with computer-driven lathes and mills. They are "subtractive," whereas 3-D printers extrude, deposit, and fuse material one microgram at a time. Even though they add material to an empty predefined shape rather than milling out material from a solid block, 3-D printers rely on the same principles of software control and multi-axis automated tooling. Their crucial advantage over CNC machines is their ability to create hollow shapes, such as curved tubes and globes, in one single piece. With regular CNC machines, comparable shapes require designing and machining multiple separate elements for later assembly. The 3-D printers are therefore considered more flexible and more efficient.

Obviously, this is not *Star Trek* technology, but one can see a strong similarity in both intent and process. While 3-D printers heat materials and deposit them layer after layer to create a predesigned three-dimensional object, replicators conjure coherent matter out of data. In a way, the improbable (if not impossible) physics is much less important than the economic model it heralds. By combining software with mechanical reproduction, additive manufacturing purports to remove human intervention from the shop floor and to reallocate it to the design office. It leads to a more optimal division of labor: to the human brain the intellect-intensive tasks of imagining and designing, and to the machines high-precision fault-free fabrication.

It is not an accident that MakerBot Industries, the leading manufacturer of consumer 3-D printers, would call its main product the Replicator. If you put the two devices side by side, you will notice a striking similarity.

In both *Star Trek* and real life, software and computing power are key. They take on all the mechanical and repetitive aspects of making an object, thus allowing human(oid) users to devote their energy and genius to creativity. Computers and software translate sketches into usable data on the fly. Then they let that data be manipulated and shared among multiple people or sites. And finally, they transmit that data to the CNC machine or the 3-D printer for production. The design data is turned into sequential commands for the robotic tools. Consumer models use plastic filaments of various colors, while industrial 3-D printers can fuse and shape metal alloys using high-powered laser beams.

Contrary to an automated production line geared to manufacturing only one type of object in great quantities, given the right design data, 3-D printers can make anything in any shape and on demand. They also remove waste and imperfections. By their very nature, handmade, one-of-a-kind objects cannot benefit from the efficiencies of scale, and they may occasionally suffer from irregularities and minute faults. But 3-D printers bring the precision and quality of mass production to single, unique items. You can have your cake and eat it too. You get the value and pleasure of a tailor-made object, with the reliability and consistency of automated industrial processes. Lastly, this setup leverages network effects: for instance, you can pick and choose any model design from publicly accessible databases, such as MakerBot's Thingiverse. Design can take place anywhere, and so can the production of the actual thing. It is distributed manufacturing.

There is no inventory, just a continually expanding database of models in the cloud, and printing stations all across the globe, either in public places or in private homes and businesses.

This is not quite Drexler's molecular nanobots nor the theoretical von Neumann cellular automatons that can make copies of themselves, not yet at least. But case in point: the longest-running open-source 3-D printing project, the RepRap, was specifically launched to develop a machine that can manufacture all of its own constituent parts, from circuit board to casing to extrusion heads. As with most open-source projects, what is learned and invented along the way is as valuable as the stated goal.

Additive manufacturing has gone mainstream: it has left the tinkerers' garages and academia's research labs for good. Serious publications such as the very staid *Economist* hail it as the harbinger of a new industrial revolution,[54] and large business conglomerates have embraced it with enthusiasm. In a recent interview, a Boeing spokesperson stated that "we have approximately 300 different part numbers on 10 different aircraft production programs, which amounts to more than 20,000 non-metallic additive manufactured parts that are on vehicles that we have delivered to our customers."[55] That is a hell of a lot of components on actual flying aircraft. Similarly, General Electric recently started

54. "A Third Industrial Revolution," The Economist, April 21, 2012, accessed February 24, 2016, http://www.economist.com/node/21552901.

55. Frank Catalano, "Boeing files patent for 3D-printed aircraft parts — and yes, it's already using them," *Geekwire*, March 6, 2015, accessed February 24, 2016, http://www.geekwire.com/2015/boeing-files-patent-for-3d-printing-of-aircraft-parts-and-yes-its-already-using-them/.

printing fuel nozzles for its LEAP jet engines.[56] The new nozzles consist of one single part instead of the nineteen used on previous models, thus increasing their resistance and durability by over five times. They are printed out of an alloy powder that is deposited layer by layer and fused with a laser (in a process known as direct metal laser melting). And that is only the beginning. Both industry behemoths plan to radically expand their use of additive manufacturing in the coming years. And you can bet they are not the only ones.

By contrast, consumer applications are still limited, mostly due to materials. Right now your home 3-D printer will only function with TPU (thermoplastic polyurethane) filaments. This confines the range of use cases to the whimsical and the artful, with the occasional headline-grabbing stunts. You can print saltshakers, Lego bricks, *Star Trek* figurines, busts of yourself. You can even make your own fully functional plastic gun out of printed parts.

That said, the 3-D printing community of hackers and hobbyists is brimming with excitement and a sense of possibilities. The toothpaste will not be put back into the tube. Nobody really knows where this is going, but it is going somewhere. You can purchase handheld 3-D scanners at your local mall to take snapshots of real-life gizmos for later printing. My kid, now in second grade, plays with 3-D modeling software like it's a video game and dreams of his very own 3-D printer

---

56. See Andrew Zaleski, "GE's bestselling jet engine makes 3-D printing a core component," Fortune.com, March 5, 2015, accessed February 24, 2016, http://fortune.com/2015/03/05/ge-engine-3d-printing/ as well as GE's own corporate literature on the topic: Tomas Kellner, "Postcards from Tatooine: Modified GE Jet Engines Give Algeria's Desert Province Power Lift," GEReports.com, September 13, 2013, accessed February 24, 2016, http://www.gereports.com/post/80701924024/fit-to-print.

to create toys. It reminds me of my elation, and my parents' complete befuddlement, when I first got my hands on a Sinclair ZX81.

Furthermore, 3-D printing technology is picking up steam. New 3-D printer projects appear on Kickstarter on a monthly basis. There are companies involved in 3-D printing desserts, clothing, shoes, musical instruments, houses, and even muscle tissues and organs.

Just to cite a recent announcement, on May 5, 2015, *Business Insider* reported: "Real-life Star Trek 'replicator' prepares meals in 30 seconds."[57] The device in question, rather unimaginatively called the Genie, can combine, reheat, and rehydrate stored ingredients:

> The Genie, similar in size and appearance to a coffee maker, can produce an unlimited variety of meals using pods, that contain natural dehydrated ingredients. So whether salty or sweet, an appetizer or a dessert, the device can create the food you crave in 30 seconds.

Based on the past experience of the personal-computer revolution, we can reasonably expect 3-D metal printing to reach every desktop in a not-so-distant future. Photonics, the scientific study of light sources, seems to be following a similar type of exponential path as computing. With the inevitable miniaturization of high-power lasers, you will be able to make and replace most everyday metal objects from the comfort of your own home. And you can count on the usual weekend political philosophers to jump at the chance to make their own automatic assault rifles. Oh well.

---

57. "Real-life Star Trek 'replicator' prepares meal in 30 seconds," Business Insider, May 5, 2015, accessed February 25, 2016, http://www.businessinsider.com/r-real-life-star-trek-replicator-prepares-meal-in-30-seconds-2015-5.

The first laser 3-D printer project hit Kickstarter in August 2014 (the Ice1 and Ice9 by a company named Norge) but failed to meet its funding goal.[58] It could only handle plastics, which may account for its unsuccessful campaign. It is only a minor setback. It is bound to happen. Just watch.

This strongly suggests that like Captain Kirk's flip phone—sorry, communicator—the *Star Trek* replicator might not be so far-fetched after all. Most likely, the real-life version of the device will in fact consist of several specialized machines. While the principle behind them is the same, *Star Trek* just happens to bundle all these different machines into one single fictional über-replicator. In that sense, the twenty-fourth-century replicator is the last 3-D printer you will ever need. Living organisms excluded, it can really make anything. It is as fast as a transporter, and it sports a streamlined user interface. Like with Captain Picard's "tea, Earl Grey, hot," you just need to proffer a vocal command and, as the French say, voilà!

THE PARETO MACHINE

As I hinted before, the replicator, a rather unassuming and pedestrian machine, has tremendous implications for *Star Trek*'s society. And not just that. It tells us a lot about where we are headed.

The replicator, as envisioned by *The Next Generation*, is the crowning achievement and the speculative end point of automation and mechanical reproduction. It is an ideal, the extrapolated sum of all the potential powers of technology. Beyond the replicator, there is

---

58. Norge Ltd, "Ice1 and Ice9 – The first low budget SLS 3D printers,"
     Kickstarter.com, accessed February 25, 2016, https://www.kickstarter.com/
     projects/1812935123/ice1-and-ice9-the-first-low-budget-sls-3d-printers.

nothing, no machine that can be conceptually better, that can more fully fulfill its purpose in the world. The replicator is the last machine. You cannot really improve on it. You ask and it makes. In that sense it bears a strong resemblance, at least in function, to Asimov's positronic robots, which free humans from toil and want.

In *Star Trek*'s twenty-fourth century, too, physical work is no longer required. The production of all the basic necessities of life, from food and clothing to toys and machines, is completely automated. John von Neumann's dream of machines making machines has finally become a reality.[59] This not only means a giant leap in living standards for all, but also a complete change in the distribution of work. Machines take care of the repetitive, energy-intensive, low-skill, high-output labor. They handle the transformation of natural resources into consumer staples. Meanwhile, humanoids can shift their focus to the high-skill, low-output end of the curve, the kind of products and services that require knowledge, education, creativity, and a personal touch, whether it be wine making, exploration, or a doctor's bedside manner. This is labor substitution on a very grand scale.

As I discussed in the previous chapter, physical labor still exists in the Federation, but as a playful and elective activity, one way among many to cultivate the self. For instance, maintaining all these wondrous machines does involve some degree of physical exertion. And nobody works harder than a Starfleet engineer. But engineering is above all an intellectual endeavor. Figuring out what is wrong with the pattern buffers or the network relays takes years of education and experience.

The replicator makes everything very cheap, and not just because *Star Trek* has cracked the problem of unlimited energy supply. Think of it in terms of inputs: to work properly the replicator only needs energy,

---

59. John von Neumann, *Theory of Self-Replicating Automata*, edited and completed by Arthur W. Burks (Urbana and London: University of Illinois Press, 1966).

matter, and data. The first two are assumed to be trivial, while model design may occasionally take time, artistry, and knowledge. Even then, the replicator uses the same utilitarian glass mug every time it serves tea to Captain Picard. In other words, it heavily relies on design standardization for most of its products. And for those things not stored in its data banks, one has to assume that it can still do it, as long as it is provided with sufficient parameters. It is only software. Code once, deploy everywhere.

Now consider the economic consequence: replicators are everywhere and can make anything on the spot, literally. This resolves most headaches that arise from mismatches between the supply and demand of goods. In our world, we generally settle these imbalances by way of markets and price-fixing mechanisms. Too much of something here, not enough of that something over there—let's trade. In *Star Trek*, on the other hand, this only happens for a very limited class of products. There is never a dearth of Earl Grey tea bags. The captain will not run out, and he will not be forced to overpay someone who is hoarding them on a far-off planet. Thanks to the replicator, there is no longer a market for tea bags, or many other things for that matter.

So to answer Captain Janeway's question, the replicator would certainly mean abundance but also profound social dislocations. Many people would find themselves out of a job overnight, including economists! There is one important proviso, however. Call it the Ferengi exception. In the hands of a profit-seeking Ferengi, the replicator is an amazing profit-making machine. The Ferengi owner of such a machine does not have any incentive to make it widely available to the competition. On the contrary, he has every reason to drive his competitors out of business one by one, by substituting real products with replicated ones. In theory, he could become the richest Ferengi that has ever lived.

Author Neal Stephenson further explores the negative implications of similar machines in his 1995 Hugo-winning masterpiece, *The Diamond Age*. In the near-future world he builds, advances in nanotechnology have led to the invention and spread of what the author calls "matter compilers."[60] In essence, they are replicators. They can assemble molecules into a multitude of objects, on demand. There are public matter compilers that provide basic necessities for free, but most other designs and objects are proprietary. One has to pay to compile them, and those who own the intellectual property rights are making fortunes.

The Diamond Age's world is one of strife and unresolved conflicts. The advent of matter compilers has not solved anything. In this scenario, replicators (or matter compilers) never fully become public goods. Only limited services are provided for free, on a sort of humanitarian basis. In that sense, Neal Stephenson's work fully embraces the notion that a post-scarcity economy is as much a matter of technological progress as it is a result of politics and collective choices.

A Ferengi cannot realize the full social benefit of the replicator within the bounds of Ferengi culture and economics. A Ferengi replicator is just a supremely profitable robot, an employee that will not unionize nor try to take the place of the boss. In the Federation, however, replicators are like air or public radio. They are public goods. They are nonexcludable and nonrival: nobody can be prevented from using them, and their usage by any given individual does not preclude any other individual from using them as well. In addition, because they can produce almost anything, replicators instantly confer their public-good properties onto all the objects they materialize out of thin air. They act on society like a beneficial virus. They are the perfect, albeit fictional, economic machine, a hypothetical instance of what is called

---

60. Neal Stephenson, *The Diamond Age* (New York: Bantam/Spectra, 1995).

in econ-babble a "Pareto improvement" (after Italian economist Vilfredo Pareto, who theorized the vast problem of the optimal distribution of goods in society). Literally, replicators make everyone better off at nobody's expense.

The status of the replicator as a public good is not disruptive to the Federation's economy. Remember that in the canon itself, its invention came after the advent of post-scarcity economics. In that respect, the replicator is not the only catalyst for what could be called "mature" twenty-fourth-century trekonomics. Its wide adoption took place in a society that had already moved on from older forms of capital accumulation. Yet it definitely made it easier and more efficient to forgo markets in most goods and to redirect work and personal pursuits toward more abstract, more elevated ends.

CHAPTER 4

"...ONLY A FOOL WOULD STAND IN THE WAY OF PROGRESS."[61]

NATURAL LIMITS AND TECHNOLOGY SUBSTITUTION

The planet Gideon has applied for membership in the Federation.[62] It is known for being a paradise: its inhabitants enjoy very long life spans because of its germ-free environment. Yet, its government is not as forthcoming as would be expected of an aspiring Federation member. The Bureau of Treaties sends the *Enterprise* to investigate. Upon the ship's arrival, the Gideons forbid any sensor sweep of the surface and demand that Kirk—and only Kirk—beam down to meet their ambassador, Hodin. No team, no accompanying party, no mission specialists, just the captain. Odd.

---

61. *ST:TOS*, 2x24: "The Ultimate Computer."

62. *ST:TOS*, 3x17: "The Mark of Gideon."

It turns out Gideon is hiding a terrible secret. The absence of disease and the Gideons' "love of life," as they put it, has led to gruesome overpopulation. The Gideons do not die of old age and do not use contraception. As a result, their planet is so densely packed that from space its surface appears to be covered in brown organic goo. Instead of a paradise, it is a festering hell where people are so numerous that they live like sardines in a can, and no privacy exists.

The heads of Gideon's government have hatched a desperate plan to solve this tragic situation. They will use Captain Kirk as a super carrier to infect their population with the Vegan choriomeningitis virus (*Vegan*, as in Vega the star system, not the organic food co-op). It so happens that ladies' man Kirk is a traveling vial of galactic diseases. He has caught the Vegan plague on one of his journeys and has developed an immunity to it. The Gideons, on the other hand, planetbound and living in a germ-free environment, are not so lucky. Kirk is promptly beamed to an empty replica of the *Enterprise* by subterfuge. In lieu of diplomatic negotiations, he is to meet and be seduced by Odona, the daughter of Hodin. Hopefully, Kirk will inoculate her with the disease through a torrid exchange of bodily fluids.

He obliges. He can do anything. He is Captain Kirk. Weird people in unitards—all Gideons—intermittently crowd behind the view screens of the fake *Enterprise*, seemingly watching over the progress of Kirk and Odona's mating ritual. I still recoil at how utterly deranged that whole scene is. It is nothing but a creepy alien peep show. Camp of the highest order.

Odona gets infected and quickly becomes quite ill. According to her father, she must die to serve as an example of civic virtue to Gideon's youth. Her death should inspire them to take responsibility and kill themselves. That nod to the 1960s' generational conflict is, shall we say, crude. In the end, Spock and Kirk discover the Gideons' stratagem and foil it, while Bones saves the young woman's life. No surprise there.

She is now a carrier of the Vegan virus herself, and is free to spread it among her compatriots if they so wish it. Gideon's admission to the Federation is put on hold. *Whoosh!* On to the next planet!

In this chapter we delve into the question of *Star Trek*'s economic Utopianism. Can we really grow to trekonomics' level of wealth? Aren't limited natural resources the ultimate barrier to a cornucopia? Does *Star Trek* fail Econ 101? Is it batshit insane?

"The Mark of Gideon" gives us the beginning of an answer, and it sure ain't pretty! It is easy to dismiss it with the benefit of hindsight, as it was an episode from the doomed third season of *The Original Series*. A write-in campaign from fans had saved the show from cancellation the year before, but network executives had basically had enough. Yet one has to be charitable and get past superficial impressions. Its main flaws do not lie in the storytelling or in the lo-fi quality of the episode (it was a so-called bottle show, where only existing sets were used in order to keep production costs down, hence the non sequitur of beaming Kirk to an empty *Enterprise* replica). It is the premise itself that is beyond repair.

Because its inhabitants abstain from birth control on moral grounds, Gideon becomes so overpopulated that its government attempts planetary self-genocide by way of foreign pathogens. That rather final solution to their population crisis is outrageous to the point of absurdity. Fans of *The Original Series* have to face it: as a plot device to illustrate the social advantages of contraception and family planning, this is terminally whacked-out. Yet it is also particularly intriguing because *Star Trek* writers and producers considered it believable and worthy of a full episode. To them, voluntary planetary-scale euthanasia probably sounded like a not-entirely implausible last-resort scenario, in case we didn't get our act together and curb runaway population growth. It was a logical, if a bit extreme, extrapolation that pushed the fictional stakes to crazy heights in order to underline the point about the actual real-world peril. At least some semblance of critical distance was preserved by ascribing that nuttiness to the alien-of-the-week instead of the Federation.

The show first aired in January 1969, in a context where fears of overpopulation had suddenly taken center stage in the public's imagination. Paul Ehrlich had published his landmark *The Population Bomb* to wide acclaim the preceding year. Strange as it may seem today, worldwide famine, economic collapse, and the exhaustion of Earth's natural resources were discussed on the nightly news as very real and immediate possibilities.

"The Mark of Gideon" was earnestly trying to address that "hot" issue in *The Original Series'* habitual brains-brawn-and-babes style. In taking up such a fraught topic, this installment broke with one of *Star Trek's* central tenets, the idea that in the future most of humanity's economic problems would be solved.

In that sense, "The Mark of Gideon" is somewhat out of character, so to speak. Usually *Star Trek* does not come across as so desperate. In fact, it is rather the opposite: *Star Trek's* sunny disposition, easygoing opulence, and reliance on technology are routinely derided as naive, unrealistic fantasies. Sometimes *Star Trek* is too optimistic for its own good. In contrast, conventional wisdom considers that in the real world, our prospects for material and social improvements are severely limited by nature. In short, there is no pie-in-the-sky, magical sci-fi techno fix to the plunder of the Earth by the billions and billions of rapacious humans who all want their cars, their burgers, and their iPhones, *now!*

This widely accepted view is completely at odds with *Star Trek's* economic optimism. Both cannot be right at the same time. To use the evocative title of John Maynard Keynes's 1930 essay, the "economic possibilities of our grandchildren" are either endless or they are not.

So who has the best argument? *Star Trek*, or conventional wisdom?

MALTHUS

"The Mark of Gideon" is undeniably a by-product of the population panic in vogue at the time of its production. The show's clunky narrative magnified something that was already in the air. To a lot of thinkers in the late 1960s, uncontrolled population increase seemed to preclude continued economic growth and the hope of abundance and welfare for all. It was taken for granted among hippies, technologists, and scientists alike that we were going to run out, and sooner than we'd thought. This made sense on a visceral level. We could not go on reproducing like rats or Tribbles forever, just as the Gideons did. We would end up consuming all of nature's bounty.

Many books had seized upon this trope of overpopulation and resource exhaustion. In science fiction, John Brunner had published his masterpiece *Stand on Zanzibar* in 1968. The story took place in a fictional year 2010, when a crowded Earth was bursting at the seams. The book gave ample space to the rise of Europe's former colonies in Africa and Southeast Asia. The title referred to the anecdote that if all of humanity's 3.5 billion individuals (at the time) were to stand side by side, they would cover the entire island of Zanzibar. The dark and gooey organic mass extending over the planet Gideon clearly suggests a direct borrowing by the *Star Trek* writing staff. Likewise, the theme was very much on Asimov's mind since his description of Earth's underground cities in *Caves of Steel*, where enormous crowds live in very limited spaces. However, while amazing books in their own right, these were marginal works by marginal authors in a marginal literary subgenre. Science fiction had not yet gained its current status as a cultural bellwether.

The demented tone and genocidal mania in "The Mark of Gideon" did not come from science-fiction literature. It was straight out of Paul Ehrlich. In his 1968 bestseller *The Population Bomb*, mentioned earlier, the Stanford biology professor warned about the threat of overpopulation. He ponderously intoned that "the battle to feed all of humanity is over. In the 1970s and 1980s hundreds of millions of people will starve to death."[63] Repeatedly referring to population as a "cancer," the book was a misanthropic exercise in doomsday predictions. With barely disguised overtones of sexual and racial hysteria, Ehrlich claimed that humanity was going to "breed itself into oblivion."[64] Some of his prescriptions were rather tame, running the gamut from free birth control and sex education for teens to voluntary vasectomies, while others were *Star Trek*–level insane. Or *Dr. Strangelove*, you pick. For instance, Ehrlich proposed to triage humanitarian food aid to developing countries based on which were more likely to survive in the long run. He also had this idea to spike US tap water with sterilizing agents, just like chlorine or fluoride, but for the gonads.

You can't really fault a biologist for being obsessed with people's reproductive functions; after all, that is the heart of the discipline. But you can take exception with the way some biologists tend to view economics and human society through the blinders of their science. These eminent and well-intentioned scientists brand humanity as the ultimate invasive predator, a swarm of rummaging wild boars who somehow stumbled upon language and atomic bombs. Ehrlich once claimed that the maximum human population hovers at around 1.5

---

63. Paul Ehrlich, "Prologue," in *The Population Bomb*, rev. ed. (Rivercity, MA: Rivercity Press, 1975), p. xi.

64. ibid., p. xii.

to 2 billion or so. Beyond that point, we exceed the planet's carrying capacity and cause irreparable harm to the biosphere's thermodynamics. And please, pray tell, how does one reduce the earth's population to its purported optimal size? Should we resort to self-inflicted epidemic holocaust, like the Gideons in *Star Trek*? And who gets to decide who should be infected and who should not? The recesses of such speculations are very dark. The only reason they are not treated as farce is because of the prestige and titles of the white men who voice them.

Ehrlich's bizarre screed of a book had a tremendous impact. It captured the Zeitgeist with accessible populist science and a knack for polemics.

Among many side effects, Ehrlich's fevered warnings about the physical impossibility of feeding teeming hordes of billions (all conveniently located in southern climes) prompted the creation of the Club of Rome. In 1972, this ad hoc assemblage of business leaders, government bureaucrats, and socialites released a landmark research report entitled *The Limits to Growth*. Based on a rough computer model, it sold more than twelve million copies worldwide and stoked a global panic about the coming collapse of civilization as we knew it. The oil shock of 1973 certainly helped popularize its main thesis. Its accuracy is still difficult to assess, especially given that its authors themselves cautioned that their simulations were predictions "only in the most limited sense of the word."[65] To date, the most notable real-world accomplishment of the Club of Rome research has been to serve as a blueprint for the one-child policy in China. Following the policy's recent rescinding, the extent and nature of its failure are the object of much debate in social science.

---

65. Donella H. Meadows et al., *The Limits to Growth: A Report for the Club of Rome's Project on the Predicament of Mankind* (New York: Universe Books, 1972), p. 92.

Of course, the cosmic irony of all this panic in the Western world was that it took hold exactly as Norman Borlaug and his colleagues were introducing new varieties of high-yielding wheat and rice to Mexico and South Asia. But very few of the self-righteous overpopulation activists had the time or inclination to keep pace with actual science. The Green Revolution completely passed them by, unnoticed.

It remains that there is a real and serious economic hypothesis underneath the hackneyed plot of "The Mark of Gideon." It is the old idea, first put forth by Thomas Malthus, that nature itself can exert checks on population and economies. Earth is supposed to have a finite carrying capacity, there are natural limits to economic growth, and economic expansion through capital accumulation and productivity gains will someday come to an abrupt halt. Once the number of people exceeds the productive capacity of the planet, poverty, war, and social upheaval will ensue, killing the excess population and restoring the old equilibrium. Not only will there be a peak oil, but also a peak gold, peak silicon, peak potash, peak phosphate, peak platinum, peak neodymium, peak dilithium (why not?), peak everything. At some point we'll run out of raw materials, and therefore we should conserve, recycle, and show restraint as a society.

Its apparent common sense and its moral undertones are the main appeals of the Malthusian worldview. It seems to jibe perfectly with our immediate, spontaneous perception of the world around us. It fits neatly into almost all of our conditioned behaviors: we all learn from an early age to cope with the fact that, to some degree, everything is scarce. We grow up to experience and understand that relative scarcity is a natural, and thus absolute, limit. After all, isn't the first truth of our own individual existence that it is finite? The knowledge of our mortality has a way of determining a lot of our ideas about the natural world.

Reality, however, is somewhat different and considerably more complex. After more than two centuries of technological and scientific advances since Malthus first published his *Essay on Population*, we have also experienced that both nature and society do not necessarily conform to our intuitions, our imagination, or our most intimate fears.

This all hinges on what we understand as natural. There is a major difference between natural resources—the generic, philosophical concept—and economically useful resources. For instance, nobody disputes that there is a physically finite quantity of dilithium crystals in the universe, or of hydrocarbons sequestered in Earth's crust. That limit is nevertheless entirely theoretical to the extent that the amount of oil or coal that can be extracted economically is much, much lower. At some point in the future, it will not make any sense, from the pure perspective of cost, to drill for additional fossil fuels because deposits will be too hard to reach and therefore too expensive to exploit. It will become markedly cheaper to develop and use substitutes. That is a very important distinction to remember. This tells us that as far as economics is concerned, there is no such thing as natural limits, only supply-and-demand curves.

Conventional wisdom clamors along with Malthus and his followers: But that's crazy! We can't grow indefinitely! We're going to run out!

To which economists retort: First, *indefinitely* is a very long time, and certainly not a useful variable or a valid frame of reference. Besides, Malthus first made his claims in 1798, and so far he has been proven utterly and decisively wrong.

Second, beware of biologists such as Paul Ehrlich when they start rhapsodizing about economic issues in biological terms, for they have an unfortunate tendency to draw panicked and misguided conclusions. Besides, this is the same discipline that brought us eugenics, the imbecilic idea that the human "race" could be "improved." Don't believe the hype or the apocalyptic predictions, even when endorsed by such reputable science-fiction shows as *Star Trek*. Humans are not cockroaches; we learn and adapt much, much faster, and in a very deliberate way. Culture, the accumulation and transmission of knowledge, is our killer app as a species. It has allowed us to escape nature's dominion over our lives. It is the only thing whose improvement yields consistent and measurable results over time. Evolutionary biology models of environmental pressure on insects or fish populations are not built to describe humans' relationship with the natural environment. They do not factor in culture. To adapt, bees and codfish only have random gene mutations and selective pressure. We have the Google.

Third, growth itself is a very fungible category: for instance, let's consider agriculture, Malthus's prime culprit in his argument for the existence of natural checks on economic and population growth. As a share of global GDP, agriculture has been declining for over a century, yet we manage to feed an increasingly large population. As a matter of fact, world population rose from roughly one billion in Malthus's time to about seven billion today. Agricultural production has experienced incredible growth in absolute terms, but not nearly as much as the rest of the economy, which is more brain intensive. Global average life expectancy and standards of living have shot up as well. We live longer, we live better, and there are many, many more of us.

And lest we forget, this is after taking stock of the horrors of the twentieth century. Two world wars; genocides in Armenia, Europe, Cambodia, and Rwanda; an economic depression—yet these world-shaking events barely made a dent in humanity's overall trajectory of progress. Population and productivity kept on grinding higher even through destruction, political upheavals, and engineered mass death. If that is not intriguing, then I don't know what is.

It may be that *Star Trek*'s optimism, its extrapolation of constant and compounding progress, is not so wide off the mark after all. It may be that, contrary to the theories of Malthus and his intellectual heirs, it is grounded in sound economic facts and theory.

And in bird poop. Yes. Bird poop.

GUANO AND TECHNOLOGY SUBSTITUTION

Our success as a species turns on our unique ability to understand the basic processes of nature. We investigate them with science, so as to refine them and multiply their latent powers to our advantage. Even the most humble of substances can be analyzed and reverse engineered to great effect. Among other benefits, science fosters technological substitution. Nowhere has it had more real-world impact than in the case of bird poop. How scientists found a better, more efficient alternative to bird poop offers a vivid rebuttal to the notion that there are natural limits to growth.

The Incas had been using the dried droppings of seabirds as a fertilizer long before the Spanish conquistadores set foot on their shores. Starting in the early nineteenth century, the virtues of *wanu* (in Quechua), or *guano* as it is known in Spanish, were rediscovered by European agronomists. They were eager to boost agricultural productivity in light of Malthus's dire predictions of looming economic and social collapse in the face of overpopulation.

The large-scale industrial extraction of guano started in earnest in the 1840s. The coasts and nearby islands of Peru and Northern Chile were methodically strip-mined of the bird poop accumulated over eons. The fine powder, rich in nitrogen, potassium, and phosphates, was not only easy to transport but also easy to spread on freshly tilled fields back in Europe and North America. It quickly became so valuable a commodity that it led to a worldwide gold (or rather, poop) rush to find other deposits, and even caused two bloody wars between Spain, the former colonial power, and Chile, Bolivia, and Peru. A law from that era, which grants exclusive concession to anybody who finds guano islands, is still on the books in the United States.

By the turn of the twentieth century, the age of easy bird poop was over. The world had reached peak bird poop. Bird poop nations and business empires were on the brink of collapse. The reserves of guano from South America were nearing depletion, while the global demand for fertilizers kept on growing.

It is under these trying circumstances that on July 2, 1909, German chemist Fritz Haber first demonstrated an apparatus that synthesized ammonia out of thin air to the BASF chemical company's principal scientist. Ammonia is a compound gas made out of three atoms of hydrogen and one atom of nitrogen. It has the advantage of combining easily with acids to form salts. The most common salt derived from synthetic ammonia is ammonium nitrate. It is used as a precursor in low-velocity explosives (such as *MythBusters'* favorite, ANFO: ammonium nitrate/fuel oil), as well as in fertilizers. Needless to say, don't try this at home.

Vaclav Smil, the geographer and historian of science, considers the synthesis of ammonia from atmospheric nitrogen the "most important invention of the twentieth century."[66] According to Smil, synthetic ammonia accounts for most of the world's population increase from

---

66. Smil has penned numerous works on the topic of the nitrogen cycle and its importance to humanity. See, in particular: *Cycles of Life: Civilization and the Biosphere* (New York: Scientific American Library, 1997)., and *Enriching the Earth: Fritz Haber, Carl Bosch, and the Transformation of World Food Production* (Cambridge: MIT Press, 2001). I believe that Vaclav Smil's extensive body of work is a necessary starting point for any student of trekonomics.

1.6 billion in 1914 to 7 billion at present. Ammonium nitrate is easy to manufacture and even easier to use by farmers. Growing crops absorb it and convert it to biomass with very high efficiency. It currently represents half of all the inputs in agricultural production and, as such, could be said to feed half of the world.

Fritz Haber won the Nobel Prize in 1921 for this triumph of science and engineering. His legacy, however, is ambiguous and tragic. Although of Jewish origins, Fritz Haber was above all a committed German nationalist. During the the first World War, this undisputed benefactor of humanity led the effort to develop explosives and chemical weapons on behalf of the German Empire. Despite his fame, his service to his country, and his medals, he had to flee the beloved fatherland after Hitler came to power. He died a broken man in Switzerland in 1934. The Zyklon-B gas, used by the Nazis in their gas chambers, was his invention.

Fritz Haber's process to synthesize ammonia is not only an epochal, era-defining invention, it is also a perfect real-world example of technological substitution. Once guano had become too scarce and too onerous, it became necessary to find a substitute. The lure of gigantic potential profits led BASF to back Haber and to invest in the first synthetic ammonia production facility in the world at its home base of Oppau (now a neighborhood of bucolic Ludwigshafen am Rhein, in Germany).

Substitution is just another way to describe technological progress in the context of a market economy. As population and the economy grow, we also grow our knowledge and human capital. We are driven by market opportunities and increasing demand to make widely available those things that were previously unthinkably scarce. Thus, the price of what is very costly today will inevitably tend toward zero in the long run, because either it becomes incredibly cheap to produce or it is replaced by something better and therefore it becomes obsolete. Think of guano, or the book you are currently reading (either in print or in digital form): at one point books were incredibly costly, very scarce luxury goods only accessible to a tiny elite. These days, paper and ink rank among the cheapest of commodities. Not to mention the actual price of storing bits of data, which follows Moore's law and declines by half every eighteen months or so. And what is true for books is certainly true for reading glasses, telephones, penicillin, fertilizer, railroads, refrigerators, flushing toilets, food, etc., etc. Empirical data suggests that given enough time, all rival goods are either substituted or become nonrival.

Technological substitution matters tremendously because it is the best way we have found to deal with limited natural resources such as bird poop. It is the primary engine of economic development and of humanity's welfare.

Its actual role over time has been the object of much investigation. How much does technology contribute to gains in productivity and overall prosperity? Based on their models, economists Robert Solow and Trevor Swan attributed about 80 percent of historical US economic growth to technological progress. In later research, economist Paul Romer in particular demonstrated that public investments in education and R & D, human capital for short, were a crucial factor in improving productivity through technology.

Robert Solow was awarded the Nobel Prize for his pioneering work, and Paul Romer has been on the short list for a while. Their research, and that of their colleagues, shows that there is no correlation between increased resource usage and economic growth. In fact, it is quite the opposite: technology and knowledge allow societies to keep producing more goods per single unit of raw materials. The total amount of raw materials used may still rise in absolute terms because of mechanical increases in demand (bigger markets, more people), but the rate of increase is significantly lower than the rate of productivity growth. This is why the share of raw inputs in every economic sector tends to shrink consistently over long periods, through vastly different rates of compounding.

In 1970 the average US resident consumed the equivalent of 2,700 gallons of gasoline per year for her total energy use. In 2012, that number was down to 2,500 gallons.[67] Another way to look at this is to remark that GDP per capita in the US more than doubled in forty years, while the total energy expended per person stayed basically flat. So much for waste, inefficiency, and Malthusian checks. It is important to note that in that particular case institutions and government regulations played a major role: energy efficiency mandates created strong market incentives for innovation and the adoption of substitute technologies.

What conventional wisdom labels as hard, unbreakable limits—in other words, the finite amount of raw materials in the universe—are not what they seem. While we may one day, in the distant future, hit them, it is highly likely that we will have reached the limit of these raw materials' economic usefulness much earlier. More advantageous substitutes will have replaced the now-dwindling commodities in the production process.

The problem is never one of the hypothetical natural limits of extractive resources such as guano or oil, or any compound or crop that comes out of the earth, for that matter. These commodities, exploited as private, capitalistic enterprises, were always subject to the iron laws of the market. If something becomes too expensive, if peak oil or peak silicon or peak phosphate happens, demand will drop. And if demand doesn't drop, if it is inelastic, as in the case of a necessary good such

---

67. Alliance Commission on National Energy Efficiency Policy, *The History of Energy Efficiency* (Washington, DC: Alliance to Save Energy, 2013). Accessed March 2, 2016, https://www.ase.org/sites/ase.org/files/resources/Media%20browser/ ee_commission_history_report_2-1-13.pdf.

as fertilizer, then the incentives to invent an equivalent ersatz will kick into full gear. In the end, what matters to us in regards to any natural resource is not the actual molecules it is made of, but the services it can provide us, once extracted and transformed. It may look like raw materials are absolutely necessary for innovation and economic growth. But looks are deceiving. Imagination, knowledge, and market demand are *always* the main catalysts and the main ingredients.

This does not imply that innovation will somehow happen painlessly by some magic of the market. On the contrary, substitution and adaptation are almost always experienced as social cataclysms. Entire industries collapse, people lose their livelihoods en masse, cities and even whole countries may crumble. There is a reason why the great economist Joseph Schumpeter famously called this "creative destruction."[68]

THE LIMITLESS RESOURCE

When combined, market incentives and human ingenuity can turn into a very potent brew. The Malthusian mind-set forgets the main resource at our disposal, one that constantly renews itself and gives back considerably more than it consumes: the human brain. That organ is a marvel of efficiency on its own. Its productivity is multiplied by its unique ability to interface with other brains, both dead and alive. Once networked through the input/output protocols of language and culture, the human brain can do almost anything. That is why I believe that, on balance, population growth is a good thing. For humanity,

---

68. Joseph A. Schumpeter, *Capitalism, Socialism, and Democracy*, 3rd ed. (New York: Harper and Brothers, 1950), p. 83.

the benefits of adding brains are nonlinear. More people means more inventions, more science, more art, and more love.

According to a recent study, the number of scientific publications increased a hundredfold within a century, and that number only includes medical and natural and engineering sciences.[69] During the same period, world population quadrupled. The growth in raw scientific output is an extraordinary marker of human development: it signals the spread of education and knowledge, the intensification of intellectual exchanges, and a rise in the number of stable research institutions that governments and private citizens are able to support. The actual difference in multipliers between population and scientific publications is staggering. Science and creativity are truly our main resource, and they show no evidence of imminent exhaustion.

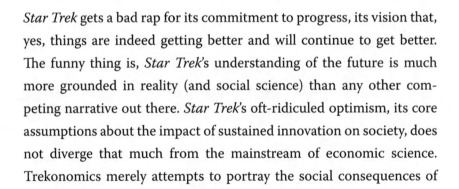

Star Trek gets a bad rap for its commitment to progress, its vision that, yes, things are indeed getting better and will continue to get better. The funny thing is, *Star Trek*'s understanding of the future is much more grounded in reality (and social science) than any other competing narrative out there. *Star Trek*'s oft-ridiculed optimism, its core assumptions about the impact of sustained innovation on society, does not diverge that much from the mainstream of economic science. Trekonomics merely attempts to portray the social consequences of

69. Larivière, Vincent, Éric Archambault, and Yves Gingras. "Long-term patterns in the aging of the scientific literature, 1900–2004." In Proceedings of the 11th International Conference of the International Society for Scientometrics and Informetrics (ISSI), edited by Daniel Torres-Salinas and Henk F. Moed, 449-456. Madrid: CSIC, 2004. http://www.ost.uqam.ca/Portals/0/docs/articles/2007/ ISSI_Aging_1900-2004.pdf

what looks like extreme wealth for all, as a result of several more centuries of scientific and technology-driven economic growth. It assumes that our future trajectory will closely resemble the elapsed three hundred years since the onset of the scientific and industrial revolutions. It is not a communist-like tabula rasa but rather the logical extension of observable processes happening here and now, right in our midst. Just like today, human capital and innovation form the cornerstones of *Star Trek* society's welfare. What that really means is trivial to compute yet almost impossible to comprehend.

In the United States, between 1870 and 2010, productivity grew by 1.6 percent to 1.8 percent annually.[70] In other words, output per worker roughly doubled every 39 years for the past 140 years. By the miracle of compounding, 100 units of goods in 1870 turned into about 800 units by 2010. Even if you extrapolate to the twenty-fourth century using the lower average rate, you still end up with an astronomically high number (in that scenario, from 2010 to 2325, output per worker roughly doubles seven times over, from 100 in 2010 to 6,400 in 2325).

Using the United States as a benchmark might be a little too optimistic, if only because the United States was truly the Goldilocks economy of the past century. If we project an even lower rate of 1 percent annualized productivity gains for the world for the next three hundred years, we will still go from 100 of today's theoretical units to 1,600 by the time *Star Trek* rolls around. Note that this can happen without any so-called singularity, whereby some magical new invention would turn us all into superhuman cyborgs who never die.

---

70. Robert Shackleton, *Total Factor Productivity Growth in Historical Perspective: CBO Working Paper 2013-01* (Washington, DC: Congressional Budget Office, 2013), accessed February 25, 2016, https://www.cbo.gov/sites/default/files/113th-congress-2013-2014/workingpaper/44002_TFP_Growth_03-18-2013_1.pdf.

These numbers make trekonomics look rather tame. It may very well be that trekonomics does not require absurd growth rates nor social revolution nor even faster-than-light travel or first contact with pointy-eared aliens. Trekonomics amplifies the better impulses already at work in our existing economic system. Its only speculative aspect resides in its description of reconfigured market incentives and transformed social relations as a result of exponential growth. That is all.

Today, we seek to exploit inefficiencies and mispricing in order to extract monopoly rents. For instance, imagine bird poop is becoming scarce and expensive. I will try my very best to invent a substitute that will be unique, hard to copy, and very popular all at the same time, so that I can corner the market and live the long and prosperous life of a rentier robber baron. My invention will have changed the world for the better. It will also have put a lot of other people out of business as an unintended consequence. That is largely unavoidable with market-driven technological substitution.

In trekonomics the incentives and motivations are not so crudely materialistic, nor are they so disruptive to people's livelihoods. And they do not need to be, because everyone in the Federation already lives like a king, thanks to the accretion of productivity gains over time. As we have seen before, in trekonomics incentives are about reputation and symbol, public recognition and glory, and what could be called self-improvement.

It is true of our world as well, but not to the same extent. Money usually precedes reputation as an index of success. Once money is no longer needed as the primary instrument for pricing and exchanging goods and information, all that is left is our existential thirst to be recognized and loved by others.

If you can ignore the gadgets and the aliens in drag for a moment, you will have to admit that *Star Trek* in fact eschews the romance of science fiction. *Star Trek*'s future is just not that exciting. It is devoid of catastrophic danger or life-threatening drama. It is very much a continuation of the present. In a way, it is not even clear that *Star Trek*'s future really deserves its usual utopian label.

NEWS OF OUR DEMISE . . .

Our culture hungers for the cheap thrills of apocalypse. Doom-and-gloom talk is exciting and sensational, and even more so in the guise of authoritative science. That does not make it right. It is the educated and liberal version of conspiratorial thinking (if the word "thinking" can apply to the reptilian part of the human brain). It is Greek tragedy for the Information Age: the almighty gods, inscrutable and hidden, are angry at us for reasons beyond our comprehension, and they are out to fuck us up. And so, like poor Oedipus, the more we try to escape our fate the closer we get to meeting it. It is exciting because it is scary as hell. It gets people riled up. Reality can't really compete with that brand of "we're all gonna die" escapism, especially when it is delivered by highly credentialed sages.

Star Trek doesn't hold a candle to that type of entertainment. *Star Trek* is boring, which is also why it is hopeful. It is the business-as-usual future.

That is not to say that our actual future will necessarily be as bright as *Star Trek* depicts. Not all is perfect in the best of all possible worlds— far from it. We all have a responsibility to be engaged and to work and fight to mitigate the most troublesome effects of our presence on Earth. After all, we are leaving a trail of mass species extinction and ocean acidification in the fossil record. Claiming our own geological layer of gunk and heavy metals, like the asteroid that ended the dinosaurs' reign, is no small feat. In light of that, the net present value of any improvement, any innovation or gain in efficiency, however marginal, is enormous and worth the effort.

Human industry and ingenuity, while incredibly beneficial, are without a doubt the cause of our current global warming predicament. They are also the remedy. We are not going to destroy ourselves as a result of global warming or overpopulation. It will not be simple or painless, but it is demonstrably within our powers. That is why alarmist popular science, along with dystopian science fiction of every stripe, should not be taken too literally. News of our imminent demise has been greatly exaggerated. Doom is highly melodramatic, and melodrama sells.

While *Star Trek* tells us that there are objective, historically documented, and economically measurable reasons not to get into a fetal position and freak out, it also warns us of the challenges ahead.

CHAPTER 5

"...THE THOUGHT THAT WARP ENGINES MIGHT BE CAUSING SOME KIND OF DAMAGE"[71]

FREE RIDING AND NEGATIVE EXTERNALITIES IN A POST-SCARCITY WORLD

Stardate 47310.2, in the seventh season of the *Enterprise-D* voyages. The USS *Fleming*, a Starfleet Medical transport ship, has disappeared in the region of space known as the Hekaras Corridor. The Corridor, several light-years in length, gets its name from the fields of tetryon particles that surround it and make it a delicate affair to traverse at warp speed (don't ask). The *Fleming's* disappearance raises suspicions. The ship is carrying a very valuable supply of biomimetic gel. The *Enterprise* goes on the hunt for the missing vessel, even though the tetryon fields appear to hamper the range and accuracy of its sensors.

---

71. *ST:TNG*, 7x09: "Force of Nature."

Upon entering the Corridor, the *Enterprise* encounters a stranded Ferengi transport ship. Although the Ferengi vessel is completely crippled and dead in space, it greets the *Enterprise* with a volley of phaser fire. DaiMon Prak, the Ferengi commanding officer, justifies his belligerence by asserting that the *Enterprise* is responsible for the verteron pulse that put his ship out of action (again, don't ask). He is nonetheless mollified by Captain Picard's offer of assistance. The plot thickens. What exactly incapacitated the Ferengi ship? And what of the *Fleming*?

Who did it?

Proceeding farther into the Hekaras Corridor, the *Enterprise* comes across a large debris field largely made of duranium parts, maybe a telltale sign of the *Fleming*'s untimely fate. As the crew begins a sensor sweep to survey the area, Data detects what seems like a "small metallic object."[72] This probe emits a strong burst of verterons, the same type of high-energy radiation that brought the Ferengi ship to a standstill (just drop it, nothing is gained by asking). Captain Picard attempts to pull back but it is too late. The *Enterprise* has lost warp propulsion, shields, and all other subspace systems. It is now adrift in space.

A small shuttlecraft approaches the *Enterprise*, and its two Hekaran occupants beam straight into Main Engineering. "What do you want?" asks Geordi. "We are trying to make you listen," replies the man. "You are killing us,"[73] adds his female companion.

The two Hekaran siblings, Rabal and Serova, are scientists. They have discovered that travel at warp speed through the Hekaras Corridor creates subspace singularities, literally tearing apart the space-time continuum. Most ominously, it would seem that the phenomenon is not limited to their region of space. In fact, it affects every quadrant of the galaxy. However, Rabal and Serova do not have definitive proof yet,

---

72. Ibid.

73. Ibid.

only their models and calculations. They have nonetheless mined the Corridor to attract the attention of the Federation.

In spite of their condemnable tactics, Captain Picard agrees to review their findings because of the seriousness of the claims. Data gets to work. His preliminary investigation turns up intriguing results. It would appear that there might be some merit to the maverick scientists' research after all. As Captain Picard summarizes their contention: "It is like pacing up and down on the same piece of carpet. Eventually you wear it out."[74]

The analogy might not be the most fortunate, but it drives the point across. Travel at warp speed is slowly destroying the very fabric of space. If warp propulsion is allowed to continue unabated, it will eventually render unsafe the environment in which it takes place. The milieu that makes possible and sustains faster-than-light interstellar travel will disappear. Put in more exact economic terms, because of overuse by warp-capable civilizations, the common resource, space-time, is at risk of becoming extremely scarce if not entirely unavailable.

THE TRAGEDY OF THE GALACTIC COMMONS

This chapter deals with negative externalities, the cost of an activity to a third party who is not involved in said activity. In this case, the activity is warp travel, the third parties are the Hekaran people—and, by extension, the entire galactic community—and the externality is the space-time continuum itself.

It turns out that every race, every civilization, is adversely affected by a few people's use of warp engines: as more and more aliens use high-energy warp travel, space-time begins to break down, reducing

---

74. Ibid.

its availability for all. It is a textbook example of what ecologist Garrett Hardin famously called "the tragedy of the commons,"[75] where groups of individuals, from villagers to entire societies, end up depleting resources they share in common. "Force of Nature" raises the question of how an incredibly opulent and absolutely free society such as *Star Trek's* manages negative externalities to avoid the tragedy of the commons.

Just like "The Mark of Gideon," "Force of Nature" is a single-issue episode. It aired in October 1993, at the beginning of *Next Generation's* last season. Interestingly, the show's original working title was "Limits." It was a deliberate attempt at doing an episode about environmental crisis, and more specifically the "ozone hole," as producer Jeri Taylor put it somewhat unartfully.[76]

Because it is so hard to turn such a complex and abstract topic into an entertaining narrative, "Force of Nature" ends up burying the lead. That is its major failure, in my opinion. It gives short shrift to the real problem at hand: collective action. Toward the end of the episode, Picard announces that, based on the preliminary evidence, Starfleet has decided to curb its use of high-warp travel. He goes on to add: "The Federation is sharing all our data with warp-capable species. We can only hope that they realize it's in their own interests and take similar action." That observation, the single-most important line of the entire episode, feels almost like a throwaway.

75. Garrett Hardin, "The Tragedy of the Commons," *Science*, n.s., 162:3859 (Dec. 13, 1968): pp. 1243–48.

76. Larry Nemecek, *The Star Trek: The Next Generation Companion*, rev. ed. (New York: Pocket Books, 2003).

The problem at hand is, of course, that not every Alpha Quadrant race is as concerned about the health and integrity of the fabric of space. The Federation's findings and recommendations about limiting speed to warp five are passed along to the Cardassians and the Romulans, but with no guarantee that they will follow them. Worf assures his comrades that the Klingon Empire will adhere to the new voluntary restrictions, but he is much less sanguine about the Romulans.

Picard's worries are legitimate. He is keenly aware that the rational choice for other civilizations, their best utility-maximizing course of action, would be to free ride on the back of the Federation's efforts at restraining its own use of high-speed space travel. This is the real challenge: the Federation's virtuous behavior can only be effective if it is adopted by all the other warp-capable civilizations without exception. Otherwise, it is both useless for the galactic environment and greatly detrimental to the Federation's welfare and standing in interstellar affairs.

The Klingon Empire will follow the Federation's lead and comply with the new curbs on warp speed. Who would have thought the Klingons were so responsible and respectful of nature? It does make some sense, though: fundamentally, Klingons are hopeless romantics. They live and die by an antiquated code of conduct that stresses honor, loyalty, and sacrifice. Usually, a quaint reverence for the enchantments of the natural world is not far behind such chivalrous ideals. But by comparison, Cardassians and Romulans are cold and shifty. And they have a cultural bias and a much greater interest in adopting a business-as-usual approach. Let the Federation and its allies shoulder all the burden of mitigating the risks of space-time's unraveling, while they will be free to gain a major strategic advantage over their foes. There will always be enough time to take care of the space-time continuum when all enemies are crippled and defeated by their own self-imposed, virtuous behavior. In galactic affairs, as on Earth, it might not pay to be good stewards of the environment.

The Federation gives itself some wiggle room by establishing an exception for emergencies. In addition, the Federation does not even attempt to unilaterally extract a price for bad behavior by other races. It correctly estimates that the cost of such a policy would be prohibitive. It would likely mean war. So the Federation does the only thing it can in the present: it hopes that by modeling good, science-based behavior, it will somehow sway the more selfish governments or shame them into doing the right thing.

If they do not, however, then the Federation will have to seriously reevaluate its policy in the face of mounting strategic losses, hence the escape hatch of the emergency provision. In that likely case, only space itself will bear the cost of high-warp travel, at least for a while. Eventually all the Alpha Quadrant civilizations will have to pay a price too, but the argument could be made that it is much better to expand and consolidate now, so as to maximize one's strength and aggressively advance one's positional advantages until the galactic environmental crisis reaches its climax. Simply put, when the time inevitably comes to impose painful restrictions on everyone, would you rather be one of those who are forcibly compelled to adjust, probably at gunpoint, or would you prefer to be the one who sets the rules and enforces the change by dint of strategic supremacy?

This is also a classic problem of collective action, where the sum of all self-interested behaviors does not lead to a positive outcome for all. It demonstrates how the long-term, optimal policy that would benefit all the Alpha Quadrant powers equally (that is, preserving the fabric of space to allow for warp travel, at considerably lower speeds) is at odds with each race's rational self-interest and objectives, which is to gain and maintain a dominant position in the game rather than share the prize equally among all participants. Rightly or wrongly, the

Romulans, the Cardassians, and others operate on the belief that the galactic environmental crisis is in fact a competition for supremacy, a zero-sum game, and that there will be winners and losers.

It is almost impossible to ascertain the validity of that premise, especially because of the unusual nature of the game. Unlike the Federation, Romulans and Cardassians are not accustomed to conducting foreign policy on the basis of altruism. To them, galactic politics is the brutal business of power and self-preservation. It falls in the category of win or lose. Mutually beneficial outcomes are not their main goal; they probably do not even appear on their list of priorities.

THE GAME

What we have here is nothing but the *Star Trek* variant of the prisoner's dilemma.

It works like this: Imagine two prisoners are being interrogated in isolation. They have no ability to communicate with each other at any point. Both are offered the same deal at the same time by the prosecutor: if you don't betray your fellow prisoner, you will get jail time, but if you betray your friend, you will get a reduced sentence. Furthermore, if both betray each other, they will both get a higher sentence than if both say nothing, and if only one betrays, he will get the maximum jail time reduction.

So knowing that the best way to minimize your jail time is to betray, and knowing that the other prisoner knows that, what do you do? (Hint: the optimal outcome is what is called a Nash equilibrium, described by John Nash of Russell Crowe fame.)

Suppose you are the Federation: knowing that the Romulans' best decision is not to reduce warp speed and therefore to damage the galactic environment, your best decision as the Federation should certainly not be to unilaterally reduce warp speed either. If you were to do that, you would get none of the benefits of environmental preservation (because the Romulans will trash space-time anyway) and you would stand to lose your long-term strategic position vis-à-vis your enemy, the Romulans. In that case your best solution is to not reduce warp speed either. The reciprocal is of course true for the Romulans.

In the end, we are in a situation where the Nash equilibrium, that is, the best possible individual decision in full knowledge of the other player's best possible decision, leads to an equally adverse outcome for all.

"Equally" is the paramount term in this case. It means that from the standpoint of the individual player, such a hideous result is not the worst possible outcome. After all, you could lose it all by playing the good galactic citizen, and without even the benefit of actually saving space-time from collapse!

If you find this dreadful, it's because it is. Game theory, another one of John von Neumann's inventions (in collaboration with economist Oskar Morgenstern),[77] is the formal logic of strategic decision making under uncertainty. It was created at the dawn of the nuclear age, to better understand utility-maximizing behaviors and, incidentally, the mechanics of nuclear deterrence and mutually assured destruction. In our speculative case, its conclusions are not easily dismissed. The fabric of space-time will be profoundly damaged, if not beyond repair, because it is demonstrably the best possible course of action for both the Federation and the Romulans.

It is not even clear that a breakthrough in space-travel technology, such as transwarp or wormhole carving, would work. If either the Federation or the Romulans came up with a nonpolluting alternative

---

77. See John von Neumann and Oskar Morgenstern, *Theory of Games and Economic Behavior* (Princeton: Princeton University Press, 1944).

to warp engines, would they be inclined to share it with every other Alpha Quadrant race? The Federation might, given its strong bias for peaceful coexistence and ethical behavior. But more adversarial regimes such as the Romulans? Hard to say. In any case, the strategic advantage would be nothing short of overwhelming, so why share?

The interesting part is that the Federation decides to unilaterally curb its use of warp propulsion. It hopes to set an example and entice others to follow.

PRISON BREAK

Some may argue that prisoner's dilemma games are too schematic, that they fail to capture the situation in its full complexity. For instance, a growing body of evidence, the so-called social heuristics hypothesis, shows that in many instances most humans opt for altruistic behavior over utility maximization. Furthermore, research in behavioral economics amply demonstrates that in the real world, rational self-interest seldom is the only factor in the decision process. However, how this may apply to large entities or state actors is more hazy.

Another, maybe more convincing, criticism of the prisoner's dilemma model outlined above, is that it is presented as a single, final occurrence. Studies have shown that when the game is repeated many times with the same players, they tend to adjust their strategy toward mutual cooperation. People do learn from adverse outcomes.

It could be said that this iterative variant of the game is a better approximation of the Federation-versus-Romulan conflict over the use of warp propulsion. In a way, the game is being replayed each time a starship exceeds the safe maximum warp speed. The game's awful results repeat and accumulate, feeding back information to each player. This must have some impact on the Federation's and the Romulans' decision makers. By taking stock of space-time's rapid decay as a direct consequence of their actions and, hopefully, learning from their mistakes, both the Federation and the Romulans might ultimately decide to jointly curb their overuse of high warp speed.

Another significant objection to this type of model comes from the work of economist and Nobel Prize–recipient Elinor Ostrom. She forcefully argues that prisoner's dilemma games and the tragedy of the commons are inadequate reductions of vastly more complex and more dynamic empirical realities. As such, they confine policy and policy makers to terms that are too generic to account for the immense diversity of situations. She suggests that a broader range of solutions does in fact arise from the self-organizing abilities of the local stakeholders.

In her seminal book *Governing the Commons*, she explores fascinating real-life experiments, where the expertise of local actors led to efficient systems of common-pool resource management with minimal intervention from higher-level institutions. From these very detailed case studies, she moves to theorize that social processes do not necessarily fit into overly schematic models of decision making. Her great contribution is to show that communities and societies can succeed in maintaining common resources. As she explains in regard to the prisoner's dilemma and the tragedy of the commons:

> "These models can successfully predict strategies and outcomes in fixed situations approximating the initial conditions of the models, but they cannot predict outcomes outside that range. They are useful for predicting behavior in large-scale CPRs [Common Pool Resources, author's note] in which no one communicates, everyone acts independently, no attention is paid to the effects of one's actions, and the costs of trying to

change the structure of the situation are high."[78]

There may be a way out of the prisoner's dilemma or "Leviathan," as Ostrom calls the brutal, top-down regulation by state institutions.

She is careful to note that her work is limited to local examples. She specifically refrains from engaging in a discussion of worldwide carbon dioxide pollution. However, her approach, rooted in empirical observations, may nonetheless hold the key to the beginning of an escape route from our dreadful predicament.

COLLECTIVE ACTION

The Federation has solved these problems. Throughout "Force of Nature," it is never once in doubt that it will do the right thing by voluntarily curbing its use of high warp speed. It is in the nature of the Federation's governance. It is hard-wired to identify and implement the best possible course of action.

The problem is always the others. Romulans, Cardassians, Ferengi, and all minor warp-capable civilizations do not share the Federation's foresight and altruistic values. The benefits to the galactic environment can only be marginal if the Federation implements warp speed restrictions on its own. For this to work, for space-time to be saved from breaking apart, each and every Alpha Quadrant civilization has to strictly adhere to the same restraints.

In that respect, "Force of Nature" provides a lukewarm reaffirmation of the Federation's wisdom. Geordi La Forge, the *Enterprise*'s resident warp-propulsion expert, has to come to terms with the fact that

---

78. Elinor Ostrom, *Governing the Commons: The Evolution of Institutions for Collective Action* (Cambridge: Cambridge University Press, 1990), p. 183. It is hands-down one of the most important books of the past fifty years.

his passion and life's work is endangering space itself. As he admits to Rabal: "I have been in Starfleet for a long time. We depend on warp drive. . . . I don't know how easy it'll be to change." To which Rabal responds matter-of-factly, with a hint of foreboding in his voice, "It won't be easy at all."

What "won't be easy at all" is to convince the Federation's friends and foes alike to share the cost of adjusting their behavior, to cooperate for the sake of the common good, and to stick to it over time. The difficulty is not technological in the least. At its heart, it is a classic political problem of collective action.

Collective action is the grab-all term for the parts of economics and political science that deal with the allocation and consumption of so-called public goods. Because it is concerned with all the things that are in limited supply and at the same time freely available to all members of society—air, oceans, knowledge, radio spectrum, fire safety, and, yes, even space-time—collective action is of particular relevance to *Star Trek* and trekonomics. And not only that—collective action is also necessary to understand how our society actually functions.

Collective-action theorists aim to analyze the choices that groups of people make when consuming public goods. Who has the most to gain, who has the most to lose, and how can institutions and governments encourage collaboration and regulate consumption of common-pool resources to prevent exhaustion?

Public land, fish stock, fresh water, and space-time, as in the case of *Star Trek*, are some of the most notable common-pool resources. While their total available quantity and natural renewal rate can vary over time, they are nonexcludable and nonrival—that is, access to them cannot be restricted, because no one has exclusive ownership rights over them, and their consumption by someone does not prevent anyone else from using or consuming them at the same time. Everyone is free to avail themselves of these resources.

This is obvious for the atmosphere and the plants and plankton that perform photosynthesis. Their nonrival, nonexcludable character as common-pool resources is indisputable. Everybody gets to share in their products or in the services they render (solar-radiation shielding, oxygen, and carbon sequestration from photosynthesis). It is a little less obvious, but nonetheless true, of public services such as fire safety, national defense, or even government. In these cases, delivery of the services is delegated to specialists, and a society-wide bargain takes place whereby a majority pays in, while a minority takes on the actual duty. Incidentally, that is called taxation, and it is a good thing, an index of civilization.

Without rules or regulations, be they self-imposed or enforced by an external instrumentality (an agency or a government), overconsumption is almost always guaranteed. Such rules and regulations are extremely hard to devise, and enforcement is very complex.

EASY RIDER

Common-pool resources are not infinite. Scarcity and depletion always lurk at the all-you-can-eat buffet. This is the heart of collective action's most persistent and vexing problem: free riding. Free riding occurs, and tragedy may befall the commons, whenever individuals, firms, and states take more of a common resource for their own private benefit than the others who share in it. They free ride because they can, and because there is little society can do to stop them. After all, the goods are plentiful, and are free for the taking.

We can point to many instances of common-resource collapse in the wake of excessive free riding. The disappearance of codfish off the coast of Newfoundland provides a stark illustration. Both local fishermen and commercial operators had every incentive to draw on a seemingly inexhaustible stock of cod. It was there, available to anyone with a trawler. And so trawl they did, until there was nothing left to fish and their economic livelihood had vanished.

The self-destruction of Nova Scotian cod fishing is a famous and amply documented example of the tragedy of the commons. But free riding can take on other, more pernicious forms. Oil companies and car manufacturers poisoned the atmosphere with leaded gasoline for half a century because it prevented car engines from sputtering. Willingly or not, we abetted their crime by our continued consumption. Thanks to science and political activism, we mustered the power to ban lead in domestic products. However, the public health consequences and the costs borne by society were enormous (including but not limited to widespread disruption of prefrontal cortex development in children, leading to significant increases in violent crime).[79] We let oil and car companies free ride on the back of society. It would have taken much longer to ban lead had it not been for the heroic work of Caltech geochemist Clair Patterson.

Due to their physical attributes, some common-pool resources can be managed and restored over time (for instance, aquifers, forests, or fish stock), while others cannot. It is relatively straightforward to substitute guano or oil, especially when fortune awaits the entrepreneurs who invent and sell the substitutes. It is difficult to replenish local fisheries or forests, but it is far from impossible and it has been done. It is orders of magnitude more complex to scrub the carbon dioxide accumulated in the atmosphere since the dawn of the Industrial Age.

The effects of self-interested market-driven enterprises, both local and multinational, spill over to the realm of common resources. Forest

---

79. In that particular case, see Lauren K. Wolf, "The Crimes of Lead," Chemical and Engineering News, accessed February 25, 2016, http://cen. acs.org/articles/92/ i5/Crimes-Lead.html.

clearing for agriculture and oil extraction and consumption have an immediate and direct impact on the largest common-pool resource, the atmosphere. Human economic activity releases greenhouse gases, like methane and carbon dioxide. Oceans and forests can only absorb so much of these, and not without unintended feedbacks such as acidification, which in turn triggers dangerous perturbations of food chains. The excess gases that cannot be absorbed by the oceans are stored in the atmosphere, leading to global warming and all manner of assorted disasters (drought, heat waves, glaciers lost, permafrost melting, and sea-level rise, among others).

According to the most recent official UN report on climate change, we are on track to add two to four degrees Celsius to Earth's mean temperature by the end of the century. The UN panel forecasts that by 2100, we would need to achieve carbon-negative energy production to stay sustainably under two degrees Celsius of warming. You heard that correctly. The main international scientific body tasked with making policy recommendations regarding global warming is now pinning its hopes on sources of energy that would actually subtract carbon dioxide from the atmosphere. That is how bad the whole thing is. But the most shocking fact that often gets overlooked is that Earth's estimated present mean temperature is fourteen degrees Celsius and has been so since the end of the last ice age twelve thousand years ago—a two- to four-degree increase in less than a century is a very big deal. It is the *Mad Max* scenario, the one single time when trashy Hollywood science fiction gets the future right.

And just when you thought it could not get any scarier, here are a few other deeply troubling facts to lose sleep over.

Free riding takes place at a myriad of points in the overall system, from individuals to corporations to states. Many private economic actors routinely engage in various forms of legal and illegal tax evasion, weakening the very same public institutions that help and guarantee their business. This is free riding, but on government. The usual self-serving argument that everybody does it anyway does not make the practice any less craven or repellent. The managers and stockholders of these multinational corporations are perfectly aware that they are breaching the contract between their companies and society as a whole. Basically, they behave no better than Third World dictators who stuff stolen cash in Swiss vaults. Only a residual sense of guilt about the extent of their free riding makes them publicize their paltry philanthropic efforts and their so-called corporate-citizenship initiatives. They operate with the dread of getting caught, and thus aggressively support political parties, economists, and opinion makers who agitate against taxes out of naive philosophical principles. The perverse result is that all too often and in too many countries, the party of the free market, which in truth should defend open society, progress, and civic spirit, ends up as the party of tax evasion, monopoly, and free riding.

It is estimated that the global fossil fuel–industrial complex, which avails itself of all the imaginable offshore tax loopholes and local market incentives, is subsidized by states and governments to the tune of $400 billion a year. In addition, oil extraction, transportation infrastructure, cement manufacturing, cattle raising, and the generation of electricity from coal and natural gas—all these activities spew out carbon dioxide and methane with abandon. And why not? The cost of doing so is minimal since the atmosphere is the largest freely available common resource, and right now, no price is paid for polluting it.

Economic takeoff in very large countries, from China, India, and Indonesia to Nigeria and Brazil, is multiplying greenhouse-gas release at an alarming rate. It would be very hard to curtail their development, both economically and ethically. For one, in a globally integrated economic system, developed countries depend on these nations for their supply of cheap goods and labor. Furthermore, it would be unconscionable to forcibly deny them the right to enjoy higher standards of living, especially considering that Western nations, which got there first so to speak, are overwhelmingly responsible for most of the atmospheric carbon-dioxide buildup in the past century. The difficulty is heightened by the fact that the cost of current free riding is deferred into the future, and will most likely not be spread equally among all people.[80] The predicted impacts are expected to vary greatly depending on geography and the level of wealth and organization of local communities. The Netherlands and New York City have more resources at their disposal to face rising sea levels than Bangladesh and the Bahamas. At least the plutocrats in the Bahamas can always relocate to another tawdry beach estate. The farmers of the Ganges-Brahmaputra delta do not have that luxury.

It could be argued that this is the ultimate case where the aggregate of all individual, self-interested actions turns detrimental to all. Fossil-fuel usage is the Big Kahuna, the most colossal form of free riding. Cheap transportation and cheap power may benefit everyone from the narrow standpoint of price in the present, but they will eventually prove very noxious to society. That is, their total price is set incorrectly by the market: the additional cost of externalities, such as global warming resulting from greenhouse-gas release into the atmosphere, is not factored in. Professor William Nordhaus, one of the foremost environmental economists, summarizes the problem: "One major lesson from economics is that unregulated markets cannot efficiently deal with harmful externalities . . . unregulated markets will produce too much CO2 because there is a zero price on the external damages

---

80. The leading authority on the economics of global warming is William Nordhaus. See in particular: *The Climate Casino: Risk, Uncertainty, and Economics for a Warming World* (New Haven and London: Yale University Press, 2013).

of CO_2 emissions. Global warming is a particularly thorny externality because it is global and extends for many decades into the future."[81]

It is as much a market failure as the result of a deliberate distortion by incumbent players. Car and oil companies, power producers—even states—have a direct, immediate, and strategic interest in passing on and deferring the cost of externalities to society. The real cost of intensive fossil-fuel use is not reflected in the actual price of coal and oil. If it were, we would probably be much closer to the limit of hydrocarbons' economic usefulness, and the pace and rewards of deploying substitutes would be much higher. In a market economy, there is nothing like price signals to awaken the creative forces of free enterprise and to put in motion titanic shifts in social behaviors. In the meantime, the stakeholders with the most to lose in the inevitable transition are sowing FUD (fear, uncertainty, and doubt) to keep public pressure at bay for as long as possible.

Even the most virulent global-warming deniers do not dispute that aggressive policy steps to curb carbon emissions will upend not only oil companies' business but the economies of entire nations. As writer and activist Naomi Klein astutely remarks in her latest book, one should listen carefully to the deniers because they spell out the thoughts and negotiating position of those who finance them.[82] Technology substitution will make some folks fabulously rich and powerful, but it sure won't be the current established players, either public or private.

In essence, to put the situation in stark terms, the scientific consensus on global warming requires rational, self-interested economic actors in cartel-like dominant positions to either pivot dramatically from what has earned them their wealth and power, or sign their own

---

81. Ibid., p. 6.

82. Naomi Klein, *This Changes Everything: Capitalism vs. the Climate* (New York, Simon & Schuster, 2014).

death warrants. As soon as we let the market function properly—that is, as soon as the leading economic powers cooperatively set a price on carbon emissions—the business of the fossil fuel–industrial complex becomes that much less attractive. No wonder they are not exactly thrilled and no wonder that it is quite difficult to convince them to get onboard with reducing their greenhouse-gas emissions. Oil and gas producers, corporations and countries alike, are fighting for their long-term survival.

As a result, it has proven impossible so far to assign a global price on externalities. Carbon pricing and carbon-tax schemes have been implemented locally to middling success. More sweeping plans are languishing in government agencies' drawers all around the world. As the prisoner's dilemma shows, in this kind of situation, it is often a much more beneficial strategy for some of the stakeholders to free ride until the bitter end.

▲

Free-market idealists have no good answer to the overuse of common goods, precisely because well-lubricated market mechanisms are the very cause of free riding. They usually argue that privatizing economic activity solves the problem of free riding: for instance, one should count on the oil companies' rational self-interests to guide the extraction of oil in the most efficient and economical manner, especially if they do not have to pay for the pollution they cause. That is, the long-term cost of their activity to society as a whole. Fundamentally, their business is built around avoiding paying for these negative externalities, the true cost of inputs. The air, on the other hand, belongs to everyone. Everyone uses it for free. One cannot easily bring it into the market's orbit. Try to imagine a market for breathable air, something along the line of the movie *Total Recall*, where the evil corporation that controls Martian mines has a monopoly on the supply of air. While this certainly makes for excellent dystopian science fiction, it is highly doubtful that in the real world it would prove either practical or beneficial to market participants.

When it comes to free riding on common-pool resources, the silence of Ayn Rand's libertarian disciples is deafening. To be perfectly fair, the essayist and libertarian god Murray Rothbard himself considered pollution an aggression against private property and as such worth shutting down (by judicial authority or by force). Obviously, like most libertarian doctrine, the practicality of such absolutist views belongs more in science fiction than policy making. It also seems to contradict the libertarians' long and successful public advocacy against regulations of all sorts.

The existence of free riding highlights the fundamental inconsistency of a certain economic idealism that regards the pursuit of self-interest as ultimately good to society as a whole. Humans have developed two types of responses to resource scarcity: technological substitution and collective action. On the one hand, market-based economics is extremely efficient at spurring innovation. It is not the sole avenue to promote technological progress, but it certainly works. When unleashed, as in the case of guano and the synthesis of ammonia discussed earlier, the animal spirits of the market can mitigate resource scarcity. But this only works as long as these resources and raw materials fall within the purview of private enterprise and the cost of externalities remains tolerable to society. In other words, as the Ferengis would say, substitution works when there is a profit in it.

Common-pool resources, on the other hand, are free and available to all. That makes them that much less sensitive to the usual market mechanisms. You cannot put air in a bottle and resell it (although I hear they sell bottles of pure Canadian air to smog-ridden Beijing citizens . . .). The incentives to exploit common-pool resources are too overwhelming: after all, they are free. Their management and consumption require a different approach. In order to preserve them for everyone's benefit, they must be made more expensive than they currently are—that is, free—and their price must be set by a cooperative effort of all parties involved. This implies negotiating binding agreements and setting up instrumentalities for monitoring the application of the contracts and for adjudicating disputes that may arise from occasional breaches. Above all, this requires institutions and the kind of trust in these institutions that only time, effort, and active participation can foster.

If any conclusion should be drawn from this quick survey, it is the following: free riding on public goods is much more of a threat to our continued welfare than the physical scarcity of raw materials. Public goods are always at risk of exhaustion because of their nonexcludable, nonrival nature. It would seem that in the absence of some form of regulation or contract, or any other agreed-upon system of pricing or rewards and penalties, free riding on public goods will inevitably occur. Designing and implementing regulation on such a scale is itself a very involved process whose ultimate success is far from guaranteed. In many ways, depressing as it may sound, in our world free riding is a feature, not a bug.

KEEP PARADISE RUNNING SMOOTHLY

Which leads us back to *Star Trek* and trekonomics. How does trekonomics manage to ward off the dangers of free riding when everything is a public good and there are no financial incentives to speak of?

Qualms and gripes notwithstanding, "Force of Nature" is a uniquely significant effort. It is the only episode in the entire canon where not only the *Enterprise* but the whole Federation has to wrestle with the central issue of our time: how to get nations, private entities, and individuals to cooperate in order to reduce their use of warp engines (or their greenhouse-gas emissions). And even more pressing: How to prevent some of them from free riding? That is, how to ensure that no one uses faster warp speeds (or emits more carbon dioxide) than all the others, thus causing much more damage to the space-time continuum (or the Earth's atmosphere) while everybody else behaves carefully.

I mentioned earlier that there seem to be surprisingly few people within the Federation that live high on the hog. The main impetus to free ride—shifting costs present and future onto the community— does not apply because thanks to technology, common-pool resources are close to infinite.

Nevertheless, as a response to free riding, a high-tech cornucopia sounds deeply unsatisfying. Even within the confines of highly speculative fiction, it is too much of a cop-out. It seems to me that technology substitution in and of itself is simply not enough. For one, public goods are not limited to natural resources. They also include the kind of services that only a society can take on collectively, such as education or security—the sphere of public power, if you will. One would think that effective public institutions, vested with the power to enact and enforce responsible resource distribution and usage, are a necessary complement to technological solutions. The problem is that the Federation does not particularly stand out for its strong, centralized, active power structure.

Apart from Starfleet, whose military status is itself ambiguous (I'll just say that Starfleet's taste for insignias and spandex pajamas makes it military-curious at best), the Federation relies first and foremost on deliberative democracy. It makes extensive use of seasoned diplomats and negotiators, and never misses an occasion to offer humanitarian assistance to whoever may need it. The Federation is almost all soft power, rather than totalitarian Leviathan. Most of the time, its institutions do not operate through any kind of overt coercion. Elective democracy is the norm. Member planets are self-governing. The president is a figurehead with funky clothes and cheesy hairstyles. And the little we see of the Federation Council, a sort of pomp-and-circumstance version of the *Star Wars* cantina, does not inspire the kind of awe the Romulan Senate and its Continuing Committee do.

Politics in the Federation is more milquetoast, more liberal administration than heroic statecraft. Elected officials may squabble here and there about marginal issues, but it is hard to imagine them representing conflicting interests or constituents at odds with each other about life-or-death issues. The occasional agitator may sometimes advocate for Spartan resolve and moral stiffness in the face of the galaxy's many alien threats, but strengthening Starfleet and building additional combat-ready starships hardly count as a revolutionary stance. At the end of the day, the Federation politicians' primary task is to keep paradise running smoothly.

Public authority does exist, but obviously it is not an object of contention for private commercial interests. Government contractors and energy companies do not need to influence politics for their own private benefit. It is not even clear whether there are energy companies or industrial concerns of any kind in the first place. These might exist if only because large organizations do make some sense when it comes to large-scale endeavors. Think of the Atlantis Project in *ST:TNG's* "Family," for example, which aims to raise the Earth's seafloor to create a new continent. Without profit motives, however, these large entities behave like Starfleet. They are akin to a public agency, one among many others, championing their respective missions, jealous of their turf and of their allocation of human resources.

In that utopian setup, political conflict can truly be an honest and open discussion between rival interpretations of what's in the public's best interest. Consensus can be reached through reason and persuasion. Granted, this is the theoretical purpose of liberal democracy as it is practiced in our day and age. The practice happens to fall short, that is all.

When private gain is no longer an ulterior motive in public debates, it is easier to include expertise in the political process. Expertise, free of outside influence and private agendas, can be leveraged as a trusted, objective arbiter. In fact, political conflict resolution in the Federation comes to closely resemble the adjudication of competing scientific claims, where merit and validity trump prior reputation.

In the Federation, experts are trusted not because they are mere experts, but because any one of their findings must withstand the unsparing review of millions of other equally qualified experts. In that respect, it could even be said that the Federation's largest public good is human capital itself. Access to knowledge, know-how, and expertise is not restricted by burdensome intellectual-property laws or institutional secrecy. Instead, it is encouraged by the reputation economy, individuals vying fiercely and constantly for prestige and fame. Everyone is welcome to throw his or her hat in the ring and take part in the great brainstorm.

Moreover, scientific, diplomatic, or technical expertise is trusted because it is largely free of outside sponsors. The process and the institutions that carry it are also trusted because they function according to the scientific values of openness, transparency, and empirical rationality. To be fair, the only factors that could potentially color advice are personal ambitions and the logic of institutional competition. For instance, individual scientists want their conclusions to prevail because of perceived reputational gains. Likewise, public agencies and institutions always seek to expand the scope of their assigned duties.

The Federation is so chock-full of topflight scientists that it is very doubtful that bad or erroneous science could prevail in an open and highly competitive debate on policy recommendations. When the crowd is wise, as it certifiably is in the Federation, its wisdom holds real power. Making the right decisions is therefore greatly facilitated, to the point of being almost trivial.

The challenge of selling these decisions to constituents remains. The armed rebellion known as the Maquis presents an interesting case study: as part of a peace treaty with Cardassia, the Federation agrees to swap control of planetary systems situated on the common border with its former enemy. As a result, some Federation planets will become part of the Cardassian Union, and vice versa. Federation settlers will have to evacuate and relocate to new systems.[83] It is a calculated decision. Federation diplomats reasoned that the overall benefits of peace are worth more to the Federation than a minor displacement of population. The diplomatic bargaining extends peace to everyone at the expense of a small minority. Some of the settlers disagree vehemently and take up arms.[84] The public good at stake here is peace, and the free riders are those who would endanger it by their refusal to comply with the terms of the treaty. This is not so strange. Services shouldered collectively by society—safety, justice, and defense—are public goods in their own right. Starfleet, for instance, is the epitome of a public goods provider. It is as much a scientific exploration agency as it is a kind of galactic fire department, with a hint of a defense force, always on call to fix random problems on random planets.

The Federation deals with the Maquis free riders harshly. Some Starfleet officers defect to the Maquis out of personal conviction,[85] but they cannot prevent the demise of the guerrillas. This signals that, while decentralized and largely harmless in most circumstances, the

---

83. See *ST:TNG*, 7x20: "Journey's End," a very strange and intriguing episode for its use of Native American mysticism.

84. *ST:DS9*, 2x20: "The Maquis, Part I," and *ST:DS9*, 2x21: "The Maquis, Part II."

85. Fan favorite Ensign Ro Laren for example, in *ST:TNG*, 7x24: "Preemptive Strike."

Federation is not afraid to use force and coercion when the situation warrants it.[86]

All technological considerations aside, we can state with some confidence that the Federation handles its collective-action problems with a high degree of rationality and public deliberation. It may not sound very dramatic or exciting, but that is exactly the point.

It is unclear whether expert policy recommendations, once considered and adopted, are implemented outright or subject to majority rule. As Mr. Spock would say, it would seem logical for a society committed to the ideals of liberal democracy to ratify and confer legitimacy on any policy decision through formal votes.

Of course, this is not nearly as simple or easy as the show would let on. Good governance is not an iPhone. It never comes prepackaged and ready to use out of the box. If you believe that it only takes sound rules of order or a constitution, you are missing the point. What you never see in *Star Trek* stories is that governance is a dynamic process, slow and painstaking. It requires time and tending. It is built over many, many years, layer upon layer. It requires considerable efforts and a constantly renewed spirit of service and friendship from all involved.

I believe that *Star Trek's* highest utopian quality lies in the way it appears to solve collective-action problems. Technology, space travel, or the absence of money do not amount to much without an economic and political system that ensures optimal resource use. This means fair and unbridled access for all as well as sustainable management for future generations. This demands active participation in the decision-making process by all stakeholders, an intensely engaged and capable citizenry, and trust in the institutions and in the deliberative process itself. Talk of utopia.

---

86. *ST: DS9*, 5x13: "For the Uniform."

Well, maybe not, actually. In the same way that the economics of *Star Trek's* future appear rather pedestrian once you can see past the gadgets and the technological wizardry, it turns out that its political arrangement, the institutions of the Federation, are equally banal. As much as we can infer from the canon, it would seem that the Federation is what philosopher Karl Popper called "an open society."[87] The concept itself is fairly straightforward and derives from Popper's notion that true science distinguishes itself by its falsifiability. When applied to society, this means that every policy and every collective decision must be open to rational challenges until proven incorrect. This obviously requires institutional guarantees of individual freedom and a commitment to constant change. Concretely, an open society such as the Federation enshrines democracy, public debate, tolerance, and the free flow of ideas as a way to make constant and beneficial adjustments. In its ideal form, it allows for conflict resolution through rational criticism rather than violence and suppression. While an open society does not accommodate the received truths of tradition or religious or scientific orthodoxy, it nonetheless rests on justice and human rights. These core values are themselves subjected to the unsparing scrutiny of citizens and amended accordingly. Thus sentient beings such as androids and holographic doctors can gain full citizenship through contradictory debate and judicial review.

The Federation's system of government is liberal democracy of the textbook variety. While it is nothing special on paper, it is in fact extraordinary in practice, considering how incredibly difficult it is to implement in the real world. After several centuries of revolutions and, arguably, progress, we are still very far away from wholesale adoption of these rather basic political principles. Show me just one country

---

87. Karl Popper, *The Open Society and Its Enemies*, 5th ed. (Princeton: Princeton University Press, 1966).

today where the administration of justice is not biased and where policy decisions are rational, informed by science rather than guided by the invisible hand of entrenched interests or the prejudices of conventional wisdom.

Of course, the role of government is greatly diminished in the Federation because of near-universal opulence. Resource allocation and distribution among competing constituencies are only issues at the margins. The absence of scarcity attenuates a lot of the violence, direct or implicit, in the political process. Abundance and technology have rendered private property largely obsolete. As a result, there is very little worth competing for, economically speaking. In short, the Federation does not have a tax policy because it does not need one.

The Federation is perfect, or at least is as good an approximation of a perfect society as one can find in the Alpha Quadrant. Only the Borg does better than the Federation at collective action and optimal decision making, and not because the Borg is radically different—on the contrary. As I will discuss later, the Borg and the Federation are startlingly similar, and that is why they are so efficient at allocating resources. As Commander Sisko muses: "On Earth there is no poverty, no crime, no war. You look out the window at Starfleet Headquarters and you see paradise. Well, it's easy to be a saint in paradise."[88] And, I should add, the only thing that really stands in the way of paradise is the rest of the galaxy.

---

88. *ST:DS9*, 2x21: "The Maquis, Part II."

CHAPTER 6

"...THAT FUTURE, THAT SPACE STATION, ALL THOSE PEOPLE—THEY EXIST..."[89]

SOURCES OF TREKONOMICS IN CLASSIC SCIENCE FICTION

"The system goes online August 4, 1997. Human decisions are removed from strategic defense. Skynet begins to learn at a geometric rate. It becomes self-aware at 2:14 a.m. eastern time, August 29."[90] And then, ka-boom.

When it comes to intelligent machines, these famous lines from *Terminator 2* are the sum of all our fears. Arnold Schwarzenegger delivers them in his inimitable, Austrian-accented drone. There is no better modern version of Mary Shelley's *Frankenstein*. Machines of our

---

89. *ST:DS9*, 6x13: "Far Beyond the Stars."

90. *Terminator 2: Judgment Day.*

own creation escape our control, find us unworthy of life, and proceed to remove us from the face of the earth. *Terminator 2* is called *Judgment Day* for a reason. As in Mary Shelley's masterpiece, there is an undeniable element of Christian mythology in *Terminator*. That is probably why dystopian science fiction never fails to capture our imaginations. It is the same old morality play—the original sin and the fall of man—but projected into the future. It is meant to terrify and to edify. And it works. You don't go around playing God with impunity, little man.

That narrative has been the bread and butter of science fiction for the past two hundred years; intelligent machines as agents of apocalypse are a trope, a tradition. In the few stories that do not follow in that tradition, robots are either peripheral or simply ignored. Their role in society, a properly economic question if there ever was one, is seldom a topic of contention.

Take for instance the biggest science-fiction franchise in the history of the world: *Star Wars*. Paradoxically, in the *Star Wars* universe both the Old Republic and the Empire use armies of clones and robots while tolerating slave labor at the same time. Uncle Owen purchases robots from the Jawas yet demands that Luke Skywalker, his impetuous nephew, postpone his plans to become a pilot in order to help with the harvest. This suggests that Uncle Owen cannot actually afford more robots and so take full advantage of workforce automation. *Star Wars'* society is unequal. Some have the means to avail themselves of robots, clones, and slaves. Other must make do and scrape by with the help of their immediate families and nephews. Such an arrangement is closer in nature to the Roman Empire or the early American republic: an oligarchic minority controlling armies of forced laborers (whether they be protocol droids, clone troopers, or slaves), and the rest of the populace seemingly surviving. In its world building, *Star Wars* is looking backward, so to speak.

Then there are those stories whose explicit objective is to explore current political-economic realities under the guise of speculative fiction. In these works, the social impact of new technology is marginal, relegated to allegory. Think of Frank Herbert's *Dune*, one of the most significant achievements in all of science fiction. *Dune* distinguishes itself by summarily excising robots and computers from its universe with a backstory sleight of hand. We are told that some kind of civil war long ago destroyed intelligent machines and established an absolute prohibition on their usage. This is to let the readers know from the start that they should not expect any of the usual gizmos of Daddy's good old sci-fi. It clears the air for Herbert's intricate portrayal of Arrakis's unique desert ecosystem and of the humans who inhabit it. *Dune* is about many things—power, religion, the colonial exploitation of scarce resources, the complex relations between people and the environment—but it is most definitely not about machines and their place in society, on purpose.

These key examples culled from classic science fiction illustrate how unique *Star Trek* truly is in both science fiction and popular culture. It is as if *Star Trek* turned away from and even flatly rejected the more popular themes of science fiction.

Trekonomics is what makes *Star Trek*. In *Star Trek*'s future, technology is not just about the gadgets or about Moore's law of exponential miniaturization, or even about efficiency and competitive advantage in the marketplace. As Gene Roddenberry, the creator of *Star Trek*, explained it succinctly in The *Next Generation*'s bible:

Technical improvement has gone beyond developing things which are smaller, or faster, or more powerful, and it is now very much centered on improving the quality of life.[91]

In *Star Trek*'s universe, technology is humanistic, if not humanitarian. Artificial intelligence, plentiful energy, and ubiquitous automation not only enable material opulence but also remove the obligation to work to sustain oneself. With that out of the way, people in *Star Trek* have more time to devote to other pursuits. For sure, when watching *The Next Generation* and its successors, the absence of money is what jumps out immediately. It is the most visible and most arresting aspect of trekonomics. Fictional post-scarcity and a more egalitarian distribution of society's wealth may be nice and appealing on paper, and can be readily grasped, if fleetingly, by our twenty-first-century minds. No work at all, on the other hand—that is less obvious.

By disentangling humanity's pursuit of happiness from biophysical and economic necessity, *Star Trek* reprises Isaac Asimov's most original and singular economic proposition. This chapter is almost entirely devoted to Asimov's formative influence on *Star Trek* and trekonomics.

ROADSIDE PICNIC AND AN AMBIGUOUS UTOPIA

Before proceeding with Asimov, it is important to note that science fiction is not uniformly dystopian. A few sparse hints of *Star Trek*'s optimistic economic vision can be found in less well-known works.

Perhaps the most remarkable of these works dates back to early-1960s Soviet Russia. As far as I know, it is more a case of serendipitous convergence than direct appropriation. Brothers Arkady and Boris Strugatsky, who wrote together as a team, gave the first known outline of a post-economic, spacefaring human civilization, which loosely

---

91. Gene Roddenberry, "Star Trek: The Next Generation Writers/Director's Guide,"
     (unpublished manuscript, March 23, 1987), Acrobat file, accessed March 2, 2016.

mirrored *Star Trek*'s. The Strugatskys are known among movie buffs for penning Andrei Tarkovsky's *Stalker* (one of the greatest science-fiction movies ever made, up there with *2001*, *Blade Runner*, and *Minority Report*). In Russia they are as famous as Ray Bradbury or Arthur C. Clarke are here.

Their first book, *Noon: 22nd Century*, is a collection of short stories published in the Soviet Union in 1962. The action takes place in a world where hunger, disease, crime, poverty, and even nation-states have disappeared. Humans explore the galaxy and routinely encounter alien species. Some planets are also mysteriously populated by humans. The World Council has tasked an Institute of Experimental History to interact with these interstellar human populations. Its agents, called *progressors*, covertly help the backward humans advance on the path to social harmony. It is often a grisly and unforgiving business, and the progressors, because of their very high ethical standards, are not immune to overstepping their mission and intervening in ways that are disruptive. There is an undeniable allusion to Asimov's Psychohistory in the Strugatskys' concept of Experimental History, as well as an early form of the Prime Directive, but presented in a considerably more tragic light than in *Star Trek*.

One finds a first sketch of most of *Star Trek*'s themes not only in *Noon: 22nd Century* but also in the Strugatskys' subsequent books as well. It is tantalizing—did Gene Roddenberry hear about them at all? (They were not translated until several years after the end of *The Original Series*' first run.) In a way it is even more intriguing to think that Roddenberry could create the *Star Trek* universe, along very similar lines, without even knowing of his Russian counterparts' existence. Same broad conclusions, from the opposite side of the Iron Curtain.

While the Strugatsky brothers may not have inspired *Star Trek* directly, their influence reaches far and wide in Western science fiction. For instance, Iain Banks's widely acclaimed Culture universe is organized around similar principles. The Culture is a post-scarcity economy, and it does maintain equivalents of the Institute of Experimental History and the progressors. The Culture's Contact and Special Circumstances agencies both infiltrate and manipulate alien societies. The Culture novels were published during *The Next Generation*'s run, and while they may have influenced it, they are profoundly different thematically. At the very least, they suggest that at that particular moment in time, the end of the Cold War, it became possible again to imagine post-economic societies and futures.

The Strugatskys' works are surprisingly devoid of robots or automation. Their depiction of a stateless, anarchistic society has strong hints of the Federation, but it only serves as a backdrop for gripping tales of love, loss, and grieving. Their protagonists make terrible mistakes, such as in the masterful novels *Prisoners of Power* and *Hard to Be a God*. Or they are faced with impossible odds and impending death, and must sacrifice themselves to save what can be saved (as in the harrowing *Far Rainbow*, my personal favorite). I would encourage all *Star Trek* fans to read the Strugatsky brothers, and not just for the sake of the franchise's archaeology. These are among the most beautiful, unusual, and exciting works of science fiction ever written.

Another major source for *Star Trek* sits in between the *The Original Series* and *The Next Generation*. It is Ursula Le Guin's monumental *The Dispossessed: An Ambiguous Utopia*. The story opposes an anatomy of contemporary political systems against an anarchist utopia. On the planet Urras, A-Io and Thu compete for supremacy. A-Io is a capitalist society, while Thu is modeled after the Soviet Union. On Annares, the other planet in the Tau Ceti system, life is organized around anarchist principles. The people of Annares do not have personal property; all of society's resources are held in common. Even in their language they try to eschew the possessive. Annares has a challenging environment: utopia is hard, and as Spock would say, the needs of the many outweigh the needs of the few. I always thought that the planet Vulcan, with its searing heat and rocky deserts, was somehow modeled on Annares. Similarly, the Vulcans themselves, and their society, seem to have a lot in common with the Annaresti—especially their disregard for material possessions and their cryptic thoughtfulness.

The Dispossessed specifically makes the case that post-scarcity is not so much a matter of material wealth or natural bounty, but an organizational option for society. Annares is a relatively poor planet compared to Urras. Despite this, its inhabitants manage to lead fulfilling lives and to create meaningful relationships. The main challenge is one of social change: the main protagonist, Shevek, a topflight scientist and a sort of maverick, creates quite a stir when he embarks on a journey to Urras to pursue his research. Annaresti people do not usually interact with Urras; they live in a self-imposed autarky. Some see Shevek's journey as a threat. This conflict is the heart of Le Guin's story: societies are dynamic constructs; Utopia is never complete; it requires constant tending and care. These themes informed not only *The Next Generation* but also *Deep Space Nine*. The problem of exchange and cultural diffusion between a utopian society (the Federation) and more run-of-the-mill nations (everyone else) is really what makes *Deep Space Nine* so exciting. The positions are reversed, however. In contrast to Le Guin's Annares, the Federation is the benevolent, infinitely powerful, and inconceivably wealthy political entity, whereas the other races are struggling in one way or another.

RED CROSS MEETS THE MIT FACULTY CLUB

As I noted before, *The Next Generation* cemented the franchise's definitive turn toward utopia. While Cold War America infused *The*

Original Series with a very distinct flavor, *The Next Generation* moved deliberately past these quaint conflicts.

The "bibles" of the respective shows highlight that change of direction. This is how, in his 1967 writers' guidelines for what became known as *The Original Series*, Gene Roddenberry describes the status of Earth in the *Star Trek* universe (emphasis mine):

> For one thing, we'll never take a story back there and therefore don't expect to get into subjects which would create great problems, technical and otherwise. The "U.S.S." on our ship designation stands for "United Space Ship"—indicating (without troublesome specifics) that mankind has found some unity on Earth, perhaps at long last even peace. If you require a statement such as one that Earth cities of the future are splendidly planned with fifty-mile parkland strips around them, fine. But television today simply will not let us get into details of Earth's politics of Star Trek's century; **for example, which socio-economic system ultimately worked out best.**[92]

One could not be clearer. This was Cold War America. Some very specific topics were not to be broached, especially those pertaining to the socioeconomic organization of *Star Trek*'s future society. In his interviews with me, Chris Black, writer and coexecutive producer of *Star Trek: Enterprise*, summarized Roddenberry's gingerly approach as "pragmatic." Chris expounded: "He's saying, look, people can have

---

92. Gene Roddenberry and Gene L. Coon, "The Star Trek Writers/Directors Guide" (unpublished manuscript, 3rd rev., April 17, 1967), Acrobat file, accessed March 2, 2016, p. 29.

whatever utopian vision of the future they want (I might even agree with them), but network politics will only let us show so much."[93]

The Original Series' real five-year mission was to denounce the prejudices and controversies of the real world: racism, bigotry, mutually assured destruction, the Vietnam War. It was a critique of the Cold War and thus it was also, necessarily, a critique of Cold War science fiction—that is, above all a critique of Robert Heinlein.

According to Roddenberry himself, no author has had more influence on *The Original Series* than Robert Heinlein, and more specifically his juvenile novel *Space Cadet*. The book, published in 1948, is considered a classic. It is a bildungsroman, retelling the education of young Matt Dodson from Iowa, who joins the Space Patrol and becomes a man. There is a reason why *Star Trek's* Captain Kirk is from Iowa. The Space Patrol is a prototype of Starfleet: it is a multiracial, multinational institution, entrusted with keeping the peace in the solar system.

Where it gets a little weird is that Heinlein's Space Patrol controls nuclear warheads in orbit around Earth, and its mission is to nuke any country that has been tempted to go to war with its neighbors. This supranational body in charge of deterrence, enforcing peace and democracy on the home planet by the threat of annihilation, was an extrapolation of what could potentially be achieved if you combined the UN charter with mutually assured destruction. And all this in a book aimed at kids.

Such was the optimism Heinlein could muster at the time, and compared to his later works, *Space Cadet* is relatively happy and idealistic, if a bit sociopathic. It makes a lot of sense that it had inspired Roddenberry. In *Space Cadet*, Heinlein portrayed a society where racism had been overcome. Not unlike Starfleet, the Space Patrol was supposed to be a force for good. The fat finger on the nuclear trigger makes

---

93. Black, interview.

it a very doubtful proposition, however. The Space Patrol, autonomous and unaccountable, is the opposite of the kind democratic and open society championed by *Star Trek*.

The hierarchical structure and naval ranks of the first *Star Trek* series were geared to appeal to Heinlein's readers and demographic, all these starry-eyed kids who, like Roddenberry himself, had read *Space Cadet* and *Have Spacesuit—Will Travel*. *Star Trek* used all the tropes of Heinlein but sanitized them. For instance, racial and gender equality were prominent features of Heinlein's stories. Nobody cared about your sex or the color of your skin as long as you were willing to sign up for the Space Patrol or the Federal service. *Starship Troopers'* Rico was Filipino, while Dizzy, a fellow private, was his (female) love interest. In that regard, Heinlein had undoubtedly paved the way for *The Original Series'* integrated crew. From *Space Cadet* onward, he made it a new norm in science fiction that people of color and women (as in *Starship Troopers*) could also be protagonists. That they were bestowed visibility and full agency in an authoritarian version of *e pluribus unum* is a different question altogether. Kirk himself, manly, resourceful, and decisive, came across as just dim enough to evince Johnny Rico. William Shatner played up to perfection the character's kitsch, his martial swagger and womanizing slightly off-kilter in a world ruled by diplomats and scientists, all eggheads and sissies, with or without pointy ears.

Later in his life, Roddenberry stated without ambiguity that he had modeled *The Original Series* on Swift's *Gulliver's Travels*, so as to get around the network's suffocating censorship. Science fiction gave him a convenient means to blow open public debate and to push against the ideological boundaries of 1960s television. Here he is, in his own words, from a 1992 interview culled by Marc Cushman and quoted in the first volume of *These Are the Voyages*:

Swift wanted to write satire on his time and went to Lilliput
in his story to do just that. He could talk about insane prime
ministers and crooked kings and all that. It was this wonderful
thing. Children could read it as a fairy tale, an adventure, and
as they got older they'd recognize it for what it really is. . . . It
seemed to me that perhaps, if I wanted to talk about sex, religion, politics, make some comments against Vietnam and so
on, that if I had similar situations involving these subjects happening on other planets to little green people, indeed it might
get by.[94]

Economics, and specifically the social consequences of automation
and artificial intelligence, would have to wait awhile longer. That does
not mean Roddenberry was not aware of the revolutionary potential
of robotics, on the contrary. He had obviously read Asimov's stories in
his youth. He had even produced a remarkable episode in which an AI
prototype temporarily replaced Kirk and the crew at the helm of the
Enterprise.[95]

Contrast the ideological tension in *The Original Series* with the
relaxed setting described in the bible for *The Next Generation*, twenty
years later. Discussing the exact same question of Earth's society in the
Star Trek universe, Roddenberry states:

We have established that most (if not all) of the major problems facing the human species have been resolved and the
Earth has since been transformed into a human paradise, with
large protected wilderness areas, grand parks, beautiful cities,
and a literate and compassionate population that has learned

---

94. Marc Cushman, *These Are the Voyages: TOS Season One*, with Susan Osborn
(San Diego: Jacobs/Brown Press, 2013).

95. *ST:TOS*, 2x24: "The Ultimate Computer."

to appreciate life as a grand adventure.[96]

The much looser tone and thematic freedom in part reflect the shifting economics of the American television industry in the 1980s. Cable channels and syndication broke the broadcast networks' monopoly on the market, making it profitable for writers and producers to cater to niche audiences. Ideological conformism receded in favor of creative daring. This is particularly true in the case of *The Next Generation*, which was sold directly to individual TV stations, thus bypassing the networks' tastemakers and gatekeepers entirely.

Wholesale utopia was no longer out of bounds. On the contrary, it turned into a compelling selling point for the show and greatly contributed to its popularity. Gone was the uneasy silence about anything that could possibly smack of a critique of a given "socioeconomic system." In broad strokes, Earth's society had become a mixture of the Red Cross and the MIT faculty club.

One cannot help but wonder how all the so-called major problems had supposedly been solved. Lieutenant Tom Paris of *Voyager* mentions that sometime in the twenty-second century the "New World Economy" was established, and that is when "money went the way of the dinosaurs."[97] *Deep Space Nine* explored twenty-first-century social unrest in a two-part time-travel episode entitled "Past Tense,"[98] and *Enterprise* covered some of the later events with great gusto but frustratingly few details. To this day, the magnitude of the elision remains tantalizing.

---

96. Roddenberry, "*ST:TNG* Writer/Director's Guide," p. 35.

97. *ST:VOY*, 5x15: "Dark Frontier, Part I."

98. *ST:DS9*, 3x11: "Past Tense, Part I"; *ST:DS9*, 3x12: "Past Tense, Part II."

PULP FICTION

Serial short stories in pulp magazines and comic books of the 1930s and 1940s are the historical forebears of scripted television. So much so in fact that the *Star Trek* franchise acknowledged and celebrated that heritage. It paid tribute to its roots with an outstanding episode of *Deep Space Nine*, entitled "Far Beyond the Stars," revolving around the figure of a black staff writer working at a pulp magazine in 1950s New York. The character of the magazine's editor displayed some of the least palatable traits of *Astounding Science Fiction*'s legendary editor John Campbell, the man who had launched the careers of Isaac Asimov and Robert Heinlein (among other luminaries). Simply put, Campbell was a bigot. *Deep Space Nine*'s episode referenced Campbell's refusal to publish one of Samuel Delany's stories because the readers would not be able to relate to a black protagonist.

Prejudice takes a long time to stamp out. Back in the 1940s, it was a given. Asimov acidly reminisced that Campbell "seemed to take for granted, somehow, the stereotype of the Nordic white as the true representative of Man the Explorer, Man the Darer, Man the Victor."[99] That is particularly ironic given the less-than-Aryan origins of most of the young writers who were in large part responsible for the success of the pulps. While E. E. "Doc" Smith had jump-started the craze in the early 1930s with his Lensman series, Jerry Siegel and Joe Shuster's *Superman* had brought it to a whole new level of popularity. These authors, inventors of the quintessential American icon, were hardly members of the Nordic master race. Had they lived in Germany at the time . . .

Series in both comics and pulps proved a boon to publishers: they left the kids hanging, anxiously waiting for the next issue, which they

---

99. Isaac Asimov, "Reason," in *Robot Visions* (New York: Roc, 1991), p. 79. First appeared in *Astounding Science Fiction*, April 1941.

purchased in droves. The narrative recipe and the economic model worked hand in hand. Each new issue of a given magazine would feature the continuing travails of a cast of regulars, set in the same familiar city or universe. No need for lengthy exposition—you could pick up right where you had left off a week or a month earlier.

A premium pulp magazine like *Astounding Science Fiction* prided itself on publishing stand-alone pieces alongside serials. Yet, even at *Astounding*, the serial format exerted an irresistible draw on both editors and writers. Asimov's classic masterwork, the Foundation cycle, was conceived from the beginning as a multipart, ongoing chronicle of the distant future. Similarly, his robot stories could be read in isolation, but they all shared the same technological parameters and the same rolling ensemble of characters (Powell and Donovan, the fixers, and roboticist Dr. Susan Calvin, the first great female science-fiction hero).

The Three Laws of Robotics, with their inherent ambiguities, provided an ironclad dramatic structure and a narrative platform. In each installment, the protagonists had to solve a conundrum raised by robots acting up or misinterpreting the Three Laws. In one of Asimov's most famous stories, "Reason," the robots working at an orbital solar collector that supplies energy to Earth refuse to obey the commands of Powell and Donovan. To the robots, the two handymen are so obviously inferior beings that they cannot be humans, the robots' creators. Powell and Donovan fear the robots are going to misalign the microwave beam carrying the energy and kill the lower life-forms inhabiting Earth. Instead, the mechanical workers perform superbly because they have reasoned that the world outside of the station is an illusion and that their true master is the beam itself, which must be maintained in its optimal state at all times. Cutie, the leader of the space station robots, calls himself the Prophet, and makes his mechanical brethren intone that "there is no Master but Master and QT1 is His Prophet."[100] The story is funny, ironic, and profound all at the same time. It deals with a theme—the social generation of beliefs—that became a trope of science fiction in general and of *Star Trek* in particular.

Asimov's robot short stories are somewhat disjointed. Contrary to most series of the time, they do not proceed sequentially, avoiding arcs or dramatic continuity. They even appeared in different magazines, as *Astounding* and Campbell did not claim exclusivity on them (and even rejected quite a few). The Three Laws and the recurring human characters, the settings, and the universe are the narrative anchor that allowed for difference and repetition across stories and imprints. In that, they resembled or rather foreshadowed the alien-of-the-week format of *Star Trek* (with the exception of *Deep Space Nine* and parts of *Enterprise*, of course).

Asimov's robot stories laid out the broad themes and parameters for trekonomics. They explored its two central assumptions: the benevolent and beneficial nature of automation technology on the one hand, and the gradual replacement of human labor on the other hand. Asimov is rightly hailed as the first author to systematically present robots and robotics in such a favorable light. Up until recently, he remained the only major science-fiction author who seriously tackled the properly economic issue of work. I take him to be the main source of inspiration for *Star Trek*'s vision of the future.

---

100. Isaac Asimov, "Reason," in *Robot Visions* (New York: Roc, 1991), p. 79. First appeared in *Astounding Science Fiction*, April 1941.

FOUNDATION

I read *Foundation* because in *Star Trek: The Motion Picture*, Isaac Asimov was credited as "scientific adviser." It was not *Star Trek* per se, but at least he was in the movie, so close enough. My friend Dina gave me the three-volume French edition of *Foundation*, three unassuming paperbacks with dark purple covers and tiny fonts. These were the longest books I had ever attempted to read. And the biggest book present I had ever received. It took less than two pages for my head to explode. Hyperspace jump. Trantor. Hari Seldon. Mathematics. *Encyclopedia Galactica*. Psychohistory. All my wishes were fulfilled, and more. I had arrived. Or rather, I was on my way.

Foundation went something like this: Hari Seldon, a brilliant mathematician, had predicted the imminent decline and fall of the ten-thousand-year-old Galactic Empire. Based on his mathematical projections, the interregnum would last for thirty thousand years, that is unless the powers that be would agree to his plan. He had proposed to establish two Foundations, one at each end of the galaxy. Their stated goal would be to compile the entirety of human knowledge in an *Encyclopedia Galactica*, so as to preserve what could be preserved and thus mitigate the chaos and hardships that the fall of the Empire was certain to bring about.

This was all a sham.

The Seldon Plan, laid out by the mathematics of Psychohistory, was much more devious. The two Foundations were to manipulate social and economic forces on a galactic scale, with the goal to establish the new empire in just under a millennium.

The three volumes covered the first three centuries of the Foundations in the form of short stories of varying length, almost like episodes. Save for the hologram of Hari Seldon popping up here and there at crucial moments, there were almost no recurring characters.

The single thread that bound the stories together was economics. It was the book's main protagonist, the grand background and driving force behind the drama. The humans in *Foundation* had no free will to speak of, their choices and their actions determined by economic necessity, the galaxy's true deus ex machina.

Everything has been said about *Foundation*, and by much more eminent people than me. I would point to Paul Krugman's idiosyncratic foreword to the latest edition of Asimov's masterpiece, where we learn that as a kid, the Professor himself dreamed of being Hari Seldon and using "the mathematics of human behavior to save civilization."[101]

Foundation's influence on the world of *Star Trek* is not as direct as Asimov's robot stories, but it is nonetheless crucial. It is on the level of psychology: *Foundation*'s characters share with *Star Trek*'s crews a similar commitment to scientific rationality for dealing with social problems. Foundationers harbor little doubt about their ability to control their lives and their circumstances. They live in peace and prosperity, thanks to their engineering prowess and their knowledge. There is nothing they cannot accomplish and nothing they cannot fix, even when the Seldon Plan seems to go off the rails. They are masters of their universe.

THE FUTURIANS

In his collections of short stories, Asimov would preface each piece with detailed, witty autobiographical sketches. He recounted his life in Brooklyn as a budding teenage fan and writer, working at his father's

---

101. Paul Krugman, "Introduction," in Isaac Asimov, *Foundation* (London: Folio Society, 2012), p. ix.

candy shop, as well as his frequent discussions with his mentor John Campbell, the editor of pulp magazine *Astounding Science Fiction*.

Asimov's narrative voice would skip back and forth between late-thirties and early-forties New York and some version or another of the future. With these dizzying spatiotemporal jumps, Asimov was letting me witness the invention of modern science fiction as it was happening, thanks to the efforts of a quite remarkable group of writers.

Asimov and his friends were the sons and daughters of immigrants from Europe who had escaped poverty and pogroms. These kids, talented and devoted fans, called themselves the Futurians. Their names are familiar to many science fiction readers: next to Isaac Asimov, notable members of the Futurians include Frederik Pohl, Cyril Kornbluth, James Blish, Damon Knight, Donald Wollheim, and Judith Merril (née Grossmann). Ray Bradbury, from Los Angeles, was a traveling companion, their man on the West Coast.

At first, the Futurians were an ad hoc gang of like-minded fans. They had met each other through the letters-to-the-editor sections of their favorite pulp magazines, the social network of their time, if you will. Because of their talent and passion, the Brooklyn posse soon became an organized force and a kind of political party within the science-fiction community. In a sense it could be argued that they invented the science-fiction community itself by getting their own stories published, and steering the genre away from the pulps' regular fare of lowbrow aliens-and-babes.

The Futurians were unabashedly progressive. They believed that science fiction was much more than entertainment. They believed in its social utility and world-changing mission. They held it as a form of political weapon against obscurantism, fascism, and even capitalism. They viewed science fiction as an instrument of persuasion and social change. Their program, adopted and brought to a much broader audience by *Star Trek*, was to influence the young readers of the magazines by spreading the militant notion that technology and science could indeed free humanity from pathology and want. In that fateful summer of 1939, the Futurians went so far as to attempt a putsch against the more apolitical organizers of the first World Science Fiction Convention. They failed, of course. Yet their brash coming out and subsequent exclusion from Worldcon I is considered the founding event of what later became known as the golden age of science fiction. Two months after these altogether minor happenings, Nazi Germany invaded Poland in a storm of steel and fire.

The Futurians had grown up on the seedy streets and alleys of Brooklyn, across the bridge yet a world away from the gleaming towers of Manhattan, in the antechamber of the American dream. There was not much of a past to hang on to, as their families had left their language, traditions, and earthly possessions behind, across the vast ocean. Upon stepping off the steamship, all they had received were new names and a future, however uncertain. And while war was ravaging Europe once again and Jews were being massacred anew, Isaac and his acolytes were fighting back as best they could. It was not much. It was just words and imagination born out of terror, a desperate commitment to science and social progress in the face of a world set ablaze.

I remember being particularly moved by Nightfall. Asimov had written it in the spring of 1941, at the darkest hour of the war, when Hitler and the Axis seemed poised to take over the world. In the story, people in a city on a distant planet are preparing to discover the night sky and its millions of stars for the first time. The celestial movement of the planet's multiple suns and moons reveal the heavens only once every several centuries. As the last sun sets, the astronomers at the observatory are recording the rising of the stars. Meanwhile, the mob, mad with fear and anguish, is torching the city below to create some fleeting illumination. The scientists themselves are descending into madness and oblivion, but with the faint hope that their newfound knowledge might survive the great holocaust and help prevent the fall of civilization the next time night comes back.

With this haunting allegory, Nightfall introduced a central theme in Asimov's work: scientific knowledge as humanity's bulwark and life raft. This narrative construct, the scientist as a wise hero, as keeper of the flame and indeed guardian of the galaxy, would form the premise of the *Foundation* series. It would also wind its way into *Star Trek*, and flourish under the guise of Mr. Spock.

USS ASIMOV

Isaac Asimov has a long history with *Star Trek*.

In the fall of 1966, he had written a blistering review of the first episode for *TV Guide*, pointing out several scientific inaccuracies in the fledgling show. Gene Roddenberry responded with a lengthy letter in which he defended his creation's science-fiction bona fides. He highlighted his hiring of renowned professional sci-fi writers such as Theodore Sturgeon, Harlan Ellison, and A. E. van Vogt. He argued with great sincerity that the show had done the impossible: getting on the air a mature kind of science fiction, without compromising or yielding to absurd studio demands, such as putting Lassie on the *Enterprise*. It was a heartfelt and passionate plea. Roddenberry was very obviously a fan himself and assured Asimov he was doing his utmost to gain his approval. From that point onward, Roddenberry and Asimov corresponded on a regular basis. Asimov became an uncredited consultant to the show, dispensing opinions and advice on plot and character development.

In the early 1970s, Roddenberry tried to launch another science-fiction show called *The Questor Tapes*. The protagonist, Questor, was a self-aware positronic robot in search of his identity, and the most likely prototype for Mr. Data. In letters to Asimov, whom he addressed as *Ike*, Roddenberry also mentioned that he was trying to shop feature films based on his stories.

In 1970, Asimov gave an address to the first *Star Trek* convention in New York City. He had grown up a fan of science fiction and had become a writer because of fandom. He saw in the burgeoning *Star Trek* community a rekindling of the values, the can-do spirit, and the moxie of the Futurians. He knew better than most that each and every fan is at heart a writer and a maker.

And last but not least, as I mentioned earlier, Asimov was credited as "scientific adviser" to *Star Trek: The Motion Picture*. The anecdote was that upon reading the original script, distraught Paramount honchos wanted it rewritten. They had to prove that Roddenberry was either completely off his rocker or high on acid (or both). So Paramount asked the most famous science-fiction author of the time to read the script and give his unvarnished opinion. To their surprise, it was positive. And the rest, as they say, is history.

Admiration and friendship, but also a recognition of what Asimov had contributed to *Star Trek* explain why *Star Trek: The Next Generation*'s Mr. Data is endowed with the same "positronic" brain as all the early robots from *Astounding Science Fiction*. Asimov had coined the term *positronic* in "Robbie," his first robot story ever to appear in print. It stands as an early example of technobabble. Positrons are the opposites of electrons and like all anti-particles, they only appear in extreme circumstances (for instance, radioactive decay or particle accelerators). The homage to Asimov's invention stops at the term. As everyone knows, Data's character is not constricted by the Three Laws of Robotics (which exist to prevent robots from harming their human creators).

Another direct homage to Asimov is the Borg. As science-fiction master and futurist David Brin remarked, the Federation's greatest enemy and mirror image draws heavily from Asimov's 1982 continuation to the original *Foundation* trilogy, *Foundation's Edge*. The book's hero, on a quest to find who is really pulling the strings of galactic affairs, stumbles upon a Borg-like planet whose agents are conspiring against both the First and the Second Foundation. The inhabitants of Gaia are all telepaths and live in a permanent state of heightened collective consciousness. Their goal is to institute a galactic empire that will function like a gigantic organism, self-aware and self-regulating, made up of trillions of individual human beings. Contrary to the predatory Borg, the Gaians are enlightened and benevolent, but the outline of the concept is there.

The name-checks are well deserved. Asimov's ideas are everywhere in *Star Trek*. Asimov cheekily claimed paternity for the very heart of the show, its conscience and its philosophical center of gravity, Spock: "Thirteen years after I had invented Daneel, the television series *Star Trek* came out, with Mr. Spock resembling Daneel quite closely in character."[102] The claim is not just blustering by Asimov, as Roddenberry himself admitted it.

The android robot Daneel Olivaw is a recurring protagonist in Asimov's novels. He first appeared in 1954, in the classic sci-fi-cum-murder-mystery novel *Caves of Steel*. His persona is built around the Three Laws: Daneel is incredibly intelligent, equanimous, logical, and protective of his human masters. He is also extremely perceptive and intelligent, and eventually he grows to generalize the application of the First Law (no robot shall cause harm to a human) to include humanity as a whole.

If anything, and in spite of all we know of his public persona, Asimov may be too modest in that case. Spock drew a lot of his disposition from the almost human R. Daneel Olivaw. In turn, the half-human

---

102. Isaac Asimov, "Introduction," in *Robot Visions* (New York: Roc, 1991), p. 15.

and half-Vulcan science officer provided the template and the broad psychological profile for the entire *Next Generation* crew. Picard, Data, and the rest, with their unflappable temper and their hyperrational approach to problem solving, are all different degrees of Spock. The lineage is obvious and goes all the way back to Asimov: a cast of future human and alien characters modeled after a robot, himself programmed to never cause harm to humans, who strives to expand his own definition of what it means to be human.

ROBOTS OF DAWN

It goes even further than characters. Asimov also supplied large chunks of *Star Trek*'s society. R. Daneel Olivaw hails from the Spacers' Worlds. The post–*ST IV: The Voyage Home* Federation is directly inspired by them. The Spacers' Worlds feature prominently in the cycle of novels that starts with the aforementioned *Caves of Steel* (1954) and which concludes with *Robots and Empire* (1985). It could be argued that the novelette *Mother Earth*, published in 1949, is the real kickoff point of the series.

The stories take place at a point in history when humanity is split between Earth and the Spacers' Worlds. The Spacers are the descendants of the first wave of robot-assisted human interstellar colonization. Since then, a profound economic and cultural divergence has occurred between the Spacers and the inhabitants of Earth.

The Spacers make extensive use of automated labor in the form of positronic robots. Agricultural production, construction, and services are all handled by robot workers. Replace Asimov's somewhat clunky robots with *Star Trek*'s replicators, advanced natural-language computers, and holographic doctors, and you have a society that looks very familiar indeed. I would argue that but for a few narrative details and funny alien species (which never appear in Asimov's body of work except in one incredible book), the twenty-fourth-century Federation is a faithful copy of his Spacers' World.

As in the Federation, the Spacers enjoy a very high standard of living as a result of widespread automation, especially when compared to the cramped and crowded underground cities of Earth. On Aurora, the leading Spacer world and backdrop for *Robots of Dawn*, the ratio of robots to humans is said to be fifty to one. On Earth, robots are banned. They are taboo.

Spacers are very proud of their way of life, which they rightly regard as the crowning achievement of human civilization. They live lives of leisure and creative exploration. In a very funny scene, Earther police-man Elijah Baley, the main protagonist of the book series, witnesses a dinner ritual where his host, roboticist Han Fastolfe, nearly knocks him out by performing a supposed artistic stunt involving a saltshaker. Every moment of daily life, down to adding salt to a plated dish, is turned into a very intricate display of self-expression, a set piece of performance art.

Understandably, Spacers view Earthers as a teeming horde of germ-carrying, backward brutes, and want to limit their interactions with them to the bare minimum. They even want to prevent Earthers from reaching back to the stars and colonizing the Milky Way. This is the conflict at the center of *Robots of Dawn*. Who shall inherit the heavens?

A bit like Dr. Soong with Data, Han Fastolfe is the sole genius and creator of R. Daneel Olivaw, the first "humaniform" positronic robot. He does not want to share his engineering secrets with the Aurora Robotics Institute, whose ultimate goal is to manufacture humaniform robots in quantities large enough to launch a new wave of galactic expansion on behalf of the Spacers.

Han Fastolfe sees Spacer culture as largely sterile and effete, too opulent and too comfortable. He believes that hardscrabble Earthers, toughened by the overcrowded and Spartan conditions on their planet, are better suited to lead humanity forward. If the Aurora Robotics Institute has its way, the future galactic empire will be built like a bunch of suburban subdivisions. Every planet will be terraformed and made ready by armies of humaniform robots, with turnkey mansions, agriculture, and industrial facilities. Such a course of action would neuter the social, cultural, and scientific dynamism that usually comes with pioneering enterprises. To Fastolfe, and by extension to Asimov himself, humanity should settle the galaxy without the help of robots.

TRUE LOVE COULD NOT HAPPEN THERE

With the Spacers' Worlds, Asimov builds a consistent robotic utopia, and knocks it down all at the same time. He imagines a dislocation of sociability and a stalling of progress as a result of overreliance on robotic labor. On Solaria, the youngest of the Spacers' Worlds, people have developed a strong collective phobia of physical contact, and prefer to interact by holographic telepresence. The only time Solarians meet in person is for the purpose of biological reproduction. The exercise is painfully awkward, even traumatic, for the parties involved. The few children that come out of these rare and unpleasant moments of intimacy are immediately left to the care of robotic nannies, learning from a very early age to avoid the physical proximity of other humans.

Solarians consider their world the best and most civilized of all. Asimov describes it as the logical extreme of a society based upon robotic labor. To him, when pushed all the way, automation leads to the implosion of society as we know it. Removing the need to work means removing the ferment that binds individuals to each other. Solaria, in effect, is no longer a society but a mere collection of monads, one human for ten thousand robots, each living in the eerie isolation of their immense estates.

Asimov's critique of automation is therefore humanistic. He speaks to the concern that far from turning against its creators *Terminator*-style, automation may in fact prove too pliable and too amenable in satisfying all of our earthly needs, displacing other humans and society itself in the process. To Asimov, the main peril is not that we will lose control of our own creations but that they will be too *nice*.

This is particularly rich stuff coming from the guy who popularized the word *robotics* in the first place. Asimov did not fear the rise of the machines. On the contrary, he provided the intellectual foundations for modern robotics. Professor Marvin Minsky of MIT, one of the inventors and leading experts on artificial intelligence, recalled that he decided to become a computer scientist after reading Asimov's robot stories in the pulps.

To Asimov, robots were not inherently uncontrollable. In his universe robots were entirely at the service of humans, which led to very different challenges than what was usually described in popular culture. Hence, despite his enthusiasm for the liberating potential of robots and artificial intelligence, Asimov came to harbor what seemed like a moral caution, if not an objection to them.

The *Robots of Dawn* cycle presents a contrasting picture of the promises of automation. It proposes a side-by-side comparison of a post-scarcity robotic utopia, the Spacers' Worlds on the one hand, and a highly structured and frugal polity on the other, Earth, where real human work and real human relationships could still exist. For all their technology and their opulence, the Spacers' Worlds are found wanting. As told in *The Naked Sun*, the most poignant novel of the bunch, true love could not happen there.

These books came later in Asimov's career. They conveyed an unmistakable sense of nostalgia. The robotic paradise is not all that it is cracked up to be. Asimov espoused the position that luxury and an evenly distributed cornucopia would neuter humanity's drive, turning people into flaccid, solipsistic bores obsessed with trifles. This marked a major departure from the willfully optimistic stories of his pulp days. They had been an antidote to the despair and terror of the war. Once the war was over, Asimov, now in his mature years, had begun to wrestle with the consequences of his own inventions. He warned that robot-assisted opulence could drain humanity of its vigor. Asimov went from wholehearted embrace to caveat emptor and, ultimately, rejection. At the end of *Robots and Empire*, the concluding novel of the whole cycle, Earthers prevail. They settle the galaxy the hard way, with no help from robots, with only their virtue and their bare hands.

I do not know what to make of such a turnabout. It can be explained in part by Asimov's grand plan to retroactively tie together the *Foundation* cycle and its preliminary novels (*The Stars, Like Dust*; *Pebble in the Sky*; *The Currents of Space*) with the robot stories. It was a way for him to address the complete absence of robots in the Foundation universe. But I tend to find his justification unsatisfying. The demands of his overall narrative project do not fully account for his disenchantment with automation.

▲

While adopting a lot of Asimov's utopian ideas, *Star Trek* differed on the central issue of automation. *Star Trek* assumes that work never stops, only its motivation changes. *Star Trek* is the business-as-usual scenario: automation merely redirects work toward the brain and the craft; it frees people from the repetitive and the mind-numbing. To

Star Trek, automation is an opportunity to change society for the better, to make it more fair, more open, more adventurous.

CHAPTER 7

"THERE ARE STILL MANY HUMAN EMOTIONS I DO NOT COMPREHEND..."[103]

THE PSYCHOLOGY OF UTOPIA

The improbability of the physics of *Star Trek* is par for the course. It is science fiction: either you accept the premise or you do not. One way or the other, there is not much to be gained by nitpicking the warp drive or the transporter or subspace communications (the ability to exchange voice and data in real time halfway across the galaxy). It will only bring you frustration, and it will detract from your enjoyment of the clever story lines, the drama, and the characters. That is how *Star Trek*, and more generally science fiction and fantasy, works. More than any other type of fiction, they demand an explicit buy-in, a leap of faith, from the audience.

---

103. *ST:TNG*, 4x11: "Data's Day."

In addition to the highly speculative physics, *Star Trek* also requires you to buy into its characters. Unlike many other science-fiction shows and universes, *Star Trek* has always been dogged by that challenge. Spock and Picard do not exactly stand out as warm or relatable. But it's not just the top brass: even the kids in *Trek* tend to be very nice and altruistic (think for instance of Jake Sisko from *Deep Space Nine*, who hides out at night to teach his friend Nog to read and write).

In this chapter we explore the consequences of cornucopia on the human psyche through one of the most baffling and contentious aspects of *Star Trek*: its characters. Why are *Star Trek* characters so seemingly one-dimensional, goody-two-shoes, and earnest? Put less generously, why are they so fucking perfect? And please do not take my word for it; it is widely known that the shows' writers themselves had many gripes and misgivings about their subjects.

The warp drive and the transporter fall under Arthur C. Clarke's famous law that any sufficiently advanced technology is indistinguishable from magic. *Star Trek*'s characters follow the human version of Clarke's law: sufficiently altruistic and ethical humans are indistinguishable from deities, or aliens. Equal and unlimited access to abundance—the good life—is the key to understanding *Trek*'s odd gallery of characters. This also yields a singular perspective on the politics of the Federation.

NO LEARNING, NO GROWING

As a rule, Starfleet people display a level of poise and mental stability that is beyond anything we know or experience in our twenty-first-century lives. As a result, they almost never bitch, bicker, jockey for position, second-guess, or double-cross each other. *Star Trek* is bereft of all the usual conflicts and workplace dramas that make up the bread and butter of episodic television. As Commander Worf aptly puts it in *DS9*, "Starfleet officers do not brawl!"[104] And that was in the aftermath of the only recorded violent disagreement between Starfleet personnel ever (and, then again, it was not shown on-screen).

By nature (and by design, obviously), Starfleet officers are level-headed, open-minded, and generally tolerant. This creates a host of complications when it comes to pure storytelling. To wit, Nicholas Meyer, hailed along with the late Harve Bennett as the savior of the franchise, recounts heated arguments with Gene Roddenberry during the development of *ST VI: The Undiscovered Country*. The film tells of the peace negotiations between the Federation and its old enemy, the Klingon Empire. Lieutenant Uhura comments on the guests' body odor. Captain Kirk, still reeling from the death of his son at the hands of a Klingon privateer, reflects that he will never trust Klingons. Admiral Cartwright, one of the heads of Starfleet, launches a tirade so racist that apparently the great African American actor (and *Deep Space Nine* regular) Brock Peters could not bring himself to say his lines. If you watch the movie again, you will notice that his speech is cut up from several takes.

Gene Roddenberry was completely against such dialogue. This is how Nicholas Meyer recalled the discussion:

> Mr. Roddenberry really believed in the perfectibility of man, of humans, and I have yet to see evidence for this (Star Trek VI) is a film in which the crew of the Enterprise has all kinds of prejudice, vis-à-vis the Klingons. And some of their remarks, including how they all look alike, and all the xenophobic things

---

104. *ST:DS9*, 4x16: "The Bar Association."

which we grappled with—that was all deeply offensive to him because he thought there isn't going to be that.[105]

Nicholas Meyer argued that there was no historical precedent or proof that humans had ever risen above their own prejudices, and that *Star Trek*'s optimism was merely a "pose." Thus Meyer insisted that his movie characters behave like actual, real humans. This in a way is both funny and telling: Meyer's feature films—the even-numbered ones—are the greatest of the entire franchise, and at the same time they are built on a complete and deliberate misreading of *Star Trek*'s psychology.

Roddenberry's objections were consistent with his idealistic vision for *Star Trek*. However, he had no creative control over the feature films. He was sidelined after the budget overruns and the relatively poor box office of *ST: The Motion Picture*. He was still credited as *Star Trek* creator, but that was it.

He did have final say for the TV show, however, and he was all over it. Instances abound of him shooting down writers' ideas because *Star Trek* characters and Federation officers would not act as today's humans. They would not bicker among themselves; they would never display pettiness or gratuitous meanness, let alone unchecked aggression. *The Next Generation* was a workplace show without any hint of the usual workplace conflicts.

Larry David, the cocreator of *Seinfeld*, boasted that in his comedic masterpiece, contra all other sitcoms, there was "no hugging, no learning." Oddly enough, the same could be said of most of *Trek*. Perfection only lends itself to very marginal improvements.

---

105. Mark Clark, *Star Trek FAQ 2.0: Everything Left to Know About the Next Generation, the Movies, and Beyond* (New York: Applause, 2013), pp. 203–4.

THE COOKIES ARE FREE

A lot of that remarkable mental stability—and indeed, perfection—can be attributed to opulence. A world without even a hint of poverty or economic scarcity literally changes its inhabitants' brains. When watching *Star Trek*, one easily forgets what poverty truly is and the kind of toll it takes. For poverty does not only consist in economic hardship. It is not just a matter of money or accounting. The debilitating effects of financial distress go well beyond limited spending power. Poverty breeds uncertainty and anxiety. It occupies your every waking thought, and it even sneaks into your dreams. It ties you down and prevents you from planning for the future, because you must worry first and foremost about meeting your immediate needs and those of your family. You might not make the rent, or you might have to choose between the rent and skipping several meals. You are constantly faced with bad choices—it is exhausting, it is scary, it is backbreaking. Poverty creeps into all aspects of your existence, from parenting, education, and opportunity to social relations, the incidence of chronic disease, violence, life expectancy, and even love. It has been shown that the many stresses associated with poverty have a direct and measurable physiological impact on children's brain development. These stresses also tend to rob people of their capacity to make rational economic decisions. In places where poverty is prevalent, it reproduces itself and gets passed on from one generation to the next. Getting into poverty is considerably easier than getting out of it.[106]

Star Trek's world has said good-bye to all that. In the Federation, abundance and post-scarcity are much more than the absence of

---

106. The scientific and economic literature on poverty is very vast and ever growing. The latest book by Robert Putnam, *Our Kids*, is the most recent notable addition, written for the civic-minded public rather than the academic specialist.

material poverty. They have a profound and lasting effect on behaviors and social relations. They lead to marked improvements in mental health. This is particularly crucial for Starfleet officers, who must maintain clarity of judgment at all times so as to better perform their duties.

That is not to say that opulence necessarily means happiness or the lack of stress. It does not even prevent the occasional bout of depression (for instance, young Ensign Wesley Crusher seems very much saddled with the weight of adults' expectations). It does not erase all the psychopathologies, but it makes it much easier to deal with them. Overall, *Star Trek* people show little of the inner conflicts and turmoil brought on by circumstances and the many accidents of life.

The presence of a therapist on the *Enterprise* is particularly notable. Those like the preternaturally shy and clumsy Lieutenant Barclay are encouraged to find help for their sometimes crippling phobias. Gene Roddenberry describes Counselor Deanna Troi's character as such in the show's bible:

> Her starship specialty might have been known in earlier days as psychologist or psychiatrist, but now in the 24th century, the science of human behavior has grown into a much more precise and important discipline. Humanity (and Starfleet) have learned that a starship is as dependent [sic] of efficiently operating human relationships as on efficient mechanisms and electronic circuitry . . . It says something about the growing maturity of humanity that Starfleet graduates actually welcome the ship's counselor's insights on even their own performance"[107]

---

107. Roddenberry, "*ST:TNG* Writer/Director's Guide," p. 28.

You almost never encounter such concern for mental health in science fiction—as a matter of fact, the only other major protagonist and therapist in science fiction I can think of is . . . a computer program (the aptly named Sigfrid von Shrink in Fred Pohl's fantastic Gateways series). While therapy is a lesser plot point in *The Next Generation*, it had a very special resonance for me. My parents and most of their friends were psychotherapists. I grew up surrounded by these strange people. As I recounted early in this book, my very dear friend Dina, the person who introduced me to *Trek* and sci-fi fandom, was a therapist herself. The ship's counselor figure meant a lot to me, and it made real sense. Deanna Troi's character conveyed a truth that most therapists know intimately, thus reinforcing the larger message of *Trek*: because the citizens of the Federation are better equipped than we are materially, they are better off mentally.

The people of the Federation think and act from the standpoint of terminal abundance. Unlike ours, their mental universe is not bounded by economic necessity. Class distinctions, profit seeking, and conspicuous consumption make absolutely no sense to them. You never see Captain Picard flaunting his collection of horse saddles or his well-appointed wine cellar. Federation citizens live in a heightened state of what economics calls *satiation*: the point at which obtaining additional units of the same product starts to decline in value. The first cookie is always better than the tenth one, and even more so if one has unfettered access to the strategic reserve of cookies. And do not forget: in the Federation, the cookies are free. Understandably, gorging on cookies is not as exciting.

The quasi-military nature of Starfleet helps in establishing this post-economic ethos. The uniform is much more than just spandex pajamas. Its simplicity embodies the only accepted and recognized social differences in *Star Trek* society: rank, based on merit. Status is earned rather than inherited, and insignias are the only visible markers of status on board the *Enterprise*. Of course, everybody knows the captain, and he is given certain privileges because of his rank. The big chair on the bridge, the large quarters, and the ready room come with the enormous responsibilities of command. Yet, it is not like the captain is living large or that he would ever like to live large.

These traits are not exclusive to Starfleet officers. But these officers are the focus of the show, and thus we draw much more information from them than from anyone else. We can glimpse more from their spouses and parents, however. The Picard family, for instance, lives a surprisingly simple and rustic existence for such celebrated vintners.

ALIENS

The difference between *The Original Series* and *The Next Generation* explored in previous chapters is also reflected in the characters themselves. That difference is both canonical and chronological, which is to say that the movies and the series that take place before the in-universe twenty-fourth century (*TOS* and *Enterprise*) feature psychological profiles that are closer to our own.

The Original Series' Kirk looks and feels very much like our present, his morality in constant conflict with his impulses and his overflowing appetites. He is the archetype of a certain American rugged masculinity: raging hormones with a veneer of civilization. Dr. McCoy is the transitional figure: he is the voice of care, reason, and moral outrage. And Spock is the inscrutable future: the normative ideal of a man (and specifically a man rather than a woman) pacified by science and compassion.

By the time *Next Generation* rolls around, the conflict between the messy present and the aspirational future has been resolved. Stoicism has won. The *Enterprise's* new crew is all Spock and no Kirk. So much so that they don't even need a Vulcan on board. Ambassador Spock himself, appearing in the two-part episode "Unification," calls Picard a Vulcan. There is probably no greater compliment from a Vulcan (even though Vulcans do not compliment other people).

The crew members of Picard's *Enterprise* are all Vulcans in spirit and demeanor save for Mr. Data, whose imperfections and desire to emulate his colleagues, to become more like them, really makes him the most human of them all. Where *Star Wars*, *Babylon 5*, *Dune*, and others say that underneath it all, we are still the same species, *The Next Generation* claims that nothing lasts forever, and that people are in fact susceptible to be fundamentally altered by their material circumstances.

That is part of why latter-day *Star Trek* characters are so alien to us—twenty-first-century science-fiction fans. In the mirror they present to us, we can't recognize ourselves. We can aspire, for sure, but that is the extent of the identification we are allowed. As a twenty-first-century human, I feel closer to the members of *Star Trek*'s extraterrestrial bestiary, the struggling Bajorans or the hilariously ignoble Ferengi or even the gung ho Klingons, than to any of the Federation crews. One of the few Starfleet officers I can actually understand is the traitor, *Deep Space Nine*'s Commander Michael Eddington, who ends up joining the irredentist Maquis rebellion. I also get James Cromwell playing Zefram Cochrane, the inventor of the warp engine, in *ST: First Contact*. He likes booze and rock 'n' roll and feels awkward and inadequate in most situations. He boasts of having invented warp propulsion for money and naked women. Good for him. And he does not even like to fly.

On the other hand, I don't get Jean-Luc Picard or his subordinates any more than I understand Mr. Spock. I love them both dearly and look up to them; they are guiding lights in my life. But their motivations, the kind of moral universe they live in, remain a total mystery to me. I can access that universe through an intellectual discussion of its economic basis, the sense of safety and satiation that comes with being raised in a cornucopian society, but there is very little in my life and my own experience that would allow me to properly identify with them. Their behavior seems logical in the context of the show and the universe it has built: disregard for material gains, indifference to possessions, total absence of conspicuous consumption. They are nonetheless baffling and close to impossible to truly understand on a deeper, more emotional level. They are ciphers.

On some level, you could say that *Trek* characters are a fundamentally alien species, but not because some of them sport a bluish skin tone or pointy ears. They are alien because they were born and raised in a radically different, even foreign environment. If at times they come across as remote and strange, it is not because they are stuck-up. Rather, it is because we, the twenty-first-century audience, cannot relate to these unfailingly reasonable and altruistic creatures. Federation citizens are alien to us because of where they come from and how they grew up. They are perfect because they can afford perfection. Simple as that.

KIRK SPARED THE GORN

In spite of their differences, both *The Original Series* and the subsequent shows share the same overarching concern for justice. To me, it is the single most striking feature of *Star Trek*'s heroes, throughout the multiple incarnations of the franchise—that they would seek justice above all else.

Captain Kirk, at the end of "Arena," spares his beaten Gorn opponent.[108] After a skirmish between the *Enterprise* and a Gorn warship,

---

108. *ST:TOS*, 1x18: "Arena."

the Metrons, a very advanced and secretive alien race, beam Kirk and the Gorn captain to a desert planet to force them to settle their dispute. They must fight to the death. Whoever wins goes free. Thanks to a few unorthodox moves, Kirk manages to outsmart the formidable Godzilla-like alien warrior. Yet, he soon comes to the realization that the purpose of the fight is senseless and that the Gorn captain probably engaged the *Enterprise* in an attempt at self-defense. It was all a misunderstanding, and violence should have been avoided. If Kirk kills the Gorn to save his own skin, as instructed by the Metrons, this will only perpetuate the cycle of aggression and reprisals between the Federation and the Gorns. Showing mercy is the right and just thing to do, even if it breaks the terms of the challenge contrived by the Metron overlords. It might even result in death for the gallant captain. But he is Captain Kirk. He does not hesitate. He puts his life on the line in the name of justice, peace, and the greater good.

Ultimately, the Metrons reward Kirk's mercy, and both he and the Gorn captain are returned to their respective ships. The lesson holds however: the needs of the many outweigh the needs of the few, as a dying Mr. Spock famously says in the climactic scene of *Star Trek II: The Wrath of Khan*. This kind of abnegation only looks heroic to us, the audience. To Starfleet officers, self-sacrifice is logical, a perfectly acceptable trade-off if the situation warrants it. This utilitarian attitude toward their own personal deaths, albeit extreme, is normal and obvious, all in a day's work.

The theme of justice is laid out even more explicitly in *The Next Generation*: the entire show is framed from the start as a trial of humanity. In the series' pilot, "Encounter at Farpoint," the godlike, mercurial entity known as Q (an obvious reworking of the Metrons) summons Captain Picard to his courtroom in the sky.

Picard has been chosen to speak for humanity. His actions in the upcoming mission will determine the fate of the human race. He will have to prove to Q that humanity is worthy of surviving. That high-stakes test of ethics becomes a recurring storyline in the show. Most episodes in fact present the *Enterprise* crew with moral dilemmas of one sort or another. Even sillier episodes like "Captain's Holiday" (where Picard takes what turns out to be an action-packed vacation on pleasure planet Risa)[109] are opportunities for a morality play.

Justice in *Trek* is intimately tied to economic prosperity. When everyone is equally provided for, when the allocation of resources among members of society is no longer a point of political contention, it is logical to infer that most causes for unrest and crimes expire. Once untethered from economic inequality, moral standards and justice become more abstract and in some way more demanding for individuals. Issues of good and bad are no longer mired in pettiness, fodder for the evening news and mass entertainment. In short, there is no *Cops* nor *Judge Judy* in the world of *Star Trek*.

Justice—the practical application of laws—ascends to the higher realm of philosophical and ethical pursuits. You can observe that in the Vulcans, whose other greeting (besides the "Live long and prosper") is "We are here to serve." Free at last from material necessity, Starfleet officers and citizens of the Federation find themselves compelled to explore what it really means to do good in the world. It is not an easy task.

PRIME DIRECTIVE

The Next Generation's third-season episode "Who Watches the Watchers?"[110] offers one of the most compelling illustrations of *Star*

---

109. *ST:TNG*, 3x19: "Captain's Holiday."

110. The episode's title is a reference to an old Latin proverb (*Quis custodiet ipsos custodes*)—it is a reference to Robert Heinlein's *Space Cadet. Quis . . . etc.* is the

Trek's ethics. The crew is dealing with cultural contamination. The *Enterprise* must rescue a team of scientists who are studying a prewarp civilization on Mintaka III. Their lab's generator has failed, disabling their holographic cloak and thus revealing their existence to the natives. It is one of the greatest perils Starfleet faces in its quest for knowledge. The sudden appearance of seemingly supernatural beings can have profound and incalculable effects on a less technologically advanced people. The creatures from space, with their instruments and their devices as well as their ability to vanish into thin air, are like magicians or even gods. This buttresses latent superstitions and may hamper the emergence of empirical science and rational thinking, the foundations for interstellar travel.

The cardinal value of Starfleet, the first article of its charter, is what is known as the Prime Directive. It states unequivocally that it is forbidden for any Starfleet officer or Federation citizen to ever intervene in the internal affairs or the cultural, social, or scientific development of a non-Federation race or species. The prohibition is particularly important in the case of prewarp civilizations. In no way can Starfleet share knowledge or technology that could hasten a species' own development. Starfleet can never take sides.

The Prime Directive is one of the most intriguing narrative rules of *Star Trek*. It indicates that the Federation is not an imperium. The Federation's first and most important law is an absolute prohibition against any form of territorial expansion or cultural hegemony. Foreign civilizations, regardless of their level of development, are to be kept at arm's length. The idea is to avoid any possibility of overpowering a less developed society.

In "Who Watches the Watchers?" we see Picard willing to die to prove to the Mintakans that he is not some immortal, godly being.

Space Patrol's motto.

Being shot dead by an arrow will nip the contamination in the bud and prevent the aliens from falling back into their superstitious ways. Just like Kirk in "Arena," Picard puts his life on the line in the name of a fairly abstract ideal: neutralizing the emergence of a cargo cult among a primitive yet scientifically inclined society. The same is true of *Deep Space Nine* and *Voyager*, and of *Enterprise* to an extent. Doing the right thing, doing the just thing, upholding humanity's values in the face of an inhospitable and imperfect galaxy is the real mission of the various captains.

If you step back for a minute, and if you overlook Patrick Stewart's on-screen presence, you must admit that this is a rather absurd modus operandi. It makes some sense within the parameters of *Star Trek*, and as the audience we follow along, but from today's vantage point it seems utterly ridiculous. Picard is willing to die for the Prime Directive. While it is an act of selfless heroism, it is nonetheless a very strange cause to risk one's life for.

Granted, comparable things happen in today's world. Needless to say, they are few and far between. I am thinking of ahimsa, the Hindu principle of nonviolence toward all living things, deployed with some measure of success by freedom fighters all over the world. In more extreme cases, Tibetan or Burmese monks, or a young vegetable merchant in Tunisia, have been known to set themselves on fire to testify to their people's suffering and yearning for freedom. These are incredibly courageous and powerful demonstrations, meant to denounce immediate and pressing injustices. Yet ahimsa, the willingness to endure violence and brutality in order to appeal to the humanity in your oppressor, the courage to self-immolate: these are unusual if not crazy behaviors.

Dying for the Prime Directive is reminiscent of such bravery. However, the injustice it is supposed to address is not so directly threatening. It is more theoretical, a matter of sociology rather than an immediate danger. It ties the Federation's hands, and prevents both the bad and the good to come from unwanted and random interactions between a primitive people and a vastly superior civilization. That show of altruism and moral rectitude on the part of Picard negates the possibility of a fruitful exchange and denies agency to the less technologically advanced. In a way, it tells us that the Federation and its officers know better and would rather stay away.

It is both admirable and baffling. The Prime Directive could be regarded as the translation of post-scarcity into foreign policy. It codifies and turns into law the absence of need. The Federation has everything, and so do its inhabitants. Satiation is a practical, everyday economic reality. It removes the necessity for territorial expansion. The Federation routinely welcomes new member planets, but on its own terms and only after a long and grueling review process (as with, for instance, Bajor, the setting of *Deep Space Nine*: at the end of the show Bajor's application to the Federation is still snaking its way through the bureaucracy—or maybe the writers just forgot about it). The Federation never forcibly conquers new worlds nor does it subjugate foreign cultures.

The underlying reason is utilitarian. The Prime Directive is a prohibition, a negative injunction, rather than a call to proactively do good in the universe. It exists to protect Starfleet officers from complex and unpredictable entanglements, while maintaining the Federation's neutrality. It is a statement of humility: the Federation should not assume that it has all the answers and cannot presume that whatever it does will result in beneficial outcomes. Thus, the Federation refuses to make history on behalf of other people. And since it has no objective needs, it does not seize nor settle new star systems for the purpose of economic exploitation. In fact, it has so little use for imperial policies that it actively discourages its officers and representatives from getting too involved in other people's business. The meaning of the Prime Directive is also that intervention is never worth the trouble. Better stick to "seek out new life and new civilizations." Just don't touch anything.

The Prime Directive came out of *The Original Series*. It was an artifact of the Cold War, a science-fictional rebuke of America's adventure in Vietnam. As time passed, it took on a larger and more central meaning in *Trek*. Yet, by today's standards, the Prime Directive is not just unrealistic, it is plain bonkers. It is completely at odds with contemporary norms, not to mention thousands of years of human history. First of all, nobody has ever cared about preserving native peoples or cultures. In fact, quite the opposite: the First Peoples of North America were brutally eliminated by European settlers (just like the Aztecs and the Incas, who were swiftly dispatched by the conquistadores' venereal diseases). Those who survived first contact with the Europeans were parked in faraway reservations and marginalized. They endured because of their own strength and fortitude, and certainly no thanks to the White Man's generosity. Enslavement and genocide have always been expedient ways to secure new territories for upstart empires.

The twenty-first century is undeniably more civilized. Market capitalism seems to have somewhat softened the brutality of past colonial empires. We make it a humanitarian duty to spread the advances of science and technology to the farthest reaches of the world. We dispense vaccines, cell phones, literacy, banking, and TV. And don't get me wrong: I take it as a good thing on balance and in aggregate. It is progress. It brings significant improvements in standards of living, opportunity, and prosperity.

But our own economic and technological view of what constitutes progress does not come without its share of trade-offs. It displaces people from their ancestral lands to make way for roads, logging, mining, and sometimes more worthy instruments, such as telescopes. It leads to the extinction of spoken languages, unplanned and chaotic urbanization, increased pressures on shaky state institutions to deliver much-needed services. It also encourages graft, bad governance, and resource exploitation by unscrupulous actors, private and public.

In that sense, the Prime Directive acts as a caution for the best of our humanitarian and philanthropic impulses. It warns us that progress is not always uniformly good.

RESISTANCE IS FUTILE

If you really want to understand the Federation's psychology, consider its most dangerous and deadliest nemesis, the Borg. The Borg in its original form (without the queen bee introduced in the movie *ST: First Contact)* is such a great villain because it is so similar to the Federation. It is opaque, it is radically strange yet uncomfortably close. It is almost like a mirror image, with slight cosmetic alterations. The voice and the will of the Borg Collective resonate in every drone's mind and spring each into action. It is analogous to the Federation's stern moral injunctions to each of its members, but made literal and manifest through brain implants and cybernetic limbs.

Similarly, and I know this may sound a bit peculiar, the Borg's economy does not fundamentally differ from the economy of the Federation. The Borg has moved beyond scarcity. Individual drones do not have to worry about providing for themselves; their basic biological and psychological functions are all taken care of by technology. The Borg Collective does not require currency or market mechanisms to produce and exchange goods. Through constant monitoring and instantaneous communication—in other words, cybernetic collective consciousness—it can know which Borg planet, vessel, or drone needs what at any given moment and can therefore direct the flow of supply and demand harmoniously. The Borg does not require central planning, just continuous feedback. Economically speaking, the Borg's only significant difference from the Federation lies in the way it accumulates capital: through the grotesque and violent assimilation of foreign bodies, knowledge, and materials. While the Borg's ultimate purpose is conquest and predation, the exact opposite of the Federation's Prime Directive, its mode of behavior enforcement is eerily similar. The loud voice of moral obligation constantly rings between the ears of every Federation citizen. The Federation is the Borg with a smile and a smattering of free will, but it is still the Borg.

The Borg hive suggests something crucial about *Star Trek*'s beliefs. It underscores the overarching psychological conception at work in the entire series. *Star Trek* considers that human psyches and behaviors— why we do what we do—are a product of the way society is organized. Give me a hypothetical world without any scarcity, where all economic necessity has been overcome, and I will return two opposite yet very similar models of self-regulating society and politics. The Borg Collective, where individual actions and desires are erased and subsumed by a technologically enabled, literal form of general will. And the Federation, loose and mildly anarchistic, where the pursuit of individual excellence and constant self-improvement combine for the benefit and prosperity of all.

Star Trek believes that material conditions are the primary determinant in people's actions. In the Federation's cornucopia, individuals' needs, desires, emotions, and activities are significantly transformed and reoriented toward noneconomic goals. This is what makes the inhabitants of the Federation so bizarre and impenetrable and sometimes even boring. They do not seem to care at all about the same stuff as us, mostly because they do not have to. And that is why they are truly from the future.

DO THE RIGHT THING

Quite reasonably, *Star Trek* predicts that once poverty is overcome, whatever the means or the process, most of the behaviors and pathologies that usually follow in its wake will disappear. Hunger, crime, war, and most forms of social turmoil will be disposed of. Having grown up in a world where material want is unknown, a thing of the past, Federation citizens can be productive, satiated, and unconcerned by death—at peace with themselves and with the universe. No wonder they cruise around the galaxy like little Buddhas.

Such obvious conclusions still raise eyebrows in some quarters, usually the same folks who call universal health care *slavery*. But there is nothing new or groundbreaking in there. Provided we can sustain the current rate of growth, and with three more centuries of runway, *Star Trek*'s extrapolations are not particularly crazy, let alone optimistic. Yet the repeated display, episode after episode, of these cumulative improvements in quality of life, mental health, and human ethics is deeply unsettling, even scandalous.

This was done on purpose and carried through the entire run of series, even after Roddenberry's death. It was the single-most important feature that was maintained throughout and that binds together all of the multiple incarnations of *Trek*. Contrast this with the J. J. Abrams reboot movies, and you will get a better appreciation for the TV series' thematic continuity.

The new alternate-timeline movies are a whole different animal. They pack a lot of excitement but obey a different market logic as feature films. They are not necessarily concerned with defending a particular normative ideal of human improvement. Characters and their motivations are anchored in our present reality, so as to make them more immediately relatable to the general audience. The radical strangeness of Federation protagonists recedes in favor of more stereotypical comic-book mythologizing of the personal and the mundane: Kirk's daddy's dead, he's got a chip on his shoulder; Spock must save the same Vulcans who bullied him when he was a kid because he was biracial; Bones is the cynic drunkard with a heart of gold; and so on. All this ponderous, melodramatic character building is more reminiscent of Marvel Comics' golden age than of *Astounding Science Fiction*. It is as much an aesthetic as a market-driven decision. What it lacks in intellectual stimulation, it more than makes up for in fun and action.

So we do not care about or identify with *The Next Generation* or *Deep Space Nine* characters in the same way that we care about or identify with their more recent versions in the J. J. Abrams movies. We know that Picard, Sisko, Janeway, and the crew will be all right and that they'll do the right thing. Their inner conflicts are not of a deeply personal nature. They are torn about the moral challenges of upholding their humanitarian ideals in an imperfect world and under unpredictable circumstances, not about their absent moms. And for their trivial psychopathologies, they have a top-notch telepath therapist on board the ship.

Socioeconomic determinism is not at all exclusive to *Star Trek*. Many science-fiction authors use it to build their speculative worlds and to populate them with characters and intrigue. What is unique to *Star Trek* (and to a few other sci-fi universes) is its resolutely optimistic alignment. If the Federation's inhabitants all appear altruistic, selfless, dutiful, rational, and (it must be said) somewhat emotionally stunted, it is a direct result of the society they live in and that molded them. It is not just crime and hunger that have been eradicated, but all the psychopathologies that arise from the stresses of want, poverty, and uncertainty. Unfortunately for the shows' writers, *Star Trek* lacks a lot of what makes for engaging drama. The only reason to go to such extraordinary lengths to gimp your characters like that is to make a point. And it had better be a good one!

At times *Star Trek* comes across as an earnest public intervention, admonition rather than entertainment. Some even see it as preachy or hokey. I prefer to call it overly sincere. *Star Trek* takes itself and its politics extremely seriously. It truly believes in its own science fiction: Spock, Picard, and Sisko behave and think like denizens of a future where, above all, Keynes's "economic problem" has been solved. Economics, or rather trekonomics, is the key to their power of attraction.

But what happens to those alien species who do not share these values but revel in scarcity and cutthroat economic competition?

CHAPTER 8

"NEVER BE AFRAID TO MISLABEL A PRODUCT"[111]

THE FERENGIS, INTERSTELLAR CAPITALISTS

No self-respecting book on the economics of *Star Trek* would be complete without a chapter on the highly entertaining and deranged capitalists of the galaxy, the Ferengis.

Those with only a passing interest in the franchise may have stumbled upon random Ferengi interlopers in a few episodes of *Star Trek: The Next Generation*. Most likely they found them annoying and ridiculous and wrote them off as yet another instance of an alien makeup fail. Think of the musical performers in the *Star Wars* cantina scene. That level of bad.

In all fairness, the Ferengis' physical appearance is not exactly endearing (to say the least). They are short with enormous lobes on

---

111. *ST:DS9*, 4x24: "Body Parts."

their bald, shiny foreheads. They have outsized ears and ridged noses. When they're not talking in a grating, high-pitched voice, their smile reveals sharp and carnivorous teeth. Their eyes are shifty and their gait is hunched, and they dress horribly. Basically, they are some kind of extraterrestrial mongrel, a cross between a slimy reptile and a rat.

Yet, what makes them awful to the casual viewer is not their troll-like physiognomy so much as their smarmy behavior. The Ferengis are the traders and the shopkeepers of the galaxy. Money and profits are their only passion. There is nothing they would not do for a quick buck, or rather a quick strip of gold-pressed latinum. They are relentless, almost fanatical, in their pursuit of riches.

There is an undeniable element of danger in the Ferengis, maybe not entirely deliberate on the part of the shows' writers. Their species' avaricious character and grotesque, swarthy physique, smattered with untoward sexual appetites directed at alien females, sometimes hew uncomfortably close to age-old anti-Semitic stereotypes. The association of greed with exaggerated facial features and bodily deformity runs deep in Western iconography.

This does not really bother me. For one, it is science fiction, and nobody could honestly mistake *Star Trek* for *Der Stürmer*, the Nazi rag. Furthermore, over the course of *Deep Space Nine*, the Ferengis reveal themselves to be much more than just money-grubbing maniacs and lecherous leprechauns. I can definitely understand the disapproval of historians and scholars, as well as the offense of some fans. But if one should have gripes about *Trek*, I think they should be focused on the bizarre and glaring heteronormativity of the twenty-fourth century rather than the Ferengis.

So there, I say it: I adore the Ferengis. Vulcans aside, they are my favorite *Trek* aliens, and not just because they provide much-needed levity to *Deep Space Nine*, an otherwise very earnest and serious TV show. Next to Spock and the Vulcans, I believe the Ferengis are the most interesting species in all of *Star Trek*. Period. I look at them as the truest and most faithful expression of *Star Trek*'s optimism. The Vulcans are role models because they have already attained stoic wisdom and enlightenment. The Ferengis are role models because eventually, with much kicking and screaming, they manage to improve their society, even if marginally. The Ferengis look ugly and act even uglier, but their story arc also demonstrates what a few tweaks in economic policy can achieve. It is not very rousing nor heroic, but that is the whole point: hard-fought, welfare-maximizing measures for Ferengi females and for Ferengi workers should not be exciting. It is plumbing rather than dramatic fireworks.

It so happens that plumbing is also our best hope in the real world. Thus, I make it a personal mission of mine to disabuse the haters and the naysayers. If, by the end of this chapter, you are not convinced of the Ferengis' pivotal role in illuminating *Star Trek*'s vision of the future, then this book will have been for naught. I will have failed.

◣

A chapter on the Ferengis is also, necessarily, a chapter on *Deep Space Nine*, the franchise's third show (sorry, the 1972–73 animated series does not count). It is the show that broke all the rules, and in doing so, breathed new vigor into the *Star Trek* universe. Instead of a starship exploring uncharted space, *Deep Space Nine* is an outpost beyond the Federation borders. The frontier is still there, but not as a moving, abstract boundary in the vastness of space. It is now a concrete physical location, an everyday occurrence. Where *The Original Series* and *The Next Generation* are seeking out new life and new civilizations, *Deep Space Nine* is preoccupied with the challenges of living in the midst of these new alien species and new cultures. It is a show about other people's beliefs and morality, and how a utopian society, the Federation, copes with a troubled and imperfect galaxy.

Commander Sisko and his crew are called to administer the space station on behalf of the Bajorans, who have just recently liberated themselves from their brutal occupiers, the Cardassians. Shortly after the arrival of the Starfleet detail, a stable wormhole leading to the other side of the galaxy opens in the immediate vicinity. From forsaken backwater, Bajor and Deep Space Nine turn overnight into the most important places in the whole entire universe. The station becomes a center of high-stakes intrigue and political machinations and, ultimately, the main prize in a galactic war to control the wormhole.

As a free port, Deep Space Nine is open to all comers: smugglers, arms dealers, refugees, and spies. These colorful characters congregate at Quark's bar and gambling establishment, a sort of twenty-fourth-century Rick's Café—the World War II–era watering hole in *Casablanca* that attracted all sorts of clientele, good and bad—and the beating heart of the show.

Quark, the Ferengi owner, is a scoundrel and a thief. Yet, we slowly discover that, underneath this grim appearance, he also has a lot of Humphrey Bogart in him. To me, Quark is the key character of the show. *Deep Space Nine* is the story of his education and, by extension, the story of how, through contact and osmosis with the Federation, the profits-obsessed Ferengis grow to abjure the most egregious and repellent of their traditions. That is the message of *Deep Space Nine*. Even Quark, biologically conditioned and consumed by his heritage to pursue wealth, can change.

Ultimately that is why the Ferengis are so important to *Star Trek*. Beyond satire and comic relief, their narrative arc in the series is an exposé and a celebration of *Trek*'s core values. Social justice and good governance can indeed happen, even to the most uncouth and greedy of species. And if the Ferengis can do it . . .

INSULTS AND EYESORES

Believe it or not, the Ferengis were initially brought into existence as the Klingons' replacements. When *Star Trek: The Next Generation* was launched in 1987, it had a big problem. Gene Roddenberry decided that the Federation's old nemesis, the Klingon Empire, would no longer be the enemy. Worf, a Klingon, was a bridge officer on Captain Picard's *Enterprise.* Fans probably ate their tricorders upon discovering the gruff and imposing lieutenant, wearing his sartorial Klingon warrior's sash over his regulation Starfleet uniform.

A Klingon on the bridge may not have been as bold as featuring a black woman and a Russian on prime time in 1967, in the middle of the Vietnam War and the Civil Rights movement. A Starfleet Klingon officer was nonetheless a resonant statement. It proclaimed loud and clear that in the time between *The Original Series* and *The Next Generation*, things had gotten better. The foes of yesteryear were now our friends. Nothing lasted forever, not even cold wars. Just like the menacing Russian bear, the Klingons no longer hid in the interstellar woods.

That new and improved state of galactic affairs removed a major cause of conflict in the *Star Trek* universe and in doing so eliminated a source of stories. To a degree, the first two seasons of *The Next Generation* were a quest to find an adversary worthy of the more sophisticated and more confident twenty-fourth-century Federation. Warriors, cold or not, had to give way to something more relevant to the pacified twenty-fourth century. What could be better, then, as an antagonist to the happy and infinitely opulent Federation, than a whole species of shifty and grotesque money-hungry weasels? The Ferengis made sense, at least on paper.

It was an unmitigated disaster. The writers could not quite make the Ferengis into a fearsome species. The Ferengis in *The Next Generation* never managed to rise above being an annoyance (and sometimes worse). Instead, thanks to a slew of terrific (and terrifying) TV episodes, as well as the movie *Star Trek: First Contact*, the fans got acquainted with the Borg. The call to arms of the cyborg hive, "Resistance is futile," reached well beyond the Trekkers' community to become a catchphrase, a pop-culture meme. The notoriety of the Borg, its deserved spot in the pantheon of great TV villains, makes it easy to forget the other, less successful candidates for Federation archenemy.

Deep Space Nine offered the Ferengis an unexpected chance at redemption. They had failed as antagonists on *The Next Generation*, but maybe they could succeed as outsiders, especially on a new show that was almost exclusively dedicated to outsiders. It was not such a big stretch, as the main characters on *Deep Space Nine* were all misfits. That in itself was a major departure from *The Next Generation*'s crew. Picard and his merry band of crack officers embodied Starfleet at its finest. Their mission was to present the Federation in the best possible light, not just to aliens and foes, but also to the audience. The *Enterprise-D* crew was the A-team: you don't get to serve on the flagship by accident.

⌃

Deep Space Nine was definitely not the flagship. It did not even look like the type of assignment that would put an officer on the fast track to glory and accolades, at least at first. *Deep Space Nine* traded the glamour of space adventure for the more standard fare of workplace drama. In the pilot episode, Sisko makes it known to Captain Picard himself that he is not happy at all about the job, that he feels he is being railroaded. Not only is the job bad for his career, but on top of that he is a single father, and the outpost is far from an ideal place to raise a preteen son.[112]

Sisko is not alone in his ambivalence. Every character has demons to contend with. Behind his youthful brashness, Dr. Bashir hides that he was genetically enhanced in his childhood (one of the few criminal offenses in the Federation, see chapter 2). Jadzia Dax, the station's science officer, is a Trill symbiont. She carries the memories of several lifetimes, thanks to the Trill worm implanted in her. Adventurous and eccentric, she particularly enjoys consorting with aliens. She spends a lot of her free time playing games of chance with Ferengis, and for real money. Not your usual run-of-the mill Starfleet science officer.

And then there is Odo, the one and only changeling creature in the entire Alpha Quadrant (until his brethren, the menacing Founders, cross the wormhole and start messing things up). He is the chief of security, the sheriff of the place. He's a lone wolf whose sense of fairness and thirst for order constantly put him at loggerheads with his superiors. Garak, the tailor and the only Cardassian left on the station after the end of the occupation, is both a traitor and a professional assassin. As a former agent of the occupiers' secret services, he is feared and loathed by Bajorans. Ironically, because of Federation protection, Deep Space Nine is the only safe place for him in the whole quadrant.

Last but not least, the Ferengis of *Deep Space Nine* are probably the truest outsiders of them all. They are the living and breathing antithesis of the Federation. In a way, they should not be there at all, they should not be on the show itself. Sisko welcomes their presence because they provide repose and entertainment to the countless aliens who pass through the station. While Quark's bar is the center of Deep Space Nine's social life, it is at the same time a major eyesore and an insult to all that the Federation stands for. The bar offers gambling tables and

---

112. *ST:DS9*, 1x01: "Emissary."

holosuites to satisfy one's sexual fantasies and serves alcoholic beverages for every species' tastes. Quark employs barely dressed hostesses to keep his customers interested. Worse still, Quark's bar is a holdover from the Cardassian occupation. There is something very unappetizing about the whole situation: Quark just changed the menu for the new landlords and did some redecorating, but otherwise business is business. Not the type of *Star Trek* hero we have come to expect.

The outsider status of the Ferengis is in fact hinted at in their name: the word *Ferengi* means "foreigner" in Farsi and has deep, mercantile origins. It derives from the Arabic *faranji*, the transliteration of "Frank" or "Frankish," used to designate European merchants in the Middle East. It is not so surprising that Roddenberry and his writers chose that name.

Everything, from their less-than-heroic appearance all the way down to their actual name, helps to establish Quark and the Ferengis as the Federation's great other. Yet, they are no longer the failed antagonists of *The Next Generation*, but complex, even nuanced antitheses to Starfleet's altruistic and satiated do-gooders.

RULE OF ACQUISITION #10: GREED IS ETERNAL

Nowhere does the Ferengis' status as the foil to *Star Trek*'s utopia shine brighter than in their sacred book, the *Rules of Acquisition*. That book and its rules are a running gag throughout *Deep Space Nine*. There is a rule for every conceivable situation, and the show makes ample use of them to move the action along. They are the touchstone of Ferengi culture and society. All 285 of them, "unabridged and fully annotated with all 47 commentaries, all 900 major and minor judgments, all 10,000 considered opinions"[113] codify life in Ferengi society. They are a mix of self-help and obligations, equal parts Ten Commandments and *How to Win Friends and Influence People* (but even more bonkers than the originals).[114] Taken all together, they give a unique glimpse into the Ferengi soul. At times, it can be very jarring to the twenty-first-century viewer.

At first, the Rules of Acquisition were a marketing gimmick. Gint, the Ferengi who had written them, wanted to find a way to sell as many books as possible. Coining them "rules" was his stroke of genius—after all, "rules" sound much more important than "random pieces of business advice from some old Ferengi."

The Rules contain such gems as the first one: "Once you have their money, you never give it back," or "Treat people in your debt like family, exploit them," as well as "Only fools pay retail." None of the Rules are particularly outrageous or irrelevant. Their comedic power comes precisely from the fact that, while a bit tawdry ("#235: A wife is a luxury, a smart accountant a necessity"), they would not be out of place in most other contexts. The Rules of Acquisition are an eruption of the less pleasant aspects of the real world into the high-minded, make-believe universe of *Star Trek*, like motivational sales seminar harangues crashing the noble science-fiction party.

Yet the Ferengis' bad taste makes us question our own assumptions as well: First of all, if as the audience we are truly committed to the Federation's tolerant ethos, shouldn't we refrain from judging other peoples' expressions of their cultural heritage? Who are we to judge in the first place?

---

113. *ST:VOY*, 3x05: "False Profits."

114. Ira Steven Behr, *The Ferengi Rules of Acquisition, by Quark as Told to Ira Steven Behr* (New York: Pocket Books, 1995).

And second: Indeed, who are we to judge, since the Ferengis' belief system and values are directly inspired by our own (even if slightly exaggerated)? Who do we dislike, who do we find annoying when we disapprove of the Ferengis? I would say that, on that account, the satire does succeed.

Much like their counterparts in the real world, the Rules of Acquisition cannot be considered a proper religion. The Ferengis do not have religious specialists (otherwise known as priests). The Rules do not come prepackaged with the supernatural trappings and cosmogony of a full-on organized religion. It is more of a civic religion, providing the kinds of public rituals and enforced behaviors that strengthen social cohesion around shared, inherited values. These ritual demonstrations of Ferengi patriotism—if there is such a thing—resemble the reciting of the Pledge of Allegiance in US schools or singing "The Star-Spangled Banner" at a baseball game.

The Rules' philosophy is very sensible: Ferengis' purpose in life is to navigate the Great River, that is, to trade, truck, and barter. It is quite literally a description of Adam Smith's cheery outlook on human motivations and the constitution of society. There is nothing reprehensible or crazy about the Ferengis' foundational beliefs. The Ferengis do have a strong ethical core: they do not enslave, they do not pillage, and they do not conquer. They certainly exploit workers and snooker customers but that, in a way, is to be expected and respected.

What makes the Ferengi civic religion so interesting is that you have to read the Ferengis as twentieth-century humans. Their funny and parodic beliefs, centered around profits and greed, are in fact a commentary on a certain archetype of present-day capitalists. But this commentary comes with undeniable complications. Ferengis' beliefs are not all parody and fun and games. There is a very serious and idealistic side to their cult of Mammon.

Next to the Rules of Acquisition, which are a sort of everyday code of conduct—think of them as kosher laws—the Ferengis also believe in the great material continuum. Nog explains it as such to a skeptical Chief O'Brien: "It is the force that binds the universe together."[115] O'Brien retorts in a thinly veiled snarky dig at *Star Wars*, "I must have missed that class in engineering school." Nog expounds: "The continuum is real. You see, there are millions upon millions of worlds in the Universe, each one filled up with too much of one thing and not enough of another, and the great continuum flows through them all like a mighty river, from have to want and back again, and if we navigate the continuum with skill and grace, our ship will be filled with everything our hearts desire."

The great material continuum is predicated on galaxy-wide scarcity (too much of a thing here, not enough there). The existence of the Federation calls into question its architecture and its epistemology, much like carbon dating terminally undermines any and all creationist fantasies.

Put yourself in a Ferengi bartender's shoes for a minute: these Federation people must be very hard to please indeed. For one, money is no object to them, which makes gambling that much less interesting. Thanks to the replicator, nothing that you carry is so special that they would spend ruinous amounts to obtain and consume it. To them, there is no such thing as "not enough" of a thing. What can you sell them that they do not already have access to? What kind of scarcity, even artificial, can you really muster to get them to bite? In a late episode of *Deep Space Nine*, Quark runs an auction of antiques at his bar.[116] Jake Sisko hopes to purchase a present for his father—an authentic Willie Mays baseball card from 1951 (he ropes his friend Nog into contributing

---

115. *ST:DS9*, 7x06: "Treachery, Faith, and the Great River."

116. *ST:DS9*, 5x25: "In the Cards."

his savings). This story is indicative: for Federation citizens, the only things really worth having are prized antiques with special meaning, rather than flashy luxuries or big-ticket items. You can't make a good living doing business with these people. You have to deal with them because they are a major galactic power, but it does not mean that you have to approve of their ways.

Ferengis regard humans (and by extension their Federation compatriots) with bafflement and disdain: "It's not my fault if your species decided to abandon currency-based economics for some philosophy of self-enhancement" the always astute Nog tells Jake Sisko when asked for money to bid on the Willie Mays baseball card. In the same vein, his uncle Quark keeps complaining that Starfleet Academy has "corrupted" and "ruined" Nog. In these sparse but hilarious pieces of dialogue, you can hear hints of the writers' unease with *Star Trek*'s utopian tenets. But not only that: at times it is as if the Ferengis take the audience's side. We share their misunderstanding and their attachment to their own beliefs. Like us, they cannot fathom that an entire species, an entire civilization, could abjure what they take to be an ontological quality of every being— a desire for profits, the lure of the deal, market competition. That is the ultimate meaning of Rule of Acquisition #284: "Deep down, everyone's a Ferengi."

RULE OF ACQUISITION #102: NATURE DECAYS, BUT LATINUM LASTS FOREVER

The Next Generation never really explained how, in the absence of money, the Federation conducts trade with other galactic civilizations. There are small glimpses in *The Original Series*. A trade dispute around grains constitutes the backstory of the famous Tribbles episode, for instance.[117] However, as we have learned from *Star Wars Episode I: The Phantom Menace*, trade disputes tend to make for rather flaccid story premises.

In contrast, *Deep Space Nine* treats economic activity and economic motives as integral parts of its universe. The confrontation between the Federation's utopian values and the Ferengis' mercantile culture drives a sizeable chunk of the series' episodes and overall narrative. And thus we are witnesses to economic exchanges, bartering, compromises, even bribes. We get to see Federation officers—gasp!—handling actual money in the form of gold-pressed latinum.

The Ferengis trade in what could be termed nonessential goods. Next to booze, Quark's bar offers gambling and holosuite entertainment. However, Ferengis' activities and interests go well beyond the hospitality business. Throughout the course of *Deep Space Nine*, we get much more than a passing glance into the Ferengis' range of enterprises. They run the gamut from soft drinks to liquor to weapons. Essentially, anything in the universe that can be bought low and sold high. However, by focusing on Quark's establishment, the series and the writers make the point that paying for what amounts to luxuries is a widely popular practice in the galaxy, and that even Federation citizens indulge in it when given the chance.

This fact barely got any mention in all of *Trek* prior to *Deep Space Nine*. In *Deep Space Nine*, luxuries do exist in the Federation and are consumed by Starfleet officers. The Federation citizens on the station are running a tab at the bar. Many times we see them giving their thumbprints to authorize transactions. This in turn is sometimes ruled as proof positive that money exists and flows in *Star Trek*. So how is that even possible given that the Federation has discarded the use of money?

---

117. *ST:TOS*, 2x15: "The Trouble with Tribbles."

This is not nearly as contradictory as it appears at first sight. It is obvious, based on the show itself, that Federation citizens are not only capable of handling money but are also empowered to do so when dealing with aliens. The thumbprints and the bar tabs point to individual accounts in the Ferengis' currency of choice, the unreplicable gold-pressed latinum. From that, we can infer that Starfleet officers are given an allowance in order to conform to alien customs. It is probably a quaint ritual or a hobby to most, a bit like being the lone gentile at a Passover dinner. It is vaguely familiar—you do not fully understand what is going on, but you nonetheless go with the flow.

By extension, it stands to reason that the Federation itself maintains foreign currency reserves so as to ease trade. In one of the funniest episodes of *Deep Space Nine*, we discover that one of the Federation's member systems, Bolias, operates a bank where customers can store their bars of latinum.[118]

This is not fundamentally different from what countries like the Soviet Union would do in the olden days of the Cold War. The Soviet ruble, like the Chinese renminbi until recently, was not convertible. The USSR preferred to exchange actual goods in bulk. When barter was not an option, it would have to resort to buying merchandise in hard currency. The Soviets would acquire it by selling commodities such as oil and gold on the world market, and then use the proceeds to purchase other goods. Contrary to modern China, the Soviet Union did not engage in much international trade, and its economy was not built as an export powerhouse or a "workshop to the world." Thus its usage of foreign currency was rather limited.

The Federation implements a similar system, except that it does not use any currency, such as the ruble, within its borders. That is where it gets a little more complicated and, perhaps, inconsistent. Let

---

118. *ST:DS9*, 6x12: "Who Mourns for Morn."

us speculate for a minute: If we assume that the Federation has close to infinite wealth, it can potentially flood the galactic market in any good or commodity (including money). It is a given that obtaining hard currency would never become a problem. The Federation could also potentially leverage its enormous wealth to corner the market in scarce commodities. In effect, the Federation can truly buy anything at any price, including influence and loyalty. It can probably buy all of its enemies outright, and lend or bribe its way to total galactic domination.

In theory, a political entity that enjoys terminal opulence can borrow an infinite amount in foreign currency and offer the ultimate guarantee of safety to those who invest in its government bonds. Similarly, it can lend infinite amounts of money to other nations or civilizations, without the need or the incentive to ever extract interest. The Federation has infinite wealth, and therefore it has an infinite ability to both repay its obligations and to absorb borrowers' defaults. It could potentially support the whole galaxy's economy and financial system without a lot of effort. It could bail out any star system at the push of a button. The interest rate on the Federation's debt would have to be zero, because there would never be any risk of default. Risk premiums and lending rates, the blood of interstellar economics, must be indexed on the Federation's benchmark. The Federation, even without a currency of its own, dominates the galactic bond market. There are profound economic and political consequences to that overwhelming financial power, and they are not fully explained in the series.

One of these consequences is that gold-pressed latinum, the Ferengis' currency of choice, cannot be nearly as important as we are led to believe. Its main attribute, what gives it value, is its nonreplicability. It is a form of specie money, the twenty-fourth-century equivalent of bullion coins. It strikes me as highly unlikely that such sophisticated capitalists as the Ferengis would adopt that type of antiquated and inefficient monetary instrument. That being said, if the Ferengis are in fact a parody of real-world libertarian goldbugs, then it makes sense that they would fall for such nonsense. Gold-pressed latinum must be another one of the Ferengis' clever tricks, probably devised by a Ferengi behavioral economist to drive customers to purchase more than they should. In a universe where computers and replicators handle most tasks, latinum still holds tangible monetary value and retains the magical ability to assign that value to the things it touches. It is a vehicle to keep alive the illusion that goods, objects, and experiences have a price and should be allocated based on individual wealth and willingness to pay for them. Latinum might be an elaborate ploy to keep alive the galaxy's markets and thus the Ferengis' almost exclusive status as intermediaries.

RULE OF ACQUISITION #19: SATISFACTION IS NOT GUARANTEED

The Ferengis represent the ideal of capitalism. Quark says that much to Captain Sisko in a monologue where he drops the mask and almost breaks the fourth wall: "The way I see it, Humans used to be a lot like the Ferengis: greedy, acquisitive, interested only in profit. We're a constant reminder of a part of your past you'd like to forget . . . But you're overlooking something. Humans used to be a lot worse than the Ferengis: slavery, concentration camps, interstellar wars. We have nothing in our past that approaches that kind of barbarism. You see, we're nothing like you, we're better."[119]

Quark's summation of his species' superiority is an explicit allusion to *doux commerce*: the Enlightenment notion that trade and commerce have the power to soften nations' mores, by making people happier through the satisfaction of their needs, whether they be important or

---

119. *ST:DS9*, 2x26: "The Jem'Hadar."

superficial. In fact, the theory of *doux commerce* supposes that the manufacturing and consumption of luxuries have a direct, beneficial political effect. It suggests that citizens, plied with available pleasures and luxuries, become increasingly less enthused by martial virtues. *Doux commerce* was to realize universal peace through free and open trade, the massive instrument of modern markets, rather than just personal cultivation and education.

That ideal was significant in that it articulated the crucial view that economic growth, consumption, and industrial capitalism could indeed serve the human pursuit of happiness. Understanding luxury was a major component in the invention of classical political economy, and I am immensely impressed that *Star Trek* directly addresses that question through the Ferengis. There is indeed a (largely) theoretical world in which the consumption of luxuries is not in fact a detriment to society, and contributes to the common good.

The political consequences are twofold: a society whose main passion is luxury and consumption is much less likely to be interested in war, and consequently, it is more likely to be interested in the best ways to procure such luxuries—that is, financial wealth. Incidentally, this was the crux of the debate between Hamilton and Jefferson during the American Revolution: Would the United States become a commercial republic, turning toward trade, manufacturing, and the pleasures of urban life, or an agrarian one, modeled on the Roman Republic, with its great patricians and its military leaders, buttressed by legions of rugged soldier-farmers and colonists.

The ideas of luxury and *doux commerce* were devised as a way to try to understand the new world of economic power and economic competition between nations. It was stunning to most at the time that incredible fortunes could be amassed so quickly by so few people, just by trading and procuring exotic goods for mass consumption (such as cane sugar, coffee, tea, and tobacco). These were goods that urban dwellers relished, and whose consumption had spurred the creation of cafés and restaurants in the great cities of old Europe. It was modern consumption, and modern life. All this new stuff ran counter to what most people knew about the world—and most notably the myth that agriculture was the main source of wealth and power. Adam Smith was very much grappling with the same type of future shock that we are experiencing today.

These utopian views, defended by the leading philosophers of the Enlightenment, had a much darker side—the pleasures of life, starting with sugar and tobacco, were in fact produced by slaves in far-away colonies. The triangular trade, forced labor, war, and genocide had brought about relative peace and prosperity in Europe and its American settlements.

The portrayal of the Ferengis as stalwarts of *doux commerce* conveniently elides that terrible reality. In that sense, this is the exact point where the fictional side of the Ferengis breaks through. While in many ways they represent our point of view, they also stand in for the dreamy ideal of a pure and enlightened capitalism, free of its historical baggage and its actual culpability.

That too is us, twenty-first-century humans.

RULE OF ACQUISITION #18: A FERENGI WITHOUT PROFIT IS NO FERENGI AT ALL

The main story of *Deep Space Nine* is the war between the Federation and a ruthless and calculating enemy, the Dominion. Like the Borg, the Dominion is an imperialist power. It seeks to bring people and planets under its rule by any means necessary. The war unfolds over several seasons, with its lot of tragedies and revelations. Under strain,

Starfleet officers must make difficult choices and ethically dubious compromises.

The climactic episode of the series is a study in the impossible choices of war.[120] Along with "Chain of Command," it is perhaps the greatest *Star Trek* episode ever produced. Captain Sisko must abandon all the ideals, large and small, he is sworn to uphold as a proud officer, so as to lure the shifty Romulans into joining the Federation's side against the Dominion. You have to be immersed in the show and attuned to *Trek* lore to fully appreciate the enormity of "Pale Moonlight." Sisko has a prominent Romulan politician killed, and his murder disguised as a Dominion assassination plot. Worse still, it is Garak, the Cardassian tailor, traitor, and spook, who orchestrates the whole affair. Sisko out-sources his immorality to his less scrupulous and shady ally. That awful trade-off, the death of an innocent man against the eventual victory of the Federation, is absolutely devastating. Avery Brooks (as Sisko) and Andrew Robinson (as Garak, and of *Dirty Harry* fame) give their finest performances in the service of a no less masterful script by Peter Allan Fields and Michael Taylor.

"In the Pale Moonlight" is *Deep Space Nine* at its most dramatic and exciting. In one of the episode's many twists, Sisko must bribe Quark to buy his silence. He does it under duress, yet another indig-nity in the name of a much higher purpose. Quark can barely contain his glee, not so much for the meager profit but because he finally suc-ceeded in forcing a Starfleet officer, and the captain no less, to show a bit of his inner Ferengi.

That little victory in the grand clash of civilizations between the Federation and the Ferengis proves to be Pyrrhic. That is what makes it so poignant. Bribe notwithstanding, the Ferengis eventually lose out. Throughout *Deep Space Nine*, the scheming and conniving

---

120. *ST:DS9*, 6x19: "In the Pale Moonlight."

profit-driven trolls are a constant challenge to the Federation's absolute mandate of cultural tolerance. Early on in the series, it is revealed that Quark is actively discouraging his nephew Nog from attending the station's human-run school. Quark strongly believes that school is not only a waste of time but also in contravention to Ferengis' customs. The only school a young Ferengi boy should attend is the school of hard knocks. Yet Nog aspires to more. Sisko's son, Jake, eventually finds a solution to Nog's dilemma, but it hardly settles the larger issue. Nog is just one single Ferengi child, and both the Federation's policy of absolute noninterference and the Ferengis' bigoted traditions remain in full force.

The penultimate episode of *Deep Space Nine* brings the great war to a close. The defeated Dominion's representatives sign a peace treaty while the various characters, from Worf to Chief O'Brien and Odo, part ways.[121] As everyone is busy celebrating and saying their goodbyes, Grand Nagus Zek, leader of the Ferengi Alliance, visits the station to announce his successor. Quark is convinced that he is the nominee. However, he grows concerned when he learns of the new laws enacted by the departing potentate. Ferengi women are now allowed to wear clothes and to join the workforce to participate in business ventures. Labor reforms and pension laws have been enacted, and an elected Congress of Economic Advisors is empowered to legislate. Even more troubling to Quark, the Ferengi State raises taxes to fund various programs and a social safety net. Things are definitely not what they used to be. Against all odds, the Ferengis have mellowed, they have become enlightened social democrats.

How did that happen?

Deep Space Nine chronicles that gradual change. Across the years, we get to witness the slow erosion of old Ferengi values. We see it

---

121. *ST:DS9*, 7x24: "The Dogs of War."

mainly through the eyes of Nog, Quark's nephew, the first Ferengi ever to join Starfleet Academy. He grows into a fine ensign, and earns his stripes by repeated acts of heroism during the war.

The turning point, however, the pivotal moment in the Ferengis' narrative arc, happens earlier in "The Bar Association."[122] In that uproarious episode, Rom, Quark's seemingly idiot brother and bar employee, starts a union and organizes a strike on the offhanded suggestion of Dr. Bashir and Chief O'Brien. There is probably no dirtier, more taboo word than *union* in the Ferengi language, so much so that neither Rom nor his fellow Ferengi employees can bring themselves to say it out loud.

The episode is a string of snarky comedic gems. In one scene in particular, Rom laboriously studies labor economics. Quark comes into his brother's quarters in an attempt to end the strike with an appropriately large bribe. Rom dismisses Quark's entreaty by retorting: "I have nothing to tell you but this—workers of the world unite, you have nothing to lose but your chains." So there you have it, the *Communist Manifesto* on prime-time TV, from the mouth of a grotesque alien.

As we have seen before, Rom is far from an idiot. But he is to Ferengis. His natural engineering talents and his compassion and generosity are wasted in his society, where the thirst and the ability to make profits is much more valued than scientific pursuits. By creating the Guild of Restaurant and Casino Employees and fighting for better pay and shorter hours, Rom finally breaks free from the ideological constraints of his own culture, centuries upon centuries of traditions and learned behaviors. He discovers that he can actually do that, and that it does not kill him—on the contrary.

Quark tries to replace his striking workers with holographic versions of himself, a bit like the doctor in *Voyager*. The holographic

---

122. *ST:DS9*, 4x16.

projectors and the software are defective, causing the virtual waiters to drop glasses repeatedly. The abject Brunt, a Liquidator with the Ferengi Commerce Authority, drops in unannounced, accompanied by a pair of menacing Nausicaan goons (a race of growling, alien mercenaries). His job is to break the strike. He threatens and cajoles the assembled employees, even acknowledging that the Ferengi Commerce Authority is willing to show them leniency: "The FCA understands that living on this station has corrupted you." The Ferengi workers have been "exposed to the twisted values of the Federation." The significance of the exposure is thus recognized: one does not live alongside utopian people without some measure of envy or inspiration. The values of the Federation are indeed contagious and threatening, because above all they are qualitatively better at maximizing people's and society's over-all welfare.

In the end, the strike succeeds. Quark relents to his employees' demands. But Rom's biggest victory arrives after that. Once better pay and working conditions are secured for his comrades, he quits his job at the bar to join the space station's engineering staff, albeit in a junior position (basically, he is hired to clean up the waste reclamation systems at night). He is beaming with pride and excitement. His real life can finally begin. His brother snarls; the Federation has definitely corrupted him.

I see a bit of *Star Trek*'s unstated mission in that final twist, the very same one that young Isaac Asimov had embraced early in his career: *Star Trek*'s and science fiction's role in the world is certainly to entertain and amaze and inspire, but it might also very well be to corrupt and change us, the real-life Ferengis.

CHAPTER 9

"I LIVE IN THE HOPE THAT YOU MAY ONE DAY SEE THE UNIVERSE FOR WHAT IT TRULY IS..."[123]

PROSPECTS FOR TREKONOMICS IN THE REAL WORLD

And now, the big question—maybe the only question that really matters: Is *trekonomics* at all possible? Is it going to happen? What do we need to reach *Star Trek*–like economic conditions here on Earth? What are the prerequisites for trekonomics?

THE ECONOMIC POSSIBILITIES FOR OUR GRANDCHILDREN

The ghost of John Maynard Keynes is never far away when thinking about the economics of *Star Trek*. It is probably because Keynes

---

123. *ST:DS9*, 7x16: "Inter Arma Enim Silent Leges."

understood all too well that economics and science fiction were joined at the hip. Their province was the future, in general, and the future of society, in particular. That is why Keynes engaged in a bit of science fiction himself, as a direct rebuke to his fellow Englishman, the popular author, inventor of modern science fiction, and erstwhile radical, H. G. Wells. To this day, his brief but incredibly prescient article, "The Economic Possibilities for our Grandchildren," sets the terms of the debate.[124]

Keynes observed that what he called "the economic problem"[125] would be solved in less than a century. In his view, that economic problem, the compulsion to make choices in the face of scarcity, had been humanity's great affair since the beginning of history. Thanks to the miracle of compounding growth, society would soon reach a point where hitherto-unfathomable abundance would become the norm rather than the privilege of a few.

Keynes had the intuition that human actions—our desires, our wants, our motivations—would be profoundly altered as a result. Overcoming the economic problem would condemn to obsolescence the entire panoply of economic behaviors that shaped our existence. Utility maximization and rational choice in the marketplace would no longer provide a usable premise for the dismal science's computations.

"The Economic Possibilities of Our Grandchildren" belongs to science fiction because of that anthropological leap. It very much describes the psychology of science-fictional characters such as Mr. Spock, whose unflappable logic is only matched by his stoicism and his absolute disregard for earthly pleasures. Economic competition

---

124. I use the version of Keynes's article reprinted in Lorenzo Pecchi and Gustavo Piga, eds., *Revisiting Keynes' Economic Possibilities for Our Grandchildren* (Cambridge: MIT Press, 2008).

125. Ibid., p. 21

is utterly meaningless to Mr. Spock. He has a much more interesting mission in life, exploring the galaxy. As far as humans are concerned, Keynes's predictions are in fact very close in spirit, if not to the letter, to *Star Trek*'s vision of a plentiful post-scarcity society—in other words, trekonomics.

Even more pointedly, if we take a step back from Hollywood's romance of space travel, with its gizmos and its aliens, we may soon come to the rather disquieting realization that we *already* live in Keynes's, and therefore *Star Trek*'s, cornucopia. Economic bliss is just very unevenly distributed, to paraphrase science-fiction author William Gibson.

Star Trek, while a science-fictional solution to Keynes's "economic problem," is anchored in the possibilities of the present, our everyday reality. Of course at first blush the organizing principles of its society seem to contradict that claim. We are very far from a world where all the necessities of life, the products of human ingenuity, are freely supplied and consumed as nonrival, nonexcludable public goods. But *Star Trek* is science fiction. Nothing more and nothing less. And therefore it is given the license to stare back at us from the other side, so to speak, from a point in a speculative future when the cumulative effects of growth, productivity gains, and automation have driven the price of most things to nil.

Yet, *Star Trek*'s evenly distributed and felicitous cornucopia is not solely a consequence of universal automation. The inspired metaphor that is the replicator arrives last rather than first. It is an easy mistake to confuse it for the catalyst that brings about terminal abundance and happiness in the show. Because it is on the screen, we tend to regard it, and all that it represents, as a necessary technological precondition for *Star Trek* society's opulence. So it bears repeating, the replicator is an end point. While it may be fictional and highly speculative, it is also consistent with the shows' premise. Its existence signifies the end of human labor.

To be precise, the replicator recapitulates the long and tortuous enterprise of the Industrial Revolution. Like Asimov's robots, the replicator is based on the observation that throughout history, humans have invented ever more powerful mechanical auxiliaries, from the steam engine to the computer, in order to replace labor as the main factor of production. And do not get fooled by the shiny machines! What really makes a difference is the accretion of knowledge and science, which precipitates into inventions and technological progress. The collective human brain, what we call culture, is far greater than the sum of its parts. Nowhere is this more true than in matters of economics.

We can observe this social process with our own eyes, the same way we can observe the slow and patient erosion of canyons by water. In *Star Trek*, we get to see a society where that secular transformation is complete.

▲

The notion that the human brain is on course to crowd out and eventually replace physical labor in the production of goods is as central to *Trek* as it is to Asimov's robot stories. Furthermore, understanding and modeling the contribution of knowledge to economic growth is a topic of paramount importance to economic science. Professor Paul Romer defined the special economic nature of knowledge in this way in his classic 1990 paper: "Instructions for working with raw materials are inherently different from other economic goods. Once the cost of creating a new set of instructions has been incurred, the instructions can be used over and over again at no additional cost. Developing new and better instructions is equivalent to incurring a fixed cost. This property is taken to be the defining characteristic of technology."[126]

To Romer, knowledge is by nature nonrival. This rather abstract concept succeeds in describing a very practical aspect of economic production. Unless protected by patents or made available at a cost to users (say, as in the case of a big-ticket university education), knowledge, the "set of instructions," has no inherent barriers to circulate and spread. It certainly has physical limitations: the means by which knowledge gets disseminated were not always as powerful and instantaneous as they are now. In our brave new world of networks and smartphones, exclusion and restriction are but policy choices. Scientific knowledge and, more generally, culture in all its forms are the secret ingredients that have allowed us to grow well beyond what was deemed possible at the onset of the Industrial Age.

Over the past three centuries, Europe and North America have escaped the tyranny of nature. This escape from necessity was painstakingly documented by the great economic historian and Nobel laureate Robert Fogel. He coined a term for this process: "technophysio evolution."[127] Fogel collected data about people's heights and weights over time. He concluded that rising prosperity, brought on by scientific and technological control over the environment, had negated the worse effects of resource scarcity and adverse natural conditions. The augmentation of human labor by science and machinery had led to unprecedented gains in health and longevity in the West. To get a better sense of this, one only needs to look at South Korea, for example,

---

126. Paul Romer, "Endogenous Technological Change," *Journal of Political Economy* 98:5 (1990): p. 72.

127. Robert W. Fogel and Dora L. Costa, "A Theory of Technophysio Evolution, With Some Implications for Forecasting Population, Health Care Costs, and Pension Costs," *Demography* 34:1 (Feb. 1997): pp. 49–66.

which zoomed from the most abject poverty to being one of the most advanced and wealthy countries in the world in less than half a century.

The direct effect of the spread of knowledge, be it restricted, patented, intellectually protected, or not, was first and foremost physiological. Now, for a small portion of the world's population, the problem of survival has been solved. According to the World Bank and the USDA, in advanced economies the share of household income devoted to food expenditures (both at home and away from home) is considerably smaller than in poor countries, hovering at around 12 percent. In the developed world, a good half of these food expenditures are in essence discretionary (spent on restaurants, on-the-go snacks, and packaged sugary water). The amount of calories available to the average US or UK consumer is well above the daily recommended two thousand per day.

The USDA estimates that in 1900, 41 percent of the US workforce was employed in agriculture. By 2000, that number had collapsed to 1.9 percent, while the contribution of agriculture to GDP was divided by ten (from 7.7 percent in 1930 to 0.7 percent in 2002[128]). By now, the production of sustenance is essentially an almost negligible economic activity. That hardly means that hunger has disappeared. To the enduring shame of the United States, malnutrition and food insecurity still afflict a staggering one-sixth of households.[129] However, scarcity

---

128. Carolyn Dimitri, Anne Effland, and Neilson Conklin, *The 20th Century Transformation of U.S. Agriculture and Farm Policy: Economic Information Bulletin Number 3* (Washington, DC: USDA/Economic Research Service, 2005), accessed February 25, 2016, http://www.ers.usda.gov/media/259572/eib3_1_.pdf.

129. Feeding America, "Hunger and Poverty Facts and Statistics," Feedingamerica. org, accessed February 25, 2016, http://www.feedingamerica.org/hunger-in -america/impact-of-hunger/hunger-and-poverty/hunger-and-poverty-fact -sheet.html.

of products cannot be blamed for the persistence of the problem. It is entirely a result of bad policy.

The case of US agriculture illustrates the impact of science on productivity gains. These are but a few among a large body of statistics that all point toward gradual improvements across the world. Poverty, child mortality, and illiteracy are down, while life expectancy is rising.

Food availability and healthy bodies are but proximate indexes of the effects of technophysio evolution. Our current state of plenty, at least in the developed world, goes well beyond nutritional safety. It could be said that the wealth of our nations—public health and public infrastructures, education, safety and good governance—is also a direct consequence of technophysio evolution.

We do live in cornucopia, if not utopia.

THE VULCANS ARE NOT COMING

Let's dispose of the whole space thing once and for all.

If you believe that *Star Trek* is about space travel, you are taking it too literally. Barring highly improbable changes in the laws of nature, there will not be faster-than-light interstellar travel or matter-antimatter reactors. *Star Trek* will not come to pass as seen on TV. And we will not make first contact with pointy-eared, benevolent aliens.

The Vulcans are not coming. They do exist somewhere, that is a statistical certainty, but for the time being, we are as much out of reach to them as they are to us. For all practical purposes, we are alone in the universe.

Star Trek's romance is predicated on the misconception that somehow we will encounter the Vulcans, because exploring the unknown is a fundamental trait of the human species. There is a convenient and self-serving narrative that exploration ennobles humankind, that our thirst for new life and new civilizations was and is and will always be disinterested, a function of our supposed insatiable curiosity.

Hogwash. This does not check out. In reality, if you look at the historical record, it is quite the opposite. We are an incredibly sedentary species. We live within a minuscule radius for such a boldly going bunch. We rarely venture beyond a few miles of our homes and workplaces. We retrace the same steps, the same commute, on most days. It is the world—its machines, its objects, its signals—that moves around us.

Save for a few exceptions, the eccentric among us, we are stunningly incurious. As a species, we are mostly preoccupied with our day-to-day affairs, subsistence and such, and we free ride on the achievements of a few crazy ones. We set out to explore and discover only if we really have to or if there is the promise of treasure at the end. And "we" is a total misnomer to begin with. Great voyages of discovery and world-changing inventions were never acts of charity or gifts to humanity, let alone collective enterprises. That is a legend we tell our kids, and usually they have none of it because they are not as delusional or full of themselves as we adults are. Christopher Columbus, Magellan, Cook—they were all conquistadores of one kind or another.

Personally I find it very reassuring, even heartwarming, that great explorers and inventors should be so typically human. They were strivers, small-minded low-rent busy bees. I like that. That means they were like you and me, just a tiny bit crazier or luckier. Of course, the native populations who were "discovered" by these gunslinging adventurers will not share my benign view of their motives, and rightly so. Colonial genocide and slavery aside, the fact remains that only eccentrics and nonconformists engage in these pursuits. A vocal and active minority, but a minority nonetheless.

With development and the considerable improvements in standards of living brought on by the Industrial Revolution, the number and proportion of people involved in research and development has shot up. At its peak, the Enlightenment's Republic of Letters amounted to no more than a few thousand white males. And look at what they did. Nowadays there are tens of millions of practicing scientists, engineers, and philosophers all over the world. And they are not hampered by slow mail or cumbersome travel arrangements. They are still a minority, but not for long, I'd wager.

This tells me that the most famous split infinitive in the history of the world, "to boldly go where no man has gone before," is more aspiration or exhortation than an empirical observation of human behavior. Wherever we are going, if we are "going" there at all, we usually go there for very mundane reasons. Boldness is seldom distinguishable from delusion, or necessity.

I want to stress that not only are we not "boldly going" there, but also that *Star Trek* has it all backward. In the canonical story, trekonomics came to be as a result of space exploration and first contact with the Vulcans. I am convinced it will be the other way around, because it can *only* be the other way around. There is no economic rationale for interstellar exploration, manned or unmanned. The costs are simply too astronomical. The distances involved make it impractical, even pointless, to envision any kind of meaningful economic exchanges, let alone empire building of any sort.

Furthermore, autarky does not work: it is baffling that we still dream of faraway outposts on inhospitable celestial bodies in an increasingly interconnected and networked world. The known, proven economic benefits of life in big cities are completely set aside in favor of space-cadet fantasies. It is as if Elon Musk and his fellow nerd plutocrats want to escape from history, on the spurious notion that humanity needs to settle other planets in order to be saved. But saved from what, exactly? One thing is for sure: Elon Musk is a brilliant and perceptive entrepreneur. He knows a good marketing gimmick when he sees one.

Since ancient times, cities have been the crucibles of civilization, the crossroads where people gather, and where goods, ideas, and arts are traded and created. It is where the combination of expertise, fun, and serendipitous encounters compounds at the fastest pace. There is a reason why universities are designed around campuses: to foster an intense social life, the ferment of invention and progress. Cities perform the same functions, but on a much grander and highly diversified scale. Furthermore, cities exist as nodes in wider networks—they rely on the spatial division of labor, they flourish on global trade and global connection with other cities, other countries. Ease of communication, safety, and reliability of transportation between cities are absolute necessity, prerequisites for growth and prosperity. All we know about the history of great cities and great nations tells us that there is nothing like trade. In light of that, it appears that settling a minuscule outpost on a faraway world, to live like rats underground because of the lack of an atmosphere, or the absence of a magnetosphere to shield us from deadly solar radiation, sounds like complete idiocy. An orbital space station might be somewhat less ridiculous, if that outpost were to actually produce some kind of tradeable goods. But if it only collected energy to beam down to Earth, then why bother with a full-on permanent settlement? We would be better off with a barebones maintenance operation or just robotic caretakers.

I don't want to discourage the fanboys and my friends in the aerospace community, but realistically, there will not be a space dock or a space elevator in our lifetimes, nor a moon base and even less of a Mars colony. As for the *Enterprise* within three hundred years? Please.

I do understand the motives of those who advocate space exploration as way to unite the world, as a sort of cultural crusade for peace through engineering. They are noble. So, what if we first used our resources to lift a billion people out of poverty? How many Einsteins or von Neumanns could we get out of that? Heck, we don't even need Einsteins—we just need thirty or forty million more engineers and programmers and medical scientists out of this one billion. That is 4 percent, tops. There is no telling what could be achieved with such an increase in raw human capital. The returns of knowledge grow and accumulate incommensurably fast.

Inspiration is a fine purpose. But the road to the stars begins on Earth, in the classrooms and the research institutions. It's not a matter of priority or allocation but a question of understanding the physics of history, so to speak. Conquering the solar system and then the stars is such an expensive proposition that it requires an amount of resources orders of magnitude greater than what is currently available. Humanity needs to be exponentially richer in order to embark on such an undertaking.

That is why *Star Trek* has it backward. The *Star Trek* canon portrays the advent of the so-called new world economy as a consequence of the invention of the warp drive. We meet the benevolent and logical Vulcans, and all our problems are solved. Well, not entirely, but that is the general thrust of the story. Oddly enough, in *ST: First Contact*, the warp engine looks like it was cobbled together by a bunch of rugged and manly mountaineers camping out next to decommissioned nuclear missile silos. As if such an engineering endeavor could actually be the product of a gang of alcoholic survivalists living in an impoverished, postapocalyptic North America.

Even a limited space program of any kind requires universities, engineering companies, experts of all sorts. In short, all manner of connected people and institutions, backed by the full faith and credit of a large and wealthy government. Sorry, even latter-day plutocrats ain't going to Mars.

I would go even further and say that faster-than-light travel and interstellar colonization are the most uneconomical of all imaginable endeavors for any civilization. You can't finance them like the Dutch or English merchants financed ships in the seventeenth century. It won't make you rich. There is no silver or sugar, no prized fruits from the pepper plant (*Piper nigrum*) to bring back from Sirius or Wolf 359 (not to mention that useless hellhole otherwise known as Mars).

For interstellar colonization to occur, money must be no object. And by the way, it can succeed: mathematical models show that it would take less than a million years to spread throughout the galaxy, even at a tiny fraction of the speed of light. But that cannot happen until we reach trekonomics, because it is just too damn expensive! As an investment it only offers a lousy risk/reward profile.

Even if we reach a point where we can afford to embark on such crazy adventures, we will have to face the paradox of progress, highlighted by science-fiction author David Brin. Each generation of starships, manned or unmanned, is bound to be faster than the preceding one. When to launch then becomes a serious question, as the first ship on its way to the next star system is bound to be overtaken by the second ship, which in turn will be overtaken by the third one and so on. As Brin argues, the funny thing about the Voyager space probes and the premise of *ST: The Motion Picture* is that the first interstellar civilization a Voyager may encounter will in all likelihood be us.

Aside from that, it may very well be that if we reach some form of *Star Trek*–like terminal opulence, it will be hard to find volunteers to travel for several decades on cramped vessels to forsaken planetoids. Who knows? I might be cynical here.

A species needs to achieve economic escape velocity first in order to spread through interstellar space. That is my addition to the growing list of explanations to the Fermi paradox. Interstellar exploration has no intrinsic economic value and therefore cannot happen until society is so wealthy that not a single person has to waste his or her time on base economic pursuits. It is a simple matter of resource allocation. When resources are quasi-infinite, we will be able to sink unbelievable amounts of time and human capital into building Alcubierre-drive ships.

Those who achieve trekonomics on one planet might not elect to spread out, especially given that leaving that one planet might entail having to start all over again in a new and less plentiful environment. Maybe post-scarcity removes both the barrier to expansion and the desire for it.[130]

In the meantime, the truly *Star Trek* thing to do, the most faithful to Roddenberry's vision, is to work to radically improve our own circumstances down here, on our pale blue dot. The gleaming cities of Earth are our life rafts, the space stations and outposts of the future.

Enough already with the space colonization nonsense! If anything, it is an expression of defeatism. It implies that this is not working out, "this" being Earth and the humans who live on it. It is an old pioneering fantasy. Let us build some kind of galactic *Mayflower* and leave this wretched and sinful place. It is as facile as it is misguided.

In any case, for a long while, there is no future but on Earth, in the cities of Earth, where soon 80 percent of humanity will live. I am convinced by economist Robin Hanson's argument that autarky is a mirage. What makes humans and Earth unique is that we are all squeezed together and we have to make do. The benefits are

---

130. See W. R. Hosek, "Economics and the Fermi Paradox," *Journal of the British Interplanetary Society* 60 (2007): pp. 137–141.

tremendous: historically, intense exchange of ideas and knowledge, along with division of labor and specialization, have led to considerable social progress.

So no, the Vulcans are not coming. We are the Vulcans. Or rather, we must become the Vulcans—stoic, rational, altruistic. To me, that is the main lesson of *Trek*.

Like it or not, for the foreseeable future the starship is Earth.

. . . BUT THE ROBOTS ARE

Robots are coming. In fact they are already here. Contrary to space travel, I believe that part of *Star Trek*'s extrapolation is indeed correct. It is inevitable that machines will substitute for even more of us in the performance of mechanical tasks, because it is inscribed in the very logic and trajectory of the past three hundred years of industrial revolution.

There is considerable and justifiable anxiety about automation. It is not a new concern. It has been with us since the dawn of the Industrial Age. However, the convergence of added computing power, progress in programming, and so-called big data is accelerating the adoption of automated work across many sectors of the economy. We are moving beyond "dumb" robots, the kind that weld car bodies together based on a fixed set of instructions. Automation is gaining ground in fields outside of manufacturing and logistics. Algorithms, software robots by another name, are now able to parse legal decisions, medical data, crime data, insurance claims.

This may not be nearly as fateful as it sounds; at least that is *Star Trek*'s take on it. The coming of the robots need not lead to impoverishment and idleness. Offloading most repetitive and mind-numbing tasks to mechanical workers, physical or digital, could prove liberating.

In a world where work is no longer compulsory, it must become truly meaningful.

The danger lies in the transition to an economy where the cost of making stuff—industry—has become more or less like agriculture today (with very few people employed and a very low share of GDP). With appropriate policies in place, developed countries can probably manage that transition. They have in the past, and therefore it is safe to assume they most likely will in the future. It does not mean that we will not experience dislocations and conflicts, but we do have old and established institutions—government, the press, the public sphere—that allow us to resolve such conflicts over time for the greater benefit of all.

The real challenge will be beyond our comfortable borders, in the developing world. In both nineteenth-century Europe and twentieth-century Asia, national development has followed a similar pattern. People moved from the countryside to urban centers to take advantage of higher-paying jobs in factories and in service professions. Again, South Korea offers a startling, fast-forward example of that: it underwent a complete transformation from a poor, rural country to a postindustrial, hyperurban powerhouse in less than fifty years. It was so rapid that most visible traces of the past have been erased and forgotten. The national museum in Seoul has a life-size reconstruction of a Seoul street in the 1950s, just like we have over here, but for the colonial era. And imagine this, China went down that very same path at an even faster clip. Half a billion impoverished people turned into middle-class consumers in three decades.

However, this may not happen again if manufacturing is reduced to the status of agriculture, a highly rationalized activity (read: employing very few people). The historically proven path to economic growth and prosperity taken by Korea and China might no longer be available to the next countries. This is what keeps many economists up at night.

The rise of the robots will probably reduce economic opportunities for emerging nations. In the developed world, we have the resources and the institutions to manage that transformation of the economic base. Countries you rarely hear about today, say Uganda and Tanzania, are projected to have two hundred million and three hundred million inhabitants respectively by the end of the century. What is going to happen to these people if there are no opportunities for work and wages because the manufacturing of goods has become a trivial, automated low-returns business? Not all of them will find jobs at Starbucks, regardless of how big their cities are.

It turns out that the reinvention of work imagined by *Star Trek* and all the social adjustments that come with it are not just some kind of pleasant philosophical exercise for overfed upper-class Western consumers of entertainment. In a world where machines produce most of the goods at a marginal cost, a just and adequate distribution of resources is a matter of life or death for billions of people yet to be born.

Developed countries will or will not enact redistributive policies in the face of growing automation. The responses are well known, from progressive taxation to universal health insurance, and from access to education to unconditional cash transfers, or so-called basic income. We possess stable institutions and the wealth to settle these matters adequately. Less developed countries do not yet. We are racing toward pervasive automation faster than they are catching up.

THERE IS SUCH A THING AS A FREE LUNCH

Robots are coming. And so is free stuff.

It is ironic that Ronald Reagan's most important bequest to the world turned out to be *Star Trek* rather than Star Wars. Not *Star Trek* the feature film nor *Star Trek: The Next Generation* (although they were contemporaries), but *Star Trek* the economics, or at least one of its precursors and cornerstones in the real world.

Reagan's much-ballyhooed Strategic Defense Initiative, the hypothetical space missile interception system, never went anywhere. It is telling that more than forty years after unveiling the project to great fanfare, engineers and military contractors are still unable to reliably knock down a rocket in midflight. And that is with all the advances in components and computing since SDI was first touted to the public. As for the lasers in low earth orbit, forget about it. Reagan's Star Wars was a propaganda coup that not only scared the hell out of the Soviets but also justified a significant rise in domestic military spending. While it may not have amounted to much in real life, it certainly put the War back into Star Wars.

Ronald Reagan ushered in the era of *Star Trek* economics by accident. On September 1, 1983, a Red Army Sukhoi-15 fighter shot down a Korean Airlines Boeing 747 carrying 269 passengers over the Sea of Japan. Nobody survived.

These were the days when westbound flights from the continental United States to Asia could not take the faster route over Siberia, due to the very stringent restrictions of Soviet airspace. As a result, airliners had to make a refueling stop in Anchorage, Alaska, before proceeding along a longer path across the Northern Pacific Ocean. In addition, past a certain waypoint somewhere off the last Aleutian Islands, civilian airplanes would find themselves out of the range of US-operated ground beacons. Once all alone in the unfriendly skies, as it were, it was paramount to be on the right heading lest one inadvertently violate Russian airspace. And the Russians did not take lightly to such incursions. And understandably so. As hard as it is to remember today, in 1983 Strategic Air Command's B-52s, loaded with their gigatons of nuclear warheads, were still prowling at the edges of Russia 24/7. Nothing had changed since Stanley Kubrick's *Doctor Strangelove*.

A minor glitch in the Korean Airlines aircraft's autopilot settings had led to a small deviation from its stated flight plan. By the time the doomed plane had reached the Western Pacific Ocean, beyond the reach of US relay stations, the minor initial deviation had widened considerably. Off its course by more than 180 nautical miles, the jumbo jet had breached Russian airspace without the pilots even noticing it. The Korean crew, flying blind over the Kamchatka Peninsula and woefully unaware of the danger, did not attempt to contact Russian air traffic control. Meanwhile, the Russian Air Force, already on high alert because of a missile test scheduled that day, scrambled fighters to intercept the wayward airliner. It was deemed hostile because it had already flown through prohibited airspace unannounced, and it did not seem to respond to repeated warning shots. The Russian pilot later recalled firing more than two hundred rounds, acknowledging that they were hardly visible to the naked eye.

Korean Airlines Flight 007 was shot down off the coast of Sakhalin. Two missiles exploded in close proximity to its fuselage, provoking a rapid decompression of the cabin. Flight recorders show that the pilots maintained control of the airplane for an additional twelve minutes, before crashing in the vicinity of Moneron Island, a mere fifty miles north of Hokkaido. It is not entirely clear whether they knew they had been shot by a Russian fighter.

▲

You might wonder what this particular Cold War incident, another in a long string of equally tragic and deadly disasters, has to do with bringing about or foreshadowing the economics of *Star Trek*. A lot, as it happens.

In the wake of the plane shooting, it quickly became obvious that a series of minute errors and malfunctions had led to a catastrophic outcome. At the root of it all, however, was a simple cause: the inability of Korean Airlines' pilots to adequately pinpoint the location of their aircraft and to make the required course corrections. Rightfully appalled and dismayed, Ronald Reagan made sure that this would never happen again. He opened the US Navy's new satellite navigation system to the public. Navstar GPS, or GPS as it is known today, overnight became the first global manmade public good.

Up until then, no technology or service of planetary reach had ever been available to everyone for free. Try as I might, I fail to come up with something remotely similar to the GPS. Water, power, health, roads, communication systems were, by definition, local affairs. In many instances, like the old AT&T, they were managed by private regulated monopolies on behalf of the public. Local governments would offload the service to a single private enterprise. In return for exclusivity and thus market dominance, the operator would agree to provide access to anyone, control its prices, and pay for infrastructure maintenance. In other cases, such as roads and highways, most of the cost was (and most of the time, still is) paid by tax revenue, whether at the city or the national level.

GPS is composed of a constellation of thirty-two satellites in medium earth orbit, about thirteen thousand miles above us. Each of them continually broadcasts its unique orbital position and that of the other GPS satellites, combined with a very precise time stamp. The satellites know their own positions thanks to the laws of celestial mechanics, which thankfully make orbital trajectories constant. As for time, each satellite is equipped with an atomic clock.

To resolve its location, a receiver unit needs to combine the position and time signals from only four different satellites in line of sight. The navigation equation is fairly straightforward and easily handled by modern semiconductors. The GPS chip has been miniaturized to the point where it is now a minor subsystem in cell phones and watches. For a faster fix, receivers in smartphones also make use of cell towers' location and time data (also obtained from GPS satellites).

The public has access to the so-called coarse signal, while high-resolution data is encrypted and reserved for military use. Signal specifications are public and open to any manufacturer, as are the navigation algorithms necessary to establish a fix. There are no restrictions on signal acquisition or known possibilities of jamming it (unless the US Navy just turns the system off).

When Ronald Reagan opened up GPS to worldwide civilian use, the system was still in its testing and prototype phase. It only reached full operational capacity in 1995, and it was up to the Clinton administration to make good on Reagan's promise. As of 2016 an estimated three billion receiving devices are in circulation, including navigation gadgets, cell phones, and advanced avionics on both military and civilian aircraft. The whole system is made up of just thirty-two satellites and costs under a billion in yearly maintenance.[131] By law, GPS is recognized as a dual-use system, for both military and civilian use. The US Department of Defense has a mandate to keep it available and operational for everyone's benefit.

GPS stands out as a perfect example of what is called a *positive externality* in economic jargon. As we saw previously, a negative externality, pollution for instance, is the cost to a third party from a transaction or an activity in which said third party has no voluntary involvement. A positive externality is the exact opposite: it consists of the benefits derived by that same third party from a transaction or an activity it did not choose to undertake. Positive externalities include

---

131. Fiscal Year 2016 Program Funding," GPS.gov, accessed October 12, 2015, http://www.gps.gov/policy/funding/2016/

public investments that indirectly increase overall social welfare, such as health care, education, and infrastructure.

Now compare locally financed roads to GPS. Both are marvels of engineering. They are free for you to use, and your personal usage does not prevent anybody else from using them at the same time (rush-hour traffic notwithstanding). But you will notice the difference: you do not have to be within the borders of any particular country to enjoy the services of GPS. GPS is available globally, as long as you have a functioning receiver in your possession.

The key difference between roads and GPS is one of reach. By design GPS is, well, global. It knows no frontiers. That is its primary purpose: getting one's accurate location in real time, anywhere in the world. And not only that, GPS was the first nonrival and nonexcludable infrastructure invention in history.

GPS is the simplest real-world analogue of a *Star Trek* replicator. Obviously the set of contraptions are not the same. Unlike it did for the cell phone, *Star Trek* never predicted GPS in any way, shape, or form. There is nothing that looks and feels like GPS in *Star Trek*. For any given planet and any away mission, the *Enterprise* crew just knows instantly which coordinates to send its red shirts to.

The Next Generation likely *copied* rather than *predicted* GPS, or at the very least the show got its inspiration from the Reagan administration *policy choice*—a case of art imitating life (and Ronald Reagan, of all people) and taking it to its extreme logical conclusion as only science fiction can. The show merely extrapolated from a political setup that was already in force in the real world. In that sense, the replicator's existence is a political decision to make a crucial technology free and available to all members of society as a public good, not some wishful utopian device.

Think for a minute on what GPS can already do. It deepens our knowledge of the world thanks to better mapping and remote sensing.

It multiplies our ability to monitor everything from harvest yields, to animal populations in the wild, to oceanic currents and global warming. In the same way, it allows for quicker and thus less polluting car trips; it makes sea and air navigation safer and more efficient. It is a crucial instrument for providing relief after a natural disaster. It is at the heart of popular services such as Google Maps, Waze, and Uber. It will make possible self-driving cars, thus enabling a profound change in personal mobility. GPS's capabilities go well beyond locating aircraft in flight. Its most significant contribution to the world is to facilitate and accelerate the production and sharing of useful knowledge.

⌃

GPS heralded the rise of worldwide free stuff. A lot of services and infrastructures were free beforehand, but nothing existed on such a scale and for so cheap—just $0.33 per year per receiving device, and its reach does not end in El Paso, Texas, or Sault Sainte Marie, Michigan. Furthermore, contrary to roads, GPS usage can double or triple at no additional cost.

There is no need to make wild predictions about a future where everything will be free. Today, GPS is part of the fabric of our lives in the same way the Internet and its amazing array of free services are. The zero–marginal cost society, as economist and essayist Jeremy Rifkin calls it, is an everyday, practical reality. While it is not the dominant form of economic interaction, it does thrive alongside the profit-oriented sector and feeds back and forth into it.

While GPS came first, it did not remain alone for long. The Internet and the World Wide Web are very similar in nature to GPS. For one, they all are products of the Cold War, public outgrowths of the US Department of Defense's secret Skunk Works. Incidentally, the network's backbone is made available and managed as a global public good, with a very interesting model of self-governance (ICANN, the Internet Corporation for Assigned Names and Numbers).

These global public goods, GPS and the services that live on the Internet, have one thing in common. They intensify the reach and possibilities of the human brain by considerably broadening the range of its network connections. Nowadays, you can carry all the world's accumulated knowledge in your pocket. This is literally mind-boggling, especially for older people like me. I still remember my first encyclopedia as a kid. It was fantastic and joyful. It was also ten volumes and sixty pounds. The long-term social and cultural consequences of such marvels are squarely impossible to foresee, just like Gutenberg could in no way imagine the kind of havoc his invention would ultimately wreak on the world.

At least we can observe that these new tools tip the balance in favor of human capital in the complex combination that makes up economic activity. Knowledge is as much a factor of production as machines and money. Knowledge not only wants to be free, as *Whole Earth Catalog*'s publisher Stewart Brand famously said, but it largely *is* free thanks to the Internet. Once released, it flows like water and seeps into every crack. It becomes impossible to contain or fence in. The genie is out of the bottle and will not be put back in.

FULL UNEMPLOYMENT

The most fortunate among us never have to actually produce what they consume. The marketplace can fulfill every conceivable need or desire. It only takes a visit to the great department store in the cloud. All that the world has to offer, from the pedestrian to the most vitally important, is available. Even cash. No money? No problem! There are institutions whose sole function is to extend credit so as to facilitate the largest purchases, from shelter to education to breast-augmentation surgery. They are called banks.

While nominally the subject of monetary transactions, everything that matters is as good as free to many of us. When allocation decisions consist in choosing between your new iPhone storage-capacity options or the trim of the car, then you know you have whittled down your ninety-nine problems to the last few marginal ones. For all intents and purposes, and save for a few minor imperfections, the global economy already acts as one massive replicator.

If we follow that line of reasoning to its logical end, then we need not do anything fundamentally different from what we are doing now. We just have to sit back, relax, and watch technological progress lift everybody up to our postindustrial level of opulence over the next three centuries. Markets in everything and the good life for all!

For my part, I see very little chance of that happening. The one thing I learned from watching *Star Trek* is that post-scarcity is not some kind of naturally occurring phenomenon or weather event. It will not fall into place. It is not preordained.

Post-scarcity is a set of policy choices. The logic of the Industrial Revolution, which points to the eventual replacement of human labor, is necessary but not sufficient. Technological progress and economic growth cannot bring us to utopia on their own. Inventions do not arise in a vacuum. They are artifacts of society, they respond to people's needs and, sometimes, demands. We cannot ask machines to distribute economic resources equally on our behalf.

While Keynes's economic predictions have proven largely accurate, his sociological insights, on the other hand, still sound as distant and far-fetched as *Star Trek*. In spite of abundance, what Keynes called the "love of money," a "disgusting morbidity" and a "semi-criminal, semi-pathological"[132] sentiment, has not completely disappeared. It is still driving both innovation and entrepreneurship, along with less efficient forms of capital accumulation. The distribution of the fruits of progress remains profoundly uneven.

The promise of the replicator, robots everywhere, and universal automation is not an engineering problem, it is a political challenge. That part is all on us. If indeed, as Arthur C. Clarke once said wryly, our "goal is full unemployment, so we get to play,"[133] then we need to imagine what such a world would really entail. This is where science fiction comes in. We must organize for post-scarcity. We must practice it in our own lives. We must be prepared for its joys and for its rigors. We must demand it of ourselves and of each other.

WHAT IS TO BE DONE?

Star Trek is not about humanity's interstellar future. *Star Trek* is a romance of postwar social democracy. This is the world it came from; this is the historical context from which it draws its belief in society's ability to improve. The improvements in question are very specific. *Star Trek* paints an ideal picture of late twentieth-century America and Europe, or rather of its expected trajectory. The political franchise has been expanded to all citizens, poverty and crime have receded thanks to rational welfare policies, and people are finally free to enjoy life without worries.

---

132. Pecchi and Piga, *Revisiting Keynes' Economic Possibilities*, p. 24.

133. Gene Youngblood, "Free Press Interview: Arthur C. Clarke" in *The Making of "2001: A Space Odyssey,"* ed. Stephanie Schwam (New York: Modern Library, 2000), pp. 258–269.

In a sense, it is more of the same, but with one significant twist: in *Star Trek*, thanks to pervasive automation, work has become elective. Thus, from the moment they are born, the immense majority of people in the Federation lead the kind of carefree, creative existences that closely resemble that of Norwegian or Japanese retirees. Not everyone is busy sightseeing on the pleasure planet Risa or volunteering or earning another PhD. In trekonomics there is also a place for the enterprising and the restless. Starfleet is their home, an institution where they can test themselves and compete for public recognition.

The elective nature of work in *Trek* is really the crux of the problem, or the policy challenge. If we assume that automation and artificial intelligence will indeed succeed in replacing most of human labor, from the factory floor to the laboratory, then wage work will no longer be a viable option to sustain oneself. According to *Star Trek*, the logic of economic and technological progress is taking us toward a world of unbounded material abundance, a cornucopia of things and objects and experiences, and without much available remunerative work for people to satisfy their desires. It does not really matter whether you are a red-diaper baby or, conversely, if you believe that greed is good. You will have to reckon with that contradiction: too many good things to consume, too many good times to be had, and not nearly enough means to afford them because work has become redundant.

We can already observe inklings of what such a world would look like. You need only consult the data compiled by Oxford economist Max Roser to see the rising tide of the market lifting all boats, on every continent. From the streets of Lagos or Nairobi to the gleaming cities of China and Malaysia, a global middle-class is coming into its own.

This is a new and remarkable achievement. Since the Renaissance and the conquest of the Americas, the same countries have monopolized economic prosperity. To this day, the core European powers remain the most prosperous nations on Earth. China and India, after a short eclipse, have regained their rightful places at the top. This is more a reversion to the historical mean than anything else: since the times of the Roman Empire, China and India had been the world's leading economies. So nothing really new under the sun with respect to the two largest countries in the world.

The great and hopeful novelty of the past hundred years, besides China and India's return to prominence, is the emergence of countries beyond the original core. Some are built on ancient kingdoms and cultures (like Egypt, Nigeria, and Thailand), while some are colonial inventions (like Brazil, Chile, or South Africa).

Taken together, these countries represent roughly half of humanity and rising. Their newfound prosperity, however, seems to duplicate the same imbalances we can observe in the West. Economic inequality remains endemic, with wealth flowing toward the very top at an increasing pace.

Besides the often dreary political consequences of a moneyed aristocracy, the concentration of wealth in a few hands is particularly worrisome in a world where automation and software are replacing formerly well-paying occupations. How do we keep people alive, literally, in a world from which work is gradually disappearing? That question is far from limited to developed countries. It is not a rich-world problem. If we wish not to squander the progress already made in expanding prosperity to all corners of the world, I believe it is inescapable that we will need comprehensive and global redistribution of wealth, along with the local democratic institutions to implement such a program.

In a nutshell, that is *Star Trek*'s romance of social democracy. The Federation can maximize the welfare of everyone, regardless of origins, talents, or appetites, because it has made the decision to make most services and products available as public goods. The mutualization of most goods and services is *Star Trek*'s solution to the contradiction of workless overabundance.

Such a world is far from a guaranteed outcome. While public goods and abundance are spreading, so is economic inequality. We will need considerable efforts, wisdom, and cooperation to steer society on a new course, so as to best adapt to the rise of our robotic assistants and brethren. The wealthiest among us will have to reallocate the bulk of their fortunes to society. In fact they already are, as many successful entrepreneurs and capitalists realize that past a certain point of accumulation, their wealth is utterly meaningless not only to them but also to the world.

Above all, we will need more public goods and more positive externalities. *Star Trek* teaches us that humanity's wondrous inventions do not fully realize their potential until they are freely shared.

As Captain Picard would say before sending off the *Enterprise* on a new adventure:

"Make it so."

CONCLUSION

"LIVE LONG, AND PROSPER"[134]

At the end of our journey through the economic intricacies of the *Star Trek* universe, a major question remains. What does the Vulcan greeting "live long and prosper" really mean?

The phrase itself, along with the hand salute, are the most iconic symbol of *Star Trek*. If you ask anyone what they know and remember of *Trek*, they usually raise their hand and spread their fingers to form the Hebrew letter *shin*. They may not know the sign is a Hebrew letter, nor its religious meaning, nor even that it comes straight out of Leonard Nimoy's pious childhood. But the greeting has stuck. It is a rallying sign, a distillation of *Star Trek*'s philosophy and values. The freeze-frame picture of Leonard Nimoy is the public face of *Star Trek*, its conscience. The Vulcan greeting has come to represent all that is good and hopeful and humanistic about *Star Trek*.

---

134. *ST:TOS*, 2x01: "Amok Time."

Some of the greatest artifacts that make American culture, comedy, music, and yes, even science fiction are largely salvaged pieces from the boats that reached these shores. They come from lives destroyed and lives rebuilt, be it after the pogroms or the middle passage. They come from West Africa and the Shtetl. They speak to us from across time of the genius and the travails of our uprooted ancestors. And thus it is more than fitting that what became known in popular culture as the symbol of the future is descended from ancient communal ceremonies, like the distant echo of a forsaken place.

This morsel of humanity, the Vulcan hand greeting, is *Star Trek* in a nutshell. It ensured that something of the old Yiddish traditions would endure. The price of survival would be the hollowing of its original meaning.

Let us hear Leonard Nimoy explain its origins again (from a post at Startrek.com):

> I grew up in an interesting inner-city neighborhood in Boston. The area was known as the West End and was written about in a book called the Urban Villagers. It was a desirable area since it was within walking distance of downtown Boston and the Boston Commons, as well as being situated along the banks of the Charles River.
>
> The population was mostly immigrants. Maybe 70 percent Italian and 25 percent Jewish. My family attended services in an Orthodox Jewish Synagogue, or "Shul." We were especially attentive to the high holidays, Rosh Hashanah, the Jewish New Year, and Yom Kippur, the Day of Atonement.
>
> Since I was somewhat musical, I was hired as a young boy to sing in choirs for the holidays and I was therefore exposed to all of the rituals firsthand. I still have a vivid memory of the first

time I saw the use of the split-fingered hands being extended to the congregation in blessing.

There were a group of five or six men facing the congregation and chanting in passionate shouts of a Hebrew benediction. It would translate to "May the Lord bless you and keep you" . . . etc.

My Dad said, "Don't look."

I learned later that it is believed that during this prayer, the "Shekhina," the feminine aspect of God comes into the temple to bless the congregation. The light from this Deity could be very damaging. So we are told to protect ourselves by closing our eyes.

I peeked.

And when I saw the split-fingered gesture of these men . . . I was entranced. I learned to do it simply because it seemed so magical.

It was probably 25 years later that I introduced that gesture as a Vulcan greeting in *Star Trek* and it has resonated with fans around the world ever since. It gives me great pleasure since it is, after all, a blessing.[135]

The hand sign tells a distinctively American story, the triumph of the poor and persecuted immigrants from across the seas. Fresh off the boat, they lived in poverty, in tenements, on the wrong side of the tracks or the river. For a long while, as with many other outsiders, they kept their language, Yiddish, and their religious customs. But their children inevitably grew up to be more American than shtetl. I look at

---

135. Leonard Nemoy, "Guest Blog: Leonard Nimoy On The Vulcan Salute," Startrek .com, September 16, 2012, accessed September 7, 2015, http://www.startrek .com/article/guest-blog-leonard-nimoy-on-the-vulcan-salute.

the Vulcan sign, the secret blessing from Leonard Nimoy's old shul, as a poetic kindred to Isaac Asimov's "Nightfall." They are cultural contraband: the vernacular idioms of outsiders that spread and flourished in the language and codes of the majority.

Beyond the significance and history of the hand sign, there is also the issue of the greeting itself. The famous catchphrase, "live long, and prosper," has a different origin. It was invented by science-fiction grandmaster Theodore Sturgeon, who had written "Amok Time," the first episode where the words can be heard. In that episode, Spock experiences Pon Farr, the Vulcans' mating period, and must rejoin his counterpart T'Pau so as to consummate. Thus at first the salute appears to be a pedestrian Vulcan affair, like when we humans greet each other with a "good day" or "how are you doing?" Nothing more than an exotic demonstration of good manners in polite, extraterrestrial society.

Certainly, that greeting cannot mean "live long and get rich." If there is anything to remember from this book, it is that *Star Trek* society and Vulcans in particular are completely indifferent to the accumulation of personal wealth.

One can infer that the Vulcan notion of prosperity has a lot to do with accomplishments and service. It is what you contribute in science and wisdom that makes you prosperous. Your prosperity is intangible: it grows out of the exchange with others, it chiefly exists and accrues in their eyes. Vulcan prosperity is something you can measure for yourself, but it is not as objective as the zeroes on a bank account statement. It is acclaim and the respect of your next of kin, your friends, your companions, society at large. As such, it is always in question.

Like civic virtue, it must be publicly demonstrated time and again by deeds.

"Live long and prosper" thus alludes to another kind of prosperity, the kind that arises from the cultivation of the mind rather than from greed, that antiquated and vulgar practice.

It is an active sentence. Instead of "long life and prosperity," it is a grammatical imperative directed at the recipient. Long life and prosperity do not befall you out of the heavens, they are not random outcomes from the lotteries of birth or of life. You must live long, that is the condition. It does not mean that you will prosper: the "and" is not a logical conjunction. You may or may not succeed. Furthermore, the phrase points to the unfinished nature of the imperative. Spock's father, Ambassador Sarek, who has arguably lived very long and prospered beyond many of his Vulcan peers, is still served the greeting. The work and the challenge to go on living and to prosper are never concluded.

In the world of *Star Trek*, prosperity has changed meaning in much the same way work has. It has become much closer to the ideals of Stoic philosophy. To Vulcans, reason and knowledge are the foundations of morality. Prosperity lies in the cultivation of the mind and in the justice of one's actions in the world. Or, as Seneca wrote: *Quam bene vivas refert, non quam diu.* It is how you live that matters, not how long.

ACKNOWLEDGMENTS

The distant origins of this book go back to a chance encounter with the late professor Robert Fogel a long, long time ago in a galaxy far, far away.

A lively and intriguing online discussion involving the most excellent Rick Webb, Matthew Yglesias, and Joshua Gans provided the initial spark.

In its actual, finished form, *Trekonomics* is the result of another, more recent, chance encounter. I am forever indebted to Chris Black, who encouraged me to just write and see what would happen. His unique insights into *Star Trek* proved invaluable. His contributions to the *Star Trek* canon speak for themselves. Just watch "Carbon Creek" again.[136]

This book could not have been published without the kind of modern epistolary friendships that only the Internet enables. There is a digital Republic of Letters, and Felix Salmon is one of its most fearless and eccentric citizens. I cannot thank him enough for his efforts on behalf of my work.

---

136. *ST:ENT*, 2x02.

It is a humbling experience to be read by your heroes:

Professor J. Bradford DeLong was an early champion of *Trekonomics*. His commitment to the values of *Star Trek* have informed his life's work in favor of a better, more equal, and more rational world. Without his help and his intellectual generosity, this book would not have seen the light of day.

Similarly, Professor Paul Krugman, himself a life-long Isaac Asimov fan, read an early and messy version of the manuscript. His notes and his wit made it much better.

It is equally humbling to benefit from the advice of incomparably more accomplished writers and thinkers: Annalee Newitz, Charlie Jane Anders, David Brin, Mark Rizzo, Dmitry Lipkin, Aaron Hill, Ben Kafka, Julie Coe, Anoush Terjanian, Ann Goldberg, Dana Simmons.

I was fortunate to take part in spirited discussions with the science, technology, and science-fiction studies group at the University of California, Riverside. I am especially grateful to Professor Sherryl Vint, whose contribution to science-fiction scholarship has been a constant inspiration and a reminder to keep it real.

Also at UC Riverside, a big thank you to Sara Stilley, who allowed me to sample some of the finest of the Eaton Collection's famous science-fiction holdings.

Larry Levitsky, cofounder of Inkshares and PiperText, brought this book to fruition. He read too many versions of it, but never once lost his cutting publisher's eye. This book is his baby as much as mine.

Using the power of the Internet to crowdfund a work on the economics of *Star Trek* was logical. In fact it was the only logical thing to do. The Inkshares team made it a breeze with its incredible technology platform. My thanks to Jeremy Thomas, Adam Gomolin, Thad Woodman, Matt Kaye, and Avalon Radys. Inkshares is leading publishing into a brighter future.

My gratitude to my editor, Matthew Patin, who helped me turn the manuscript into a real book; to Brittany Dowdle, who edited the copy; to John Powers for his artwork and Jennifer Bostic for her cover design; and to Emily Zach, who orchestrated it all.

In Paris, my oldest and best friend, Laurent Perreau.

In Hawaii, my other old friend, Manu Greif.

In Washington, DC, (and globe-trotting), Aurelia Antonietti.

In Tel Aviv, my father Yossi.

In Davis and Cambridge, the Simmons family.

In San Francisco, Jan and Basab Basu.

In San Diego and Berkeley, the Dillons.

In Los Angeles, Dana Simmons and Lazare Simmons-Saadia (who, I hope, will eventually turn into a *Star Trek* fan).

Those all over the world who made this book possible by preordering it at Inkshares.com.

Finally, I must thank my other hero, Sujatha Baliga, for taking time from her much more consequential work to read the manuscript. Her tireless advocacy for restorative justice is making *Star Trek* a reality right here and right now. She is proof that Spock is alive in each and every one of us.

Live long, and prosper.

Los Angeles, Paris, Hilo, March 2014–January 2016

FURTHER READING

ECONOMICS AND POLITICAL SCIENCE

Brynjolfsson, Erik, and Andrew McAfee. *The Second Machine Age: Work, Progress, and Prosperity in a Time of Brilliant Technologies.* New York: W.W. Norton, 2014.

Deaton, Angus. *The Great Escape: Health, Wealth, and the Origins of Inequality.* Princeton: Princeton University Press, 2013.

Fogel, Robert W. *The Escape from Hunger and Premature Death, 1700–2100: Europe, America, and the Third World.* Cambridge: Cambridge University Press, 2004.

Fogel, Robert W., and Dora L. Costa. "A Theory of Technophysio Evolution, With Some Implications for Forecasting Population, Health Care Costs, and Pension Costs." *Demography* 34:1 (Feb. 1997): pp. 49–66.

Ford, Martin. *Rise of the Robots: Technology and the Threat of a Jobless Future.* New York: Basic Books, 2015.

Hardin, Garrett. "The Tragedy of the Commons." *Science,* n.s., 162:3859 (Dec. 13, 1968): pp. 1243–48.

Hirschmann, Albert O. *The Passions and the Interests: Political Arguments for Capitalism before Its Triumph.* Princeton: Princeton University Press, 1977.

Hosek, W. R. "Economics and the Fermi Paradox." *Journal of the British Interplanetary Society* 60 (2007): pp. 137–41.

Nordhaus, William. *The Climate Casino: Risk, Uncertainty, and Economics for a Warming World.* New Haven and London: Yale University Press, 2013.

Ostrom, Elinor. *Governing the Commons: The Evolution of Institutions for Collective Action.* Cambridge: Cambridge University Press, 1990.

Pecchi, Lorenzo, and Gustavo Piga, eds. *Revisiting Keynes' Economic Possibilities for Our Grandchildren.* Cambridge: MIT Press, 2008.

Piketty, Thomas. *Capital in the Twenty-First Century.* Translated by Arthur Goldhammer. Cambridge: Belknap Press, 2014.

Polanyi, Karl. *The Great Transformation: The Political and Economic Origins of Our Time.* New York: Farrar and Rinehart, 1944.

Pomeranz, Kenneth. *The Great Divergence: China, Europe, and the Making of the Modern World Economy.* Princeton: Princeton University Press, 2000.

Popper, Karl. *The Open Society and Its Enemies.* 5th ed. Princeton: Princeton University Press, 1966.

Romer, Paul. "Endogenous Technological Change." *Journal of Political Economy* 98:5 (1990): p. 72.

Schumpeter, Joseph A. *Capitalism, Socialism, and Democracy.* 3rd ed. New York: Harper and Brothers, 1950.

Skidelsky, Robert. *John Maynard Keynes: 1883–1946; Economist, Philosopher, Statesman.* New York: McMillan, 2003.

Terjanian, Anoush Fraser. *Commerce and Its Discontents in Eighteenth-Century French Political Thought.* Cambridge: Cambridge University Press, 2012.

Veblen, Thorstein. *The Theory of the Leisure Class.* New York: B.W. Huebsch, 1924.

Von Neumann, John, and Oskar Morgenstern. *Theory of Games and Economic Behavior*. Princeton: Princeton University Press, 1944.

ON *STAR TREK* SHOWS

Clark, Mark. *Star Trek FAQ 2.0: Everything Left to Know About the Next Generation, the Movies, and Beyond*. New York: Applause, 2013.

Cushman, Marc. *These Are the Voyages: TOS Season One*. With Susan Osborn. San Diego: Jacobs/Brown Press, 2013.

—— *These Are the Voyages: TOS Season Two*. With Susan Osborn. San Diego: Jacobs/Brown Press, 2014.

—— *These Are the Voyages: TOS Season Three*. With Susan Osborn. San Diego: Jacobs/Brown Press, 2015.

Erdmann, Terry J. *The Star Trek: Deep Space 9 Companion*. With Paula M. Block. New York: Pocket Books/Star Trek, 2000.

Hurley, Maurice. "The Neutral Zone." Unpublished script, 2nd rev. final draft. March 17, 1988.

Gerrold, David. *The World of Star Trek*, Rev. Ed. New York: Bluejay, 1984.

Gross, Edward, and Mark A. Altman. *Captains' Logs: The Unauthorized Complete Trek Voyages*. New York: Little Brown & Co., 1995.

Roddenberry, Gene. "Star Trek: The Next Generation Writer/Director's Guide." Unpublished manuscript. March 23, 1987.

Roddenberry, Gene, and Gene L. Coon. "The Star Trek Writers/Directors Guide." Unpublished manuscript, 3rd rev., April 17, 1967.

Ruditis, Paul. *The Star Trek: Voyager Companion*. New York: Pocket Books/Star Trek, 2003.

Sternbach, Rick, and Michael Okuda. *Star Trek The Next Generation Technical Manual.* New York: Pocket Books, 1991.

WORKS ABOUT *STAR TREK*

Behr, Ira Steven. *The Ferengi Rules of Acquisition, by Quark as Told to Ira Steven Behr.* New York: Pocket Books, 1995.

Decker, Kevin S., and Jason T. Eberl. *Star Trek and Philosophy: The Wrath of Kant.* Chicago: Open Court, 2008.

Kraemer, Ross, William Cassidy, and Susan L. Schwartz. *The Religions of Star Trek.* Boulder, CO: Westview Press, 2001.

Krauss, Lawrence M. *The Physics of Star Trek.* New York: Basic Books, 2007.

Pearson, Roberta, and Maire Messenger Davies. *Star Trek and American Television.* Los Angeles: University of California Press, 2014.

Nemecek, Larry. *The Star Trek: The Next Generation Companion.* Rev. ed. New York: Pocket Books, 2003.

MEMOIRS, BIOGRAPHIES

Asimov, Isaac. *The Early Asimov; or, Eleven Years of Trying.* New York: Doubleday, 1972.

Alexander, David. *The Authorized Biography of Gene Roddenberry.* New York: Penguin, 1995.

Fern, Yvonne. *Gene Roddenberry: The Last Conversation.* Los Angeles: University of California Press, 1994.

Meyer, Nicholas. *The View from the Bridge: Memories of Star Trek and a Life in Hollywood.* New York: Viking, 2009.

ENVIRONMENT

Alliance Commission on National Energy Efficiency Policy. *The History of Energy Efficiency*. Washington, DC: Alliance to Save Energy, 2013. Accessed March 2, 2016. https://www.ase.org/sites/ase.org/files/resources/Media%20browser/ee_commission_history_report_2-1-13.pdf.

Ehrlich, Paul. *The Population Bomb*, Rev. Ed. Rivercity, MA: Rivercity Press, 1975.

Klein, Naomi. *This Changes Everything: Capitalism vs. the Climate*. New York: Simon & Schuster, 2014.

Kolbert, Elizabeth. *The Sixth Extinction: An Unnatural History*. New York: Henry Holt, 2014.

Larivière, Vincent, Éric Archambault, and Yves Gingras. "Long-term patterns in the aging of the scientific literature, 1900–2004." In *Proceedings of the 11th International Conference of the International Society for Scientometrics and Informetrics (ISSI)*, edited by Daniel Torres-Salinas and Henk F. Moed, 449-456. Madrid: CSIC, 2004. http://www.ost.uqam.ca/Portals/0/docs/articles/2007/ISSI_Aging_1900-2004.pdf.

Meadows, Donella H., Dennis L. Meadows, Jørgen Randers, and William W. Behrens III. *The Limits to Growth: A Report for the Club of Rome's Project on the Predicament of Mankind*. New York: Universe Books, 1972.

Oreskes, Naomi, and Erik M. Conway. *Merchants of Doubt: How a Handful of Scientists Obscured the Truth on Issues from Tobacco Smoke to Global Warming*. New York: Bloomsbury Press, 2010.

Sabin, Paul. *The Bet: Paul Ehrlich, Julian Simon, and Our Gamble over Earth's Future*. New Haven: Yale University Press, 2013.

Smil, Vaclav. *Cycles of Life: Civilization and the Biosphere*. New York: Scientific American Library, 1997.

———— *Enriching the Earth: Fritz Haber, Carl Bosch, and the Transformation of World Food Production.* Cambridge: MIT Press, 2001.

FUTURE VISIONS

Asimov, Isaac. *Foundation.* London: Folio Society, 2012.

———— *Robot Visions.* New York: Roc, 1991.

Bould, Mark, and Sherryl Vint. *The Routledge Concise History of Science Fiction.* New York: Routledge, 2011.

Diamandis, Peter H., and Steven Kotler. *Abundance: The Future Is Better Than You Think.* New York: Free Press, 2012.

Drexler, K. Eric. *Engines of Creation: The Coming Era of Nanotechnology.* New York: Doubleday, 1986.

Kotler, Steven. *Tomorrowland: Our Journey from Science Fiction to Science Fact.* New York: New Harvest/Houghton Mifflin Harcourt, 2015.

Lafargue, Paul. *Le Droit à La Paresse.* Paris: François Maspéro, 1969 (original, 1880).

McCray, W. Patrick. *The Visioneers: How a Group of Elite Scientists Pursued Space Colonies, Nanotechnologies, and a Limitless Future.* Princeton: Princeton University Press, 2012.

Newitz, Annalee. *Scatter, Adapt, and Remember: How Humans Will Survive a Mass Extinction.* New York: Doubleday, 2013.

Rifkin, Jeremy. *The Zero Marginal Cost Society: The Internet of Things, the Collaborative Commons, and the Eclipse of Capitalism.* New York: Palgrave/MacMillan, 2014.

Smith, George O. *Venus Equilateral.* New York: Prime Press, 1947.

Stephenson, Neal. *The Diamond Age.* New York: Bantam/Spectra, 1995.

Toffler, Alvin. *Future Shock*. New York: Bantam, 1970.

Vint, Sherryl. *Bodies of Tomorrow: Technology, Subjectivity, Science Fiction*. Toronto: University of Toronto Press, 2007.

Von Neumann, John. *Theory of Self-Replicating Automata*. Edited and completed by Arthur W. Burks. Urbana and London: University of Illinois Press, 1966.

Youngblood, Gene. "Free Press Interview: Arthur C. Clarke." In *The Making of "2001: A Space Odyssey."* Edited by Stephanie Schwam. New York: Modern Library, 2000.

STAR TREK EPISODES CITED

Throughout this book, I use the following notation to point to various episodes of the show: "season" x "episode number" in chronological order of air date.

Star Trek: The Original Series
1x18: "Arena." (season 1, episode 18)
1x26: "Errand of Mercy."
2x01: "Amok Time."
2x15: "The Trouble with Tribbles."
2x24: "The Ultimate Computer."
3x17: "The Mark of Gideon."

Star Trek: The Next Generation
1x01: "Encounter at Farpoint, Part I."
1x02: "Encounter at Farpoint, Part II."
1x04: "Code of Honor."
1x26: "The Neutral Zone."

2x03: "Elementary, Dear Data."

2x09: "The Measure of a Man."

2x11: "Contagion."

3x04: "Who Watches the Watchers."

3x19: "Captain's Holiday."

3x21: "Hollow Pursuits."

4x02: "Family."

4x11: "Data's Day."

5x07: "Unification, Part I."

5x08: "Unification, Part II."

6x09: "The Quality of Life."

6x10: "Chain of Command, Part I."

6x11: "Chain of Command, Part II."

6x12: "Ship in a Bottle."

6x20: "The Chase."

7x09: "Force of Nature."

7x15: "Lower Decks."

7x20: "Journey's End."

7x24: "Preemptive Strike."

Star Trek: Deep Space Nine

1x01: "Emissary."

2x20: "The Maquis, Part I."

2x21: "The Maquis, Part II."

2x26: "The Jem'Hadar."

3x03: "The House of Quark."

3x11: "Past Tense, Part I."

3x12: "Past Tense, Part II."

3x14: "Heart of Stone."

4x11: "Homefront."

4x16: "The Bar Association."

4x22: "For the Cause."

4x24: "Body Parts."

5x05: "The Assignment."

5x07: "Let He Who Is Without Sin . . ."

5x09: "The Ascent."

5x13: "For the Uniform."

5x16: "Doctor Bashir, I Presume."

5x21: "Blaze of Glory."

5x25: "In the Cards."

5x26: "A Call to Arms."

6x07: "You Are Cordially Invited."

6x09: "Statistical Probabilities."

6x12: "Who Mourns for Morn."

6x13: "Far Beyond the Stars."

6x15: "Honor among Thieves."

6x18: "Inquisition."

6x19: "In the Pale Moonlight."

7x06: "Treachery, Faith, and the Great River."

7x16: "Inter Arma Enim Silent Leges."

7x24: "The Dogs of War."

Star Trek: Voyager

1x11: "State of Flux."

3x05: "False Profits."

5x15: "Dark Frontier, Part I."

5x16: "Dark Frontier, Part II."

6x10: "Pathfinder."

6x24: "Life Line."

7x20: "Author, Author."

Star Trek: Enterprise

1x25: "Two Days and Two Nights."
2x02: "Carbon Creek."

STAR TREK MOVIES CITED

Star Trek: The Motion Picture
Star Trek II: The Wrath of Khan
Star Trek IV: The Voyage Home
Star Trek VI: The Undiscovered Country
Star Trek: First Contact

SCIENCE FICTION FOR FURTHER READING

In lieu of a list of books, I am encouraging readers to look for novels by the following authors. Their works are representative of the utopian undercurrent in science fiction, and thus deeply relevant to *Star Trek*.

H. G. Wells
Isaac Asimov
Arthur C. Clarke
Arkady and Boris Strugatsky
Ursula K. LeGuin
John Brunner
Iain M. Banks
Kim Stanley Robinson
Octavia Butler
Samuel R. Delany
Charlie Stross

ABOUT THE AUTHOR

Manu Saadia was born in Paris, France, where he fell into science fiction and *Star Trek* fandom at the age of eight. He studied history of science and economic history in Paris and Chicago. His work on *Trekonomics* has been featured in the *New York Times*, the *Washington Post*, the *Financial Times*, the *Wall Street Journal*, and *Business Insider*. He also appeared on the panel "The Amazing Economics of *Star Trek*" along with Paul Krugman at the New York Comic Con in 2015. Manu Saadia is a contributing writer for Fusion.net. He lives in Los Angeles with his son and his wife.

LIST OF PATRONS

This book was made possible in part by the following grand patrons who preordered the book on inkshares.com. Thank you.

Aaron W. Seymour

Adam Drake

Adam Gomolin

Adam Lebovitz

Alain Cimino

Alex Rosaen

Alexander D. Head

Andy Walters

Anthony Adamiuk

Anthony Ivan

B. J. Murphy

Bill Maurer

Brandy R. Hill

Brett Joseph Ellingson

Brian Blaisse

Brian Cechnicki

Bruce Hall

Buster Keenan

Carl Bell

Chelsea Lohr

Christopher Weiture

Damon Dash

Dana Simmons

Daniel and Charlene Simmons

Daniel Cartwright

Daniel Hahesy

Daniel Jensen

Darryl R. Walker

David R. Burke

David Yarrow

Deanna De Loach

Don J.

Dougall Liechti

Eric Cahoon

Eric Jensen

Frank Hamm

Fred Vigot

Furuzonfar Zehni

Gail Stockwell

Geoffrey Bernstein

Greg Dizzia

Gyoung Yoon

Hamish Hughes

Harry A. Layman

Helmholtz Watson

Ian Kenley

J. B. Filipi

James Rainsley

James S. Schaefer

Jason Delaney

Jesper Stage

Jim Reilly

Joe Park

Joel Noble

John Colley

Jonathan Arrender Smith

Joseph Terzieva

Joshua Gallaway

Judith Moores

Justy Burdick

Kai-Erik Thomenius

Kevin Cummines

Kevin P. Heaney

Kody Stone

Larry Levitsky

Laura Horn

Lauralynn Rogers

Lisa K. Little

Lock McShane

Marcos C. S. Carreira

Marianne Levitsky

Mark Dillon

Mark Rizzo

Marshall Cottrell

Martin Meunier

Maryann Hulsman

Matt Levine

Matthew R. Goolsby

Matthew Rossi

Matthew Yglesias

Meghan K. Love

Michael Kelly Oxford

Michael Robert Miles

Michael Wade

Naju Mancheril

Patrick L. Gerini

Patrick Ryan

Rich Wong

Richard Austrum III

Robert E. Smith III

Roger Thornhill

Rosemary Krimbel

Ross Crawford-d'Heureuse

Steve Williams

Steven Bien Samera

Steven De Birk

Steven Rod

Steven Schohn

Susan McEwen

Thaddeus Woodman

Tim Robertson

Trea La Brada

Zac Miller

INKSHARES

Inkshares is a crowdfunded book publisher. We democratize publishing by having readers select the books we publish—we edit, design, print, distribute, and market any book that meets a preorder threshold.

Interested in making a book idea come to life? Visit inkshares.com to find new book projects or to start your own.